PETER MELHUISH

PETER MELHUISH

The Book of
WITHERIDGE

A Parish Through the Centuries

PETER AND FREDA TOUT

AND JOHN USMAR

HALSGROVE

This book is dedicated to the people of
Witheridge, past, present and future.

British Library Cataloguing-in-Publication Data.
A CIP record for this title is available from the British Library.

ISBN 1 84114 253 0

HALSGROVE

Halsgrove House
Lower Moor Way
Tiverton, Devon EX16 6SS
Tel: 01884 243242
Fax: 01884 243325
email: sales@halsgrove.com
website: www.halsgrove.com

Frontispiece photograph: *Outside the Mitre during George V's
silver jubilee celebrations, 1935.*

Printed and bound by CPI Bath Press, Bath.

Contents

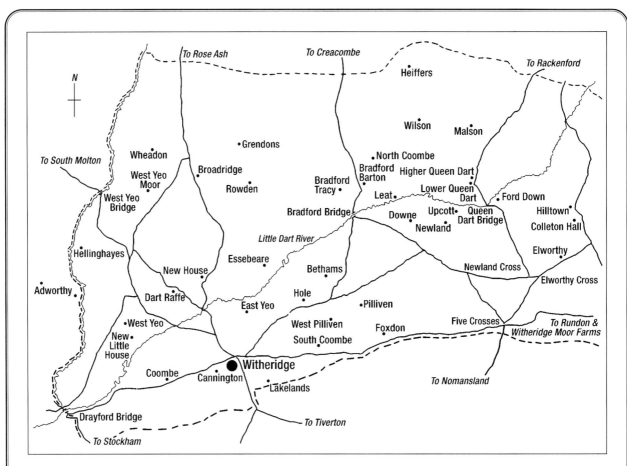

Sketch map of parish.

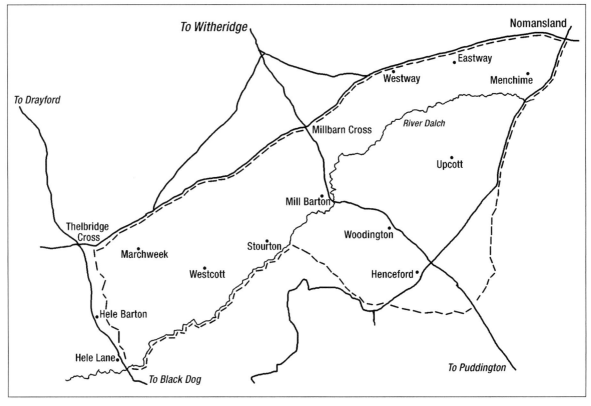

Sketch of old outliers.

Introduction

Witheridge lies on the southern edge of North Devon and people have been living here for several thousand years. Our rolling countryside is linked by two rivers, the Little Dart and the Adworthy Brook. Our original outliers were situated along the River Dalch. Many of our farms were listed in the Domesday Book of 1086. In earlier times Bronze-Age people grew crops and raised their funeral mounds on Witheridge and Dart Raffe Moors and, before them, Stone-Age folk left flint flakes in the soil, which we have since found.

This book covers the centuries with a range of events – in the thirteenth century there were a couple of grim murders, in the fourteenth we felt the effects of the Black Death, and the Reformation saw us acquire five church bells from a priory in Barnstaple. Some Witheridge men played a part in the Civil War and at that time others lost their lives in an attempt to steal hidden treasure. The eighteenth century saw a local man, William Chapple, describe the parish in detail in his reply to the Milles Inquiry.

At the end of the 1700s our first school was established and in the 1830s an extra section was added to the church tower. About that time our Union Society was formed and we were linked by turnpike road to South Molton and Tiverton. In 1848 new Church and Chapel Schools were built. Later, in spite of our efforts, the railway never came, but this led to the success of our two carriers and the transport company they formed together.

The First World War hit us hard and afterwards some emigrated, following in the steps of those who had left during the reign of Edward VII. The Second World War is remembered by locals and evacuees alike. Afterwards, the population fell below 700 for the first time in 200 years. Since then it has doubled, and in 2003 we have a thriving community, with employment, new housing, community facilities and a range of organisations. People here have always had a certain independence of mind and we look forward to the future with confidence.

We, the authors, can muster 175 enjoyable years here between us, but in addition we have been marvellously helped through the years by very many people – too many to list here. We must, however, particularly thank Mike Sampson for his work on the earliest period, Jenny Bidgood for her illustrations, and the late Revd J.A.S. Castlehow for his years of research. We thank those who have shared their memories and photos with us; we are indebted to them, and we have appreciated their enthusiasm and pleasure in contributing. We are grateful to the *Mid Devon Gazette* series for permission to use excerpts from their newspapers dating from 1857, and we thank the Parish Council and the Amory Trust for their financial support.

What we have included in this book is to the best of our knowledge accurate. For any errors that have crept in we offer our sincere apologies.

The authors

The original packhorse bridge at Drayford is marked on Donne's map of 1765,
but dated long before that. It carried what was known as 'The Great Road to Exeter'.
It was so narrow that carts had to use the ford.

Chapter 1

THE MISTS OF TIME

The last ice age ended in about 10,000BC and the glaciers, which had reached south-west England, began to retreat northwards. The temperature rose, causing the ice to melt and rivers to form. Around the area we now call Witheridge, the water carved channels recognised today as the valleys of the Little Dart and Sturcombe Rivers, and the River Dalch, as well as the Adworthy Brook. These, with their smaller streams, all drain south and westwards off the higher ground that stretches out like a finger from the southern slopes of Exmoor. The cold bleak landscape, resembling present-day Siberia, gave way to dense forests where oak and hazel were most common. Migrating herds of reindeer, which had been almost the only animals seen in the area during the ice age, followed the glaciers, while the warmer temperatures encouraged a wider range of species. Wild cattle, deer and boar walked the woods, birds flew above and beavers and fish were plentiful in the rivers and streams. At this time bears and wolves would not have been rare in the area.

Humans had probably visited the Witheridge area on rare occasions during the ice age, to hunt the reindeer, but they left no trace. However, the warmer climate and better hunting drew larger numbers of people. Their presence is revealed only by chance finds of stone tools, which are occasionally spotted in ploughed soil. Archaeologists have dated the different types of tool and told us more about their uses. The time that followed the ice age is known as the Mesolithic period and the most commonly used tools are known as microliths. These have been found scattered near Cannington Farm and on the Drayford side of West Yeo Farm. They are made either of chert or flint, both very dense stones which give incredibly sharp edges. Although often less than an inch long, they were ideal for setting on harpoons or arrows.

Mesolithic people are often called hunter-gatherers;

Stone-Age fishing.

they lived on whatever food they could obtain by hunting and gathering – fruits, berries and nuts. They had no permanent settlements, but moved around in small groups, making temporary shelters out of whatever came to hand. As they were nomadic they carried very little with them, but their stone tools were of great importance. Although they also used wood, bone and antler, it is primarily just the stone that has survived. There are no natural deposits of flint or chert near Witheridge, but some chert is to be found to the east of Tiverton. However, more substantial amounts occur in the Vale of Taunton. As such, all the stone for tools must have been brought from elsewhere and so would have been highly prized. As the Mesolithic period developed chert was largely replaced by the more easily worked flint.

At about 4,000BC growing numbers of the Mesolithic bands left their precarious nomadic way of life and began to establish permanent settlements. First, areas in the forest had to be cleared; trees were felled with flint axes. A blade of such an axe, made of a fine, pinkish flint has been found near Rackleigh, Worlington. It measured about 5in. in length, was tapered, and had a cutting edge that was 3in. wide. It would have been fixed into a wooden handle. (Practical experiments have shown that very smooth, highly polished axes, such as the one found at Rackleigh, are more efficient than rougher examples.) Once clearings had been made, wild animals, including cattle, sheep and pigs, were attracted by the grass that grew there and, over hundreds of years, they were domesticated. The clearings were gradually enclosed by hedge banks, fences or ditches. Another possibility once clearings had been established was to grow cereals, a practice which began in the Middle East and spread to Britain around this time.

The establishment of fields meant that the original settlement became more spread out and although their

Bronze-Age barrow funeral.

extent and the remains of dwellings are often not visible from the ground, archaeologists can sometimes spot them from the air as crop marks. Ditches and pits that have been filled in still retain moisture and show up as greener and more luxuriant growth in crops or grass. On the other hand, buried stone features hold less moisture than the surrounding ground, so show up as paler marks – they often appear as parched areas in the summer. Aerial photography has revealed a few such sites around Witheridge. There are signs of enclosures near Woodington and Stourton Barton (Thelbridge), as well as at North Coombe (Templeton). However, none of the sites have been investigated on the ground, so their date cannot be confirmed.

The change in lifestyle, especially the keeping of animals, led to important changes in the settlers' range of tools that, in turn, gave rise to the name by which this period is known – the Neolithic, or New Stone Age. Better quality flint, from South Devon or even further afield, seems to have replaced the coarser chert. It appears that it was brought in rough lumps and worked into the required tools once on the settlement sites. After the tools had been removed what was left of these lumps is referred to by archaeologists as 'core' and considerable amounts have been found on or near Neolithic settlement sites. A scatter of flint pieces picked up on Upcott Farm contained no fewer than 12 cores, so it is likely that there was a settlement in the immediate vicinity. The pieces removed from the cores were worked into a variety of tools, with a large proportion of blades and scrapers. Blades were used to cut up animals and the large number of scrapers, which were common at this time, were used to scrape hides to be used for clothing and shelter. The Upcott Farm scatter also contained at least seven scrapers, while single examples have been discovered near South Coombe (Templeton) and Bourne Park (Meshaw). Other flakes, less easily dated, have been found on the fields around West Yeo Farm. So far, well over 50 pieces have been found, implying a considerable amount of activity nearby.

It must be said that neither the sites nor the finds mentioned thus far reflect the full extent of prehistoric activity in the Witheridge area. They simply show the places where people, mainly archaeologists, have looked for evidence. There are doubtless many more sites yet to be discovered. Walking in almost any

ploughed field will turn up some pieces of worked flint. The only way a more accurate map of prehistoric activity could be drawn would involve a systematic walking of the fields. However, this can only be carried out where the soil is made available; woodland, permanent pasture, rough moorland and built-up areas cannot be investigated by this method.

The flint scatter at Upcott Farm, apart from the cores and scrapers, also revealed three arrowheads. Whereas these could have been made solely for hunting, they would have been equally useful in conflict. Warfare between local groups became a feature of the Neolithic period. This was probably a natural progression: settlement had made possible the accumulation of a greater amount of possessions, animals and, probably more important, land, so competition for these things became endemic and often led to violent conflict. The situation was made worse by the introduction of metalworking to Britain from the Continent. The first items were produced in about 2,000BC in gold, then in copper. Both metals were too soft to produce goods of great practical use, so the objects made were probably considered to be luxury goods owned only by the wealthier members of society.

A more durable product resulted when copper was combined with tin to produce bronze, which marked the dawn of a new era: the Bronze Age. An élite warrior class can be distinguished at this time, seen mainly through their burial customs. When members of this class died, they were usually cremated and their ashes placed in urns. Large mounds were built over the remains and examples of these can be seen on Witheridge Moor and Dart Raffe Moor, as well as Gibbet Moor and near Gidley Cross. The mounds are generally known as barrows. Alongside the remains, many exotic and prized possessions have been excavated from such sites, underlining the fact that these were the tombs of the uppermost class of Bronze-Age society. None of the local barrows have been investigated – at least, not legally – so we have no clues as to who lies buried there. Their survival in large numbers on higher ground could be due to the simple fact that in most cases this land has not been used for agricultural purposes, therefore they have remained largely undisturbed. They also probably served as boundary markers between different tribal groups and could have been placed so that the spirits of the dead warriors were able to defend the territory of the tribe.

There are three barrows on Dart Raffe Moor, lying parallel to, and south of, the road from Doorpark to Wheadon Cross. The smallest measures 27 paces across, and the largest 36, while the two smaller ones are about 3ft high. The largest stands at about 5ft and shows signs of the original surrounding ditch. Barrows were constructed by digging a circular ditch and after the remains had been placed in the centre, the soil was piled up to form the mound. Over time mounds become worn away and the ditches fill up. The other group of barrows in Witheridge is usually described as being on Witheridge Moor, although the westernmost example is on agricultural land west of the road that runs from Five Crosses to Elworthy Cross. This group is of similar size to the Dart Raffe examples, ranging in width from 28 to 35 paces across and from 3ft to 6ft in height, apart from one which is only just over 1ft high. At some point in the past this barrow appears to have been ploughed over, which resulted in the mound being spread.

One thing that sets the Witheridge Moor barrows apart, is that one of them, the easternmost, is associated with two, if not three, large stones. Standing stones were by no means unusual in the Bronze Age – we have only to consider the most famous, such as Avebury and Stonehenge, but it is not so common to find them so close to barrows. The Witheridge stones have remained largely unnoticed because they lie flat on the ground, often hidden by vegetation. Of the two stones which lie close to the barrow, the largest is over 6ft long and nearly 5ft wide, while the other measures about 4ft by 2ft. The third stone is to be found further to the east, across the north–south road that divides Witheridge Moor. Doubt has been cast on its links with the other two, but for no apparent good reason. Although pure speculation, it has been suggested that these stones could have formed part of a larger ritual monument, perhaps even a stone circle.

If there were once more barrows on lower ground more suited to cultivation, their chances of survival would not have been good. Aerial photographs have shown signs of three ring ditches near Bourne Park at Meshaw, which have been interpreted as the sort that surround barrows. It is worth noting that barrows were not the only means of burial. In 1980, a chance discovery was made while ploughing was taking place on Lower Ash Moor Farm, Rose Ash: an urn of 12in. containing the cremated remains of an adult human, dated to c.1050BC (placing it firmly within the Bronze Age). The urn had been placed in a small pit and covered by a capstone, but there was no suggestion of a covering mound. However both of these types of burial would have been reserved for the warrior classes and their families; the rest of society would probably have been accorded little, if any, ceremony. Unfortunately, despite all this evidence, no settlements of the people who built the barrows have yet been discovered. That said, some flint tools have been found close to the Gibbet Moor barrows, suggesting a nearby habitation site.

About 750BC the bronze-based culture was gradually replaced by one based on iron. One feature which seems to dominate the Iron-Age landscape, but probably originated earlier, is the hill-fort; an enclosure, sometimes covering many acres, surrounded by ditches and banks and, as the name indicates, usually sited on the summit of a hill or very near the top.

Cranmore Castle overlooking Tiverton, Huntsham Castle and probably the earthworks at Stoodleigh Beacon and Berry Castle near Black Dog are almost certainly among this type, the most famous of which is Maiden Castle in Dorset. Their purpose is hotly debated. Originally thought of as purely military in character, the current belief is that they perhaps served as meeting-places, markets, corrals for animals in times of danger, or even the 'capitals' of tribal groupings. Witheridge seems to lack such a hilltop enclosure, or does it? The ideal location for such a site would be in the area of the present village, lying, as it does, on a spur with wide views over the surrounding countryside. If there was such a site here, then it is almost certain that any signs of it, in the form of banks and ditches, would have been destroyed centuries ago. What is certain is that small farmsteads would have peppered the landscape around Witheridge.

In AD43 Britain was invaded by the Romans who set about bringing the native tribes under their control. They achieved this by making their chiefs swear allegiance to the Roman Emperor or, if they refused, by ruthless military force. Until the 1950s very little was known about the Romans in Devon, but our knowledge has grown considerably since then, and is still growing. There was a legionary fortress at Exeter, complete with bathhouse, mosaics and other typically Roman features, as well as a string of forts stretching to the north. These have been identified at Bury Barton (Lapford), above Bolham outside Tiverton and near Clayhanger, as have several small forts on the North Devon coast. More recently extensive ironworkings have been discovered near Brayford, which more than likely originated under Roman control. So, on many occasions the Devon countryside would have echoed to the clinking of Roman armour and cavalry harness.

Communications between the various Roman units were of paramount importance and the prehistoric tracks in the county would have been adapted and new roads built to link the military sites. It seems that only the most commonly travelled routes were laid with stones. It was suggested by a Victorian antiquarian that one such road ran from Exeter, by way of Crediton, through Woolfardisworthy and Witheridge, by Knowstone to Molland, 'but it has not been distinctly traced in this part of its course.' Similarly, the same source records that in 1844 a silver coin of the Roman Emperor Antoninus Pius (who reigned from AD138–61) was dug up in Witheridge, but we have no other record of this discovery.

More intriguing and, potentially more exciting, is the earthwork known as Berry Castle, which lies in a field beside the road from Bradford Mill to Queen Dart Cross. It is possible that this site is all that remains of a Roman watch-tower or look-out post.

Background: *Roman watch-tower at Berry Castle.*

It is typically Roman in that it is almost square in shape, measures 95ft by 98ft, is surrounded by a wide ditch and the interior is defended by a rampart. Although the height from the bottom of the ditch to the top of the interior rampart is now just over 3ft, in the 1860s it was said to be about 13ft high. There is now a clear entrance to the interior across the ditch on the east, but this was apparently not in evidence as late as the 1890s; it was suggested at this time that:

... the entrance must have been on the south side, and cut away in making the road to Bradford Barton, as there are no indications of an entrance through the remaining entrenchments.

It has also been suggested that Berry Castle is a moated site of a later period, but hilltop locations for such structures are rare; there is no way of feeding water into the moat apart from natural rainfall.

Throughout Britain local people continued to live and farm with little disruption in the shadow of the Roman occupation. An added bonus for some was that in the vicinity of military sites there would have been opportunities to supply provisions to the troops. Perhaps this was the case for the local Witheridge farmers if the site near Queen Dart was indeed a watch-tower. Aerial photography might have discovered some of the sites of the local farms. There are possible sites at Lewdon near Thelbridge, and nearer still at Dart Raffe Farm. The most likely example is that revealed near Drayford, where marks in the crops show three joined rectangular enclosures, the middle of which is double-ditched with a south-facing entrance.

By the beginning of the fifth century the Romans had withdrawn almost all of their troops from Britain. Before their departure they had invited Saxon mercenaries from Germany to defend the east coast of England. These people seized the opportunity to summon their fellow countrymen. Before long Saxons, together with Angles and Jutes, had arrived in sufficient numbers to make it possible to push the native British westwards towards the Atlantic. Their advance was often halted by military defeat, but by about AD700, the British had been restricted to Devon and Cornwall. This is not to say that they had been isolated from outside contact. On the contrary, there is mounting evidence that the British had important trade contacts with the Mediterranean area. In addition, the type of Christianity practised along the Atlantic fringe originated directly from the Holy Land as opposed to that later encouraged by the Saxons, which was more closely linked with Rome. Holy wells were a feature of this Celtic Christianity, often linked to the travelling saints so beloved of western Britain. Although Rackenford, Cruwys Morchard and Washford Pyne all have holy wells, Witheridge seems to be lacking. The longstone, near Stone Farm, Worlington, could well date from this period. It seems to be an example of a prehistoric standing stone which, with the advent of Christianity, had crude crosses inscribed on each of its four faces and on its top.

By about AD750 the inevitable had taken place: Devon was in Saxon hands. Yes, there were occasional skirmishes and battles, and large numbers of the native population of the South West crossed the seas to join their Irish, Welsh and Breton brothers, but the great majority continued farming under Saxon domination. One important change was that of language. Saxon slowly replaced the Celtic tongue, which was similar to modern Welsh, Cornish and Breton. Whereas these three aforementioned areas retain many Celtic place names, Devon has few, except the names of many of its rivers. The name of the River Dart has a Celtic root meaning 'oak', and Dalch derives from 'dark stream', which is, curiously, the same origin as the place name Dawlish. Many Witheridge places are almost certainly translations into Saxon from original Celtic words describing features in the landscape: Henceford comes from 'hengest' meaning stallion, plus ford; Stourton is 'stroda tun', farm of the marshy places; Bradford, broad ford; Heiffers is 'hiewe fyrs', place where furze is cut; Rowden is 'ryh dun', or rough hill; Yeatheridge or 'ierth rig', meaning ridge of plough land or arable land. Witheridge itself was 'wethra hrycg', which translates as ridge of the wethers, implying that Witheridge was a good place to raise sheep. Another group of place names give Saxon personal names, perhaps those of the original settlers who dispossessed the Britons. For example, Chapner was Ceatta's mere or marsh; Woodington was Odda's Farm, as was Adworthy (whether they were the same person or different people, we do not know), Pillaven was Pila's marshy land, Cannington belonged to Canna and Elworthy to Illa. Another farm name has a relevant meaning for the Saxon times: Horestone, from the Saxon 'har stan', meaning boundary stone. The farm stands on the parish boundary between Witheridge and Rackenford and there was probably a stone marking the limits. This has either been lost or it is still lying undiscovered in a hedge bank.

Parishes were set up as early as the eighth century, although their boundaries were not finally established until some time in the twelfth century. Witheridge Parish covered a very large area, originally over 11,000 acres which, as well as the present parish, in the early days included the lands which constitute the modern parish of Templeton as well as three outliers. These were detached parts of Witheridge: Yeatheridge, Little Witheridge and the area later known as 'the South Quarter'. The latter included land at Nomansland, Menchine, Eastway, Westway, Upcott (with Batson and Shillaton), Berrycleave, Little Newhouse, Woodington, Henceford, Mill Barton, Stourton Barton, Westcott, Marchweeke, Hele Barton, Hele Lane hamlet and land at Canns Mill – although, it must be emphasised, not all of these farms would have existed during Saxon times. Templeton was included in Witheridge until the fourteenth century, when it was made a separate parish, but the outliers remained a part of Witheridge until the nineteenth century when they were incorporated into the surrounding parishes.

As well as becoming a parish, Witheridge was also made the head of a hundred of the same name by the Saxons. This was an administrative unit, probably used for taxation purposes. Witheridge Hundred covered over 80,000 acres and stretched from Bishops Nympton to Chulmleigh, eastwards to Cruwys Morchard, then north to Oakford. It was governed by a hundred court which usually met once a month and was originally attended by all the free tenants within its boundaries. It is a great compliment to the Saxons that these two organisations, parishes and hundreds, remained fundamental to the administration of England for so long.

Saxon society became deeply divided into six classes; each provided services to the class above in exchange for protection. At the top were the royal family and earls, below which were the nobles or thanes who were expected to perform armed service, as well as repair bridges and fortresses. Next came a group who acted mainly as bailiffs or reeves on the thanes' estates. Then came cottars who, although they held a minimum of five acres of land, were required to do at least one day's work a week for the lord of the manor, and sometimes three during harvest. The duties of the next rank, the geburs, were even more onerous. They were expected to work for perhaps two days each week on the manor and to pay an annual rent of about 10d., as well as a tribute of barley and two hens in the autumn, plus a lamb or 2d. at Easter. In return, on first entering his property, each gebur received two oxen, one cow, six sheep and seven acres of land sown with corn. However, when the gebur died the lord of the manor could take what was left. The lowest of all the social orders were the slaves, but even they were accorded rights. Their food allowances were prescribed by the customs of the manor.

Ownership of land was based on the manor, which could consist of a single farm or an estate of many farms. It seems that the lands around Witheridge by the mid-eleventh century had been divided into a dozen manors belonging to lords of varying importance. As with most heads of hundreds, the manor of Witheridge itself was in royal hands, having passed to Gytha, the mother of Earl Harold (who later became King Harold). This lady also held other valuable manors in Devon, including North Molton, South Tawton, Hartland and Tiverton, as well as properties in other parts of England. A Saxon called Aelmer, as well as Bradford Tracy, had 51 other manors in Devon, while an important noble named Brictric held lands in all the counties of the South West, amongst which he counted Queen Dart.

With the Norman Conquest in 1066, land ownership changed. Almost all our local knowledge of this

NOTES BY REVD J.A.S. CASTLEHOW

Domesday: cattle, sheep and pigs at Bradford.

Witheridge was Wiriga (now celebrated in the street-name Wiriga Way) and probably included Combe, Cannington, Betham, Hole and Yeo (the area around Yeo Copse), as well as the land where the village now stands. The Domesday Book states that the lands of two Saxon thanes had been added to the manor since the Conquest – these were Woodington and Henceford, now in Thelbridge.

Odeordi represents Adworthy and Hellinghayes.

Bradeforda, one of two manors of the same name, refers to Bradford Tracy which, as well as Bradford Barton, contained the lands of Leat, Downe, North Coombe, Pillivan and Foxdon. Toredona had been added and this probably equates to Rundon, which had possibly just been carved out of the moor. The other Bradeforda almost certainly means Menchine, as this was once known as Menchine Bradford.

Draheforda is clearly Drayford and, from the size of the holding, could have included the outlier of Little Witheridge as well as lands in the present parish of Thelbridge.

Revd Castlehow adds the manor of Ratdona which he cites as being West Yeo.

The manor of Labera is Essebeare, together with Rowden, Grendon, Broadridge and Newhouse.

Welisedinge probably represents Wilson and Heiffers.

Revd Castlehow also includes the manor of Hilla which, he asserts, refers to Hilltown and Colleton.

Derta is the name of three Domesday manors in the Hundred of Witheridge, of which one can firmly be established as Dart Raffe. Another Derta was probably based on Queen Dart and included Malson, Ford Down, Newland, Rose Moor and Elworthy. The remaining Derta was held by a man called Theobald, who also owned three small manors called Wesforda, or Washford. Consequently the Revd Castlehow has suggested that his property included Upcott, Eastway, Westway, Marchweeke and the outliers of Yeatheridge and the South Quarter, which included Stourton and Westcott.

period comes from the Domesday Book, compiled in 1086 almost certainly so that the Norman King William could see who held what lands and how much they should pay in tax. The Domesday Book has probably had more written about it than any other book apart from the Bible, but still a lot of the detail is not understood. The entries give the name of a manor, its owner in 1086 and in the year of the Conquest, how much land there was for a certain number of ploughs, the amount of meadow, pasture, and woodland in acres, stock numbers, and the value of the land at both dates. Even from the start we are in trouble as identification of the manors proves very difficult, but, with the help of the notes of Revd J.A.S. Castlehow, vicar of Witheridge for 40 years from 1925 and a much-respected local historian, most of the problems can be overcome.

Within a few years of the Norman invasion, William the Conqueror had dispossessed almost all of the Saxon landowners and proceeded to share out the lands in England among his Norman supporters. As in the case of the manor of Witheridge, he kept most of the royal lands for himself. Of the other local manors, the King's shire reeve or sheriff in Devon, Baldwin, held the small manor of Wilson. Sometimes lands were handed out to members of the same family. This was the case with Queen Dart and Essebeare, both of which were given to Odo FitzGamelin, while the Theobald who owned the 'Washford' Dart was Odo's father-in-law. It is worth noting that Theobald's tenant at the latter was Alwold, the Saxon who held the manor before the Norman Conquest. He must have been considered no threat to the new regime. Dart Raffe was owned by William de Poilli, whose tenant was Ralph, after whom the farm was named.

How big were the Witheridge manors? Any idea of exact acreages must be forgotten, as the Domesday manors give areas in 'land for x number of ploughs', and each plough is generally taken to cover anything between 100 and 200 acres. As such, the sizes given below are for 150-acre ploughs. The Witheridge manors varied greatly in size, as one would expect. For example, Adworthy and Essebeare had about 75 acres of arable land, while the combined holding of Bradford Tracy and Rundon was about 700 acres, and Drayford and Witheridge closely followed with approximately 600 each. The Domesday Book gives acreages of meadow, pasture and woodland as well arable land, and the only notable figures in the Witheridge totals are the 100 acres of woodland in the manor of Drayford and the 100 acres of pasture at Hill. As far as animals are concerned, no one seems able to explain the numbers given in the document as, in some cases, even half a sheep is recorded. Perhaps the figures represent a tax assessment rather than an indication of stock on the properties. Probably the best way to use the information is to compare the numbers given for the different manors.

This way we find that Wilson had the most cattle, followed by Bradford Tracy, which had most pigs. On the seven manors where animals are recorded sheep are most plentiful, with 26 being given for Witheridge, and 20 each for Bradford Tracy and the Washford Dart. Goats are only mentioned in three cases: the Washford Dart had 25, Bradford Tracy 11, and Essebeare 5.

Probably the most annoying and difficult statistic is that concerning people. The only figures we are given are the heads of households and, even then, they are not all listed. For example, no people are recorded for Essebeare. A ready reason is that they could have worked on the Queen Dart manor, but more likely they were simply not recorded. Slaves, that is those who had no land and worked exclusively for others, were widespread on the Witheridge manors, with Queen Dart having three. Of course, these three represent not individuals but families, possibly as many as 15 or 20 individuals. Perhaps surprisingly, Witheridge manor did not contain the greatest number of families; that honour went to Bradford Barton and Queen Dart. Altogether there appears to have been 56 families counted on the Witheridge manors. Each would probably have consisted of a husband, a wife and an average of three children. So, in total, we could expect just over 200 people in these manors. It must be remembered there would have been no schools, so as soon as a child was capable of performing work, from the age of six or seven, he or she was out in the fields tending animals or crops. Therefore, apart from babies and toddlers, everyone would have been contributing to the local economy, that is, the lord of the manor's pocket.

Physically, eleventh-century Witheridge would have been largely recognisable to us. The valleys and hills had been carved out of the frozen ice-age wilderness and the River Dart flowed through the parish just as it does today, although its banks would have been more heavily wooded than now. Indeed, the woods of the parish would have echoed with the sounds of snuffling pigs and the calls of the swineherd, for it was here that pigs were kept, feeding off acorns and whatever else they could find. Here and there, smoke would be seen rising from the simple houses made of mud walls and thatched roofs. Perhaps the richest farms in the area were built of stone, but it is likely that only the village church was built in this way. Here, surrounded by vivid wall paintings, on Sundays and holy days the vicar, probably the only person in the parish who could read and write, would deliver his warnings of hell-fire for those who sinned and promises of paradise for those who performed their daily tasks well. There would have been little sign of 'heaven on earth' for the villagers. Their lives would have consisted of endless toil, from childhood to grave, with little reward apart from just enough food to make sure they could go to work the following day.

Chapter 2

THE EARLY CENTURIES

Incumbent & Patrons

The following information was compiled by the late Revd Castlehow. He took all names (except the first three) and dates directly from the printed Bishop's registers and from the work of Mr W.H. Bowers, who extracted the Witheridge Institutions from the Bishop's registers.

1154–89: Occurs Ralph. All we know of this rector is his name. He is described in an Assize Roll of 54 Hen III as being rector in the time of King Henry grandfather of the present Lord the King.

1255: Occurs (1) Robert Terry Patron – Margery la Payne. In 1256 Robert Terry seeks to gain possession of one furlong of land in Parkarigg as frankalmoign of his church of Wytherigg, (2) against Robert de Crues. He fails to get the land but received one pound of wax at Michaelmas. In the Assize Roll of 1238 a witness concerning the lordship of the Hundred is Robert, son of Terri, who had been seneschal of Roger, son of Pain, who died just before 14 October 1237.

1269: Occurs Robert of Totton who brought again the action against Robert de Crues. He also failed to get possession of the land, but recovered 10 marks of arrears.

1282: 2nd November. Thomas de Gorges, to whom Bp Quivil gave the custody of the church. Patron – Sir Robert Fitzpayne. He was also Precentor of Wells, and in 1292 he was one of those who brought news of the death of Robert, Bp of Bath and Wells to the King, and returned with license to elect (3).

1317: Sir Wm De Wengrave instituted in commedam. Patron – Sir Robert Fitzpayne. Through the neglect of the predecessor the church and the rectorial buildings and the benefice generally had suffered great injury. He had license of non-residence and to put out his benefice to farm in 1329, 1324 and 1333. Occ. Sir John Perour. In Bp Grandson's register, page 1208, there is this entry partly in Latin and partly in French. Item written in the hand of the Lord Bishop 'Help for God and charity the feeble, poor and simple'. Parson of Wytherugge against the rich and proud Hospitaller. It is written in the Scriptures, Eccles III, 'All things have their time'.

1361: 24th March. Sir Robert atte Crosse. Patrons – The Prioress and Convent of Cannington in Somerset who were patrons to the Dissolution. They last exercised their right in 1521. The Institution of Crosse was at Chudleigh and letters of Institution and Induction were addressed to the Dean of Molton and the Rector of Church Stanton, Master John Thelbrugge.

1362: 10th February. Henry de Littone, rector of Spraxton, Somerset in exchange with Crosse.

1379: 6th October. Master Edmund Demalmeshulle, rector of Stormouth Kent in exchange with Henry de Litlyntone.

1391: 17th September. Sir William Vexford, chaplain on the death of Malmeshalle.

1396: 14th May. John Luffewyk, rector of March, dio. Of Lincoln in exchange with Vexford.

1425: 16th September. Master John Hody, Bachelor of Laws, on the death of Sir John Lowicke. Master Philip Polton of Lovecok, the last rector, who's Institution is not recorded. He was the last rector and after him the priory of

Cannington sent their vicars, the rectory being appropriated to the priory the deed which endows the vicar against the impropriators being signed by the bishop at Bishop's Clyst on 16th December 1428, and by the prioress in chapter on the 13th of December.

1429: 16th March. Sir Walter Hoggis, chaplain, instituted. Sir Thomas Bowring occurs, his institution not recorded.

1431: 6th or 3rd October. Robert Sir Gaunt in exchange with Bowring for the chantry of Walton Glanville in the diocese of Salisbury.

1448: 4 June. Sir John Wolmere on the death of Gaunt.

1451: 16 July. Sir William Clyffe on the resignation of Wolmere.

1474: 17 June. Sir John Wynd on the death of Clyffe.

1476: 15 March. Sir Richard Facy, on the resignation of Wynd.

1517: 15 February. Thomas Tremayne MA, admitted to the vicarage then void. Fellow of Exeter College, Oxford.

1521: 23 September. George Verney, brother of Cecilia Verney, the last prioress of Cannington. Prebendary of Exeter. He is described in 1561 in Bishop Alley's return as 'non conjugatus, nec concubinarius, bene doctus, non predicat quia senex est, et ob defectum memoriae'. He also held Jacobstow. Died 1562. At the Dissolution the rectorial property and advowson was first granted on lease to Rogers who had also the Cannington property. The reversion was sold with other monastic lands to a syndicate, who divided up their purchase, the Witheridge share going to Lewis Stuckley of Affeton, whose widow married Thomas Melhuish of Witheridge and whose son sold the rectory to his stepfather.

1562: 9 October. Henry Squire on the death of Verney Patron – Lewis Stuckley, gent.

1587: 6 April. Ralph Nycolson, Patron – Queen Elizabeth.

1587: 14 August. John Gaydon. Patron for this turn George Southcomb of Rose Ash, gentleman, by reason of the advowson granted to him by Thomas Melhuish of Witheridge, gentleman, and which Melhuish had purchased of Lewis Stuckley of Afton and John Stuckley, Esq., son and heir of the said Lewis (Dr Oliver) Lewis Melhuish, brother of Thomas calls Gaydon, brother-in-law.

1620: 19 February. William Tyler (or Taylor). Patron – James Dinham, gentleman, this turn by grant of Lewis Melhuish of Chawleigh, gentleman. Tyler quarrelled with his wife, to whom he would not pay alimony, and who brought an action against him in the Court of High Commission. He was committed to the Gatehouse until the alimony was paid (April 24th – June 26th 1634). The case was finally settled 27th November 1634:

Defendant about thirteen years ago intermarried with his wife who brought him a portion of £1450. He held the vicarages of Witheridge and Bishop's Nympton worth 200 marks a year, and possessed besides lands and tenements worth £90 a year. Proof was given of great violence and cruelty of conduct on the part of the defendant towards his wife with scandalous speeches; and on the other side there was evidence of great provocation and of very wicked and outrageous speeches on the part of the wife. The Court condemned them both, but laid the greater blame upon Tyler in respect of his holy function, and therefore for the present allowed his wife £40 per annum towards her necessary alimony, but declared if she continued to live with her sister Elizabeth Gator, who kept a common alehouse, the alimony would not be continued.

[See *Acts of the Court of High Commission, Calendar of State Papers, Domestic, 1633–34*, p.481, and 1634 p.336.]

1643: 19 September. John Radford instituted, patron Robert Lehuish of Witheridge, gentleman.

1644: 15 November. John Radford, same patron. Mr W.H. Bowers suggests that this is probably a re-admission of John Radford of 1643 owing to the benefice having become vacant in some unexplained way by this Institution to Puddington on 28th March, 1644. Dr Oliver gives his second Institution to Witheridge in 1643, and says

'Perhaps son of the above'. John Radford was instituted to Thelbridge on 22nd October, 1632.

1650: 27 February. Hugh Shortrudge, same patron.

1661: 27 February. William Borough on Shortrudge's resignation. Patron – Thomas Melhuish of Hansford, Ashreigney, gentleman.

1672: 5 March. Samuel Shebbeare, Magd, Hall, Oxford, MA, 1669 on Borough's death. Patron – Thomas Melhuish of Northam whose daughter, Elizabeth, married Shebbeare in 1673.

1717: 4 December. John Shebbeare, Queen's College, Cambridge, BA, 1702, MA 1707 on the death of his father Samuel Shebbeare, presumably John Croker, LLB, rector of Wolfardisworthy who married Gertrude, daughter of Thomas Melhuish of Northam (above).

1742: 5 January. Charles Earle, All Soul's College, Oxon, BA, 1732, on death of John Shebbeare. Patron – Roger Melhuish of Northam, gentleman.

1745: 23 September. Thomas Melhuish, Exeter College, Oxon, BA, 1741, MA 1744, on Earle's resignation. Patron – William Melhuish of Northam, Esq. (Elder brother of Thomas).

1793: 14 June. Pery Dicken, Ball College, Oxon, BA 1790, on Thomas Melhuish's death. Patron – Richard Melhuish of Bradford.

1832: 3 April. William Prockter Thomas, LLB, Trinity Hall, Cambridge (grandson of the Revd Thos Melhuish, and nephew of Richard). Patron – himself. He was also prebendary of Holcombe in Wells Cathedral, vicar of Wellington, Somerset, and for a short time rector of his prebendal church, Holcome Burnell in Devon.

1843: 22 March. John Peter Benson, Exeter College, Oxon (son-in-law and stepson of W.P. Thomas). Patron – W.P. Thomas on his resignation.

1876: 26 January. Prockter Melhuish Benson, MA, Oxon (son of J.P. Benson) on the death of J.P. Benson. Patron – Mary Melhuish Benson.

1893: 7 June. John Peter Benson, MA, Exeter College, Oxon (brother of P.M. Benson). Patron – himself.

1921: 6 January. Mark William Melrose, MA, Oxon. Patron – Prebendary J.P. Benson of Bradford.

1925: 20 May. John Allen Scott Castlehow, BA, 1912, MA, 1916. Exhibitor of Selwyn College, Cambridge on the session of Melrose who became vicar of St Matthew's Exeter. Patron – Prebendary J.P. Benson of Bradford.

Revd Andrew Theodore Hugh Jones – 20 March 1966 – 16 January 1977, last service was Evensong and Presentation.

Revd W Reginald Hudson – Licencing Tuesday, 17th October 1978 – 30th July 1986. (Did a Burial Service Thursday 23rd October 1986 for a Mr Kenneth Albert Stone after he had retired.)

Revd Laurence Meering – Induction and Institution at 7.30pm on 30th April 1987. Last Service 3rd July 1994.

Revd Vernon Ross – Licenced 12 November 1994. Last service 30th July 2000.

Revd John Hanna – Induction and Institution on 3rd August 2002. In post in 2003.

Map made for the purpose of illustrating the boundaries of the ancient borough of Witheridge. Made from the 6in. OS map on information given in 1937 by Mr H.H. Churchill. Starting from the two houses on the main Tiverton Road called Providence Place, along the north side of the orchard until a hedge is reached which continues the line of Fulford Water and Hole Lake to the river. Then down the river to a point where a continuous line of hedge begins, which runs south-eastwards to the starting point at Providence.

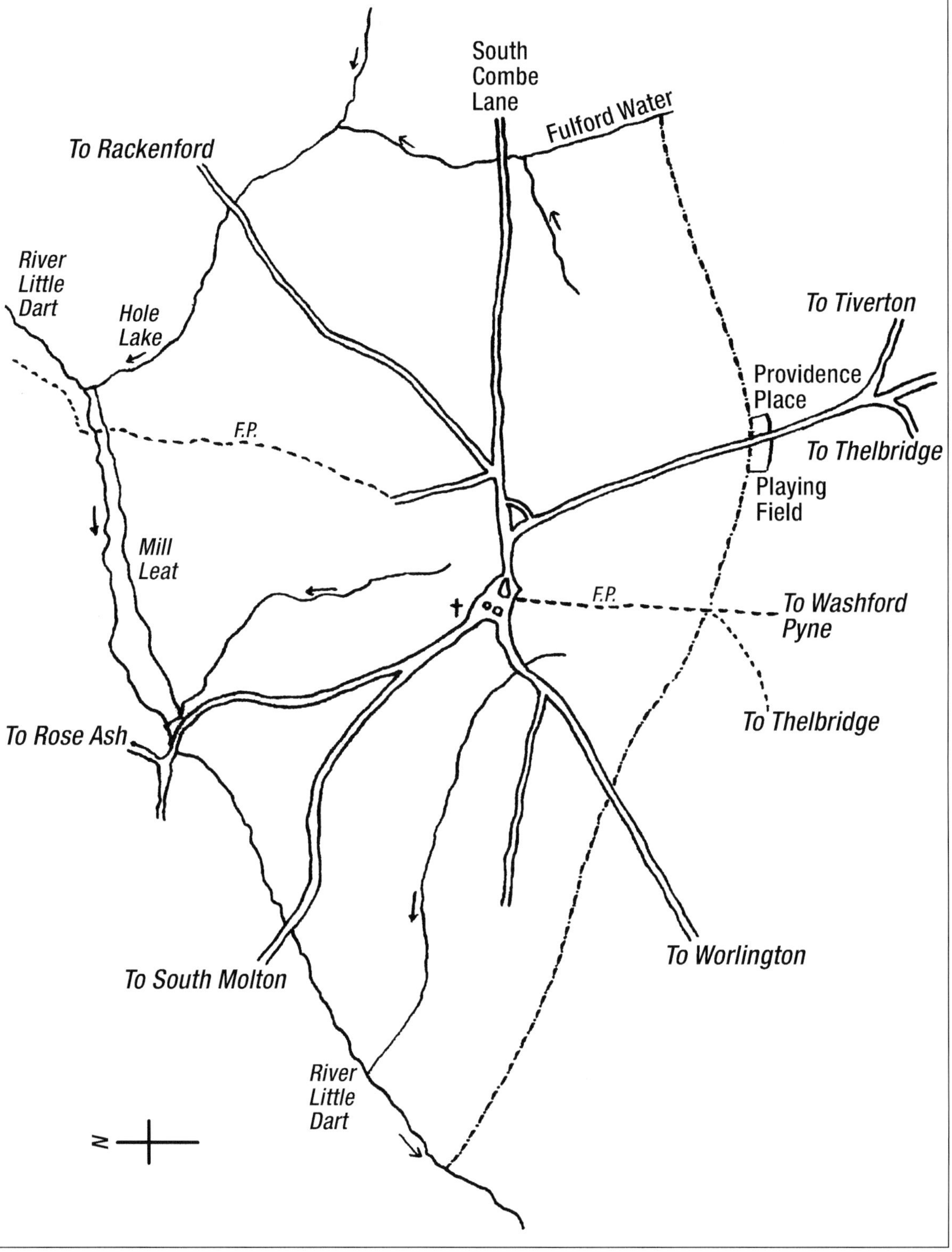

South Combe Lane

Fulford Water

To Rackenford

To Tiverton

River Little Dart

Hole Lake

Providence Place

To Thelbridge

F.P.

Playing Field

Mill Leat

F.P.

To Washford Pyne

To Thelbridge

To Rose Ash

To Worlington

To South Molton

River Little Dart

N

STORIES REVEALED BY THE LATE REVD J.A.S. CASTLEHOW

A Witheridge couple, Henry le Hoper and his wife Agatha, were arrested at Chulmleigh after stealing goods. They were put in prison there, but killed their gaoler while he slept at night. They escaped and Henry sought sanctuary in St Mary's Cheldon, confessed and abjured the realm. His chattels were worth 9s.5d. His wife Agatha fled and was outlawed. She had no chattels.

(*The Pleas of the Crown of Exeter Assize No. 175*, 1243–44, during the reign of Henry III.)

The murder of a Chulmleigh jailer, 1243.

In 1280 Bradford Tracy was the scene of a remarkable murder case, in which two women, Alice and Margery, combined to kill Alice's husband. They were tried and found guilty. Margery was hanged. Alice was sentenced to be burnt, but accomplices helped her to escape from Exeter Prison and take sanctuary in Heavitree Church.

George Southcombe from Rose Ash was a constable of the Hundred of Witheridge. He was riding his colt to Witheridge Fair on midsummer's day when he came upon two men fighting with swords. He tried to intervene and call for peace, but his colt reared and threw him and he was killed. He was buried at Rose Ash on 27 June 1595.

(*Devon Transactions Vol. XXXII*, Rose Ash.)

THE PARISH & THE BOROUGH

The parish of Witheridge is smaller today in area than it has been at any time in its history before 1890. At the time of the Domesday Book in 1086 Witheridge included Templeton, a large area now part of Thelbridge, as well as two small areas (comprising Yeatheridge and Little Witheridge) now incorporated into Worlington. The part of Thelbridge included two cottages at Nomansland, Menchine, Eastway, Westway, Woodington, Henceford, Stourton, Marchweek, Hele Lane and a cottage at Canns Mill. Templeton achieved independence in the fifteenth

century and the other parts were reassigned in 1885.

The Domesday Book used the name 'Wiriga', but there were 28 variations in all before the present spelling was agreed in the nineteenth century. Most authorities agree that the name derives from 'ridge of the wethers', stemming from the fact that the village lies at the end of a ridge (and there are still plenty of sheep in the parish). The Revd J.A.S. Castlehow identified 12 manors in the old parish, in addition to the manor of Witheridge itself; he never identified the site of a Witheridge manor-house. In 1248 King Edward I granted to Robert Fitzpaine, lord of the manor, the right to hold a weekly market on Wednesdays and a yearly fair 'on the vigil, feast and morrow of the Nativity of St John the Baptist.' In 1274 this was confirmed, together with the right of free warren, right of gallows and assize of bread and ale. The title lord of the manor passed through various families, including the Chichesters, the Fellows (earls of Portsmouth) and the Luxmoors. In the 1980s the title was sold at auction.

No information is available regarding how Witheridge became a borough. Revd Castlehow believed it came about through the connection of Witheridge with the Duchy of Lancaster. There was no borough here in 1316; the first reference occurs in 1499 and later references have been found from 1540, 1555, 1561, 1585, 1602, 1631. Revd Castlehow, referring to the year 1755, wrote that 'at that time the Borough enjoyed the common privileges of the Duchy of Lancaster, viz. exemptions from Tolls and Customs at Fairs and Markets etc.' He noted that in 1755 William Chapple had written:

The present lord of the first manor and borough of Witheridge is Coulson Fellowes Esq, in whose Court Leet the Portreece and other officers of the borough are appointed and sworn.

White's Directory of 1850 spoke of Witheridge as 'anciently a borough governed by a portreeve, with a weekly market disused before 1774.' Revd Castlehow believed that the bounds of the borough, not the parish, were formerly beaten. He included a map with his notes (opposite).

Since boroughs thrived on trade, it is possible that with the successful boroughs of South Molton and Tiverton only ten miles west and east respectively, there was not enough trade to sustain a Witheridge borough.

WITHERIDGE & THE CANNINGTON CONNECTION

In the twelfth century the Fitzpaines were an enterprising family who acquired great landholdings in the South West, particularly in Devon, Somerset and Dorset. Some places still carry the family name, such as Cheriton Fitzpaine. The family held the

Robert FitzPayne
(1225–1281)

1225   Robert born.

1227   Robert's father Roger dies.

1238   Order to Robert's free tenants to contribute to the marriage of his sister.
Robert's mother, Margery, to pay back £66.13s.4d. that King Henry III allowed her for keeping her husband's lands.

1241   Gift from the King to Robert's mother of six fallow bucks and two does to stock her park of Poole Keynes in Wiltshire.

1242   Robert holds **Witheridge** from the heirs of William Brewer, in return for 60s. when required.

1244   The King, on the insistence of Robert, pardons the inhabitants of **Witheridge** for letting Roger Caillewe, a thief, escape.

1245   The Treasury ordered to pay 12s. to buy a silken cloth to place in St Katherine's Chapel at Westminster for the soul of Robert's daughter.

1246   Robert comes of age.

1248   The King gives Robert three bucks from Braydon Forest in Wiltshire.
Grant to Robert and his heirs of free warren in **Witheridge** manor, and of a weekly market on Wednesdays, and an annual fair on the vigil, feast and morrow of the Nativity of St John the Baptist.

1249   The King gives a tun of wine to Robergia, Robert's wife, and a stag from the park at Purbeck.

1252   Robert goes on a pilgrimage to Santiago de Compostela in northern Spain – the burial place of St James the Apostle.
The sheriff of Devon ordered to pay Robert's wife £3.6s.8d. to buy herself a palfrey.

1254   Protection given to Robert who is going with the Queen on her journey to join the King in south-west France.

1256   Robert summoned to fight against the Welsh.

1281   Robert died holding Stoke-in-Teignhead, Cove and Mere and **Witheridge** in Devon, as well as lands in Dorset, Somerset and Wiltshire.

Information taken from the publications of the Public Record Office.

Compiled by Michael Sampson BA (Hons)

manor of Witheridge and Robert Fitzpaine was granted a charter to hold a midsummer fair for the village in 1248. This Robert was the son of Roger, who died shortly before 1237. There followed a succession of Roberts and it is difficult to distinguish their individual dates, but in 1299 the family was raised to the peerage and became the Lords Fitzpaine. Shortly after this they acquired the lands and properties, which had belonged to the de Courci family of Stoke Courci (now Stogursey) in Somerset. This land included the nearby manor of Cannington, where, in 1138, Robert de Courci had founded a small nunnery and endowed it with 3 acres of arable land and 3 acres of meadow. The 'foundership' of a religious house became part of the estate and became the 'property' of either his heirs or future purchasers or grantees. In this way, the Fitzpaines became founders of the Convent of Blessed Virgin Mary, to give it its full title, although it is often referred to in documents of the period as Cannington Priory.

A Robert, probably grandson of the first Robert, is mentioned in several documents connected with the convent, in particular with reference to matters concerning the election, appointment and installation of a prioress from 1317 to 1336. Election procedures were very strictly laid down – in a 'secret ballot', with each member of the community giving a verbal vote privately to the adjudicator. Two elections were held in 1317 because the legality of the first procedure was contested.

In 1326 Robert sought, and was granted, the permission of the King to purchase 24 acres of land in

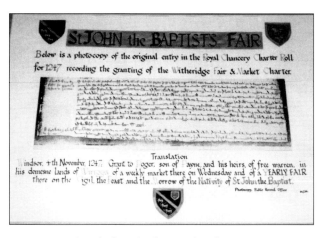

St JOHN the BAPTISTS FAIR

Below is a photocopy of the original entry in the Royal Chancery Charter Roll for 1247 recording the granting of the Witheridge Fair & Market Charter.

Translation

...indsor, 4 th November 1247. Grant to ...oger, son of ...ayne, and his heirs, of free warren, in his demesne lands of ... of a weekly market there on Wednesday and of a YEARLY FAIR there on the ...igil, the feast and the ...orrow of the Nativity of St John the Baptist.

St John's Fair charter dated 1247.

Cannington and Radweye. This 'gift' was made to support a chaplain to celebrate Mass every day for the good of his souls, the souls of his ancestors and inheritors, and all the faithful departed. It added to the wealth of the priory, but not to that of the nuns who were responsible for ensuring that the terms of the gift were faithfully executed. The community, like many others, had considerable wealth for which they were responsible, but much of it was for specific purposes and could never be used for 'living expenses'. The nuns made vows of poverty, chastity and obedience; indeed, they had little option but to keep the first. Sometimes they received small personal bequests, but very often it is recorded that they were excused paying taxes because they were so poor.

The Lords Fitzpaine did not survive for very long, for the last Lord Robert died in 1354 leaving no male heir. His only daughter was his heiress and she took all the lands to her marriage with John de Chidiok who became the new founder of the convent. It is said that during the period immediately before Robert's death the Black Death had raged through the country causing the demise of around a quarter of the population. Everywhere was in disarray and even at the convent discipline broke down. Robert had been required to help restore order and the Bishop attended a hearing when the disobedient nuns were disciplined. The prioress herself was also held to account for granting Corrodies. This was a kind of 'get rich quick' insurance policy whereby for a one-off payment, a non-religious woman would be allowed to live with the community for life. The fact that such events took place point to the extent of desperation felt by these women – not only was it against the law, but it also reveals the level of chaos and shortage of food caused by the Black Death (much farmland remained neglected because of a lack of labour). It was shortly after this that the heiress of Robert, through her husband, made a gift of 12d. of rents in Witheridge. The priory was also granted the advowson of the Church, which allowed it to present suitable prospective incumbents to the bishop. The advowson brought with it obligations to defend the rights of the Church. This gift must have come as a great relief as well as being a significant boost to morale.

The first rector recorded as being presented by the priory is Robert Crosse. He had only been in the village for a year when he asked if he might change places with Henry de Lutton, the vicar of Spaxton (near Bridgwater). He described the parish as 'large and widespread' and said that he found 'the cure of Witheridge great and onerous', which he could not rule according to his conscience because of the diverse occupations he had with the Bishop of Bath and Wells. Henry de Lutton's reason for accepting the post was not so much from a desire to move to a 'large and widespread' parish, as to get away from his next-door neighbour. He said he was in dispute with Lord James de Audelegh over a land matter and he 'dare not pursue the case while in the neighbourhood by reason of his (Audelegh's) deadly hatred' for him. Ralph of Shrewsbury, Bishop of Bath and Wells, agreed to the exchange and the matter was duly recorded in the bishop's register. The exchange took place during the Feast of the Conversion of St Paul, 25 January 1362, both vicars being instituted in their new parishes on the same day. Parson Henry de Lutton remained at Witheridge until 1379 when he exchanged again, this time with Edmund Demalmeshulle, rector of Stormough, Kent. There followed a succession of rectors of whom we know little except their names.

Cannington lies a short distance from the estuary of the River Parrett and most of the village and convent lands lay close to the flood plain. In 1427 disaster overtook the area when it was engulfed by high tides and floods, which took away much of the priory land. Consequently the pope was petitioned for more and in 1428 lands were granted in Witheridge. This part of the village became known as Witheridge-Cannington, the rest being Witheridge-Bradford. The fact that the pope and bishop were concerned with the grant would indicate that the lands were already Church property. To ensure that the vicar received sufficient funds from the lands to fulfil his obligations to the Church and support himself, the bishop set out in great detail which land belonged to the nunnery and which to the vicar. From this document we learn something of the agriculture of the time. The vicar received the tithes of beans, peas and apples growing in the ancient gardens, the tithe of coppice wood and that of calves, colts, lambs, suckling pigs, kids, geese, pigeons, eggs, wool, milk, cheese and butter, plus flax and hemp growing in the ancient gardens. The document also describes the boundaries of the lands, but without a map it is difficult to understand. We do know, however, that he was to have 'the dovecote within the garden' and a 'certain meadow of one acre

19

at the upper end of which a certain fishpond is situated'. The house in which the vicar lived was known as the manse; the Vicarage was not simply a building but rather all the lands, gardens and tithes which were assigned to him to enable him to support himself and carry out various Church obligations. The document endowing the nunnery with the Witheridge lands and setting out the conditions, was signed and sealed by the prioress, Johanna Childeldon, in her Chapter House at the priory on 16 December 1428 and by the bishop three days later.

The guide books for the churches at Witheridge and Cannington suggest that both buildings were rebuilt in the fifteenth century. On the outside they look very different – Witheridge is built from the grey bedrock stone that befits a rugged, upland parish. The present tower was not an original feature, as it was not begun until 1574. There might have been a tower attached to the previous building, but it was not retained. At Cannington the new building was added to the existing tower. The church is constructed of local red sandstone. Inside the churches there are similarities. In each there are two arcades of arches, five on each side at Cannington and four at Witheridge. The Cannington arches are taller and more slender, but the carving on the capitals does not bear comparison with the fine and beautiful work at Witheridge. Each church has a single spanned roof that covers both nave and aisle, and all ceilings contain many carved wooden bosses.

By 1440 the priory had another founder, Robert Poynings. His family badge appears on the new work on the church at Cannington, so he must have been responsible for some of the rebuilding along with the prioress. She would also have been informed about progress at Witheridge through the vicar and her steward. In the document defining the Vicarage the vicar was charged with the responsibility of 'the continued repair of the church and if need shall so require shall restore and rebuild the same.' However, this did not negate the obligations of the patrons of 'charitable giving to the church and embellishing and expanding its fabric.' The vicar then, as now, would have been into 'fundraising'; money would come in from bequests, thanksgiving offerings, individuals, guilds and communities such as the priory. There were also 'church ales', which were medieval versions of the church fête, but were not quite so genteel – they 'brewed up' ale instead of tea.

Although the priory had an interest in the rebuilding of both churches, it is unlikely that any of the nuns would have seen Witheridge. They were enclosed in their own part of the monastery and needed the bishop's permission to leave the outer wall that surrounded it. Their main work was prayer, but many activities went on within the outer walls – there were barns and workshops, houses for workers and guest-houses for travellers. The nuns were an integral part of the society of the time.

The last appointed prioress was Cecilia Verney in 1504. She came from a very religious family; her uncle, Alexander Verney was a vicar , as was was her brother George. In addition, her niece, Joan, was a nun at Buckland Mynchyn near Taunton. In 1521 she presented her brother George to the living at Witheridge, a position which he held for the rest of his life. In 1536 the Dissolution of the small monasteries took place. A survey of the values of all the religious houses throughout the land, the Valor Ecclesiasticus, had been compiled two years earlier, and now all those with a value of less than £200 were forcibly closed.

It appears that members of the community at the time of the Dissolution were given the option of leaving penniless or moving to a larger, surviving house; prioresses were the only ones to receive pensions at this stage. The nuns of Cannington were said to have gone to Shaftesbury Abbey, a most prestigious institution, and the names of some of them appear on later lists of the nuns there. Cecilia Verney is not one of them, so she might have died before the final list was drawn up, or gone to Fairfield in Stogursey to her younger brother, or even moved to Witheridge to stay with George. Two of the nuns, Dorothy Cooke and Radegund Tilley had the same surnames as tenants of Cannington Priory and might well have been local girls; they went to Polsloe Priory in Exeter as their names are on the pension list of that house. Their humble origins probably forced them to go to Polsloe either because they were not acceptable at Shaftesbury or they might have felt out of place there.

The two Cannington nuns at Polsloe kept the link of Witheridge with monasticism alive for two extra years. The word 'mynchym' was a medieval word for nun; no explanation is forthcoming as to its origin. In some places it still remains, in a corrupted form, such as at Polsloe where it has changed over the years and become 'mincing'. A stream running alongside the boundary of what was the priory is still called Mincing Lake (lake being an old word for stream). In Witheridge it became Menchine and the land held by Polsloe is now Menchine Farm.

The last link with the priory was the vicar, George Verney. He remained vicar throughout the reigns of Henry VIII, Catholic Mary and Protestant Edward VI, but died four years into the reign of Good Queen Bess. He died in 1562 after 41 years in office unmarried and highly respected. He did not hold office quite so long as the vicar of Morebath, from whose writing we learn so much about a country parson of the time. Nevertheless, he must have given the parish a sense of security in very changing times as well as a continuity which carried it through from the end of the medieval period into a new age.

Pilton Priory bells were brought to Witheridge in 1540.

DISSOLUTION OF THE MONASTERIES

The Dissolution brought one bonus to Witheridge. In the late 1530s priory, abbey and monastery property was sold off. It is known that the 'five bells of Barnstaple' were bought by a John Stephens of Witheridge. It has been suggested that the religious house for Cluniac monks was the source of these bells. John Stephens paid over the going rate for them, so it is unlikely that they were a speculation. The probability is that he gave them to the church at Witheridge; indeed the church certainly had five bells by 1552. John Stephens was a man of strong traditional views, for in 1549 he took up arms for the old Catholic religion as part of the Prayer Book Rebellion, which began in Sampford Courtenay. John was 'killed in the Rebellyon Time', probably at the Clist Heath Battle near Exeter in the August of that year, when the rebellion was crushed.

The five bells were replaced in 1754. A bell was added in 1800 and two further bells came in 1889. All were rehung in 1926.

WITHERIDGE, TEMPLETON & THE GREAT PESTILENCE OF 1348–49

The two orders of knighthood established in the aftermath of the early Crusades had very different fates. The Knights Hospitallers of St John continue today, whereas the Knights Templars lost sight of their original noble aims and became so worldly that they were dissolved by papal order in 1312. It is thought that Templeton was named after the Knights Templars. At the time of the Dissolution some lands became the property of the Knights Hospitallers and among the evidence given to an inquiry in 1440 by Bishop Lacy was a statement that the prior of the Hospital of St John of Jerusalem gave the Chapel of Templeton to a clerk by the name of Thomas Coggerstone. Several witnesses affirmed that the

The Black Death: corpses from Templeton, 1248.

chapel hamlet and domain was within the bounds and limits of Witheridge Parish. One witness was sure that the Chapel of Templeton was 'dependent on the Mother Church of Witheridge' and that the Witheridge incumbent received both great and small tithes from Templeton. No less than ten local clergy confirmed this view, supported by two laymen. John Webber of Witheridge said he had his information from a John Certyn, who had been born in Witheridge in 1322 and had lived 100 years! The other lay witness was John Palfreyman (born in Witheridge in 1368) who said that burials of Templeton people in Witheridge was confirmed by a story he had heard from his father. It seems that at the time of the 'Great Pestilence' of 1348–49, the then rector of Witheridge, William Wyngave, sent his servants with a cart to collect the bodies of those killed by the plague in Templeton and carry them to Witheridge for interment. When they returned they realised that one corpse must have fallen off en route as a result of the cart being overfilled. A William Atteybere was sent off next day to search for it and bring it back, which he did, 'and had for his pains one penny'.

The chapel was confirmed to the vicar of Witheridge by a deed of 1428. In 1439, however, a pretended foreign bishop had consecrated a burial-ground around the chapel at Templeton and introduced an Irish curate. Bishop Lacy's 1440 Inquiry found the 'foreign bishop's actions unlawful' and annulled them. The people of Templeton had enjoyed their independence from Witheridge and when Richard Melhuish came to remove a corpse, he found two graves dug, one inside and one outside Templeton's chapel. In the face of what he described as 'the excessive violence of the inhabitants' he returned to Witheridge empty handed. At some time between 1440 and 1542 Templeton received its own parochial rights and was free of Witheridge.

THE DUCHY OF LANCASTER

Neither Revd Castlehow or John Benson were able to clarify how the relationship between Witheridge and the Duchy of Lancaster began. The court rolls tell us that, in addition to the manor and hundred courts, a Duchy of Lancaster court was held in Witheridge from 1396 to 1624. The court continued from there and the last reference occurred in *White's Directory* of 1850, although no records survive. Below are some examples of the cases which the duchy court heard:

1396: *The bailiff presents that John Fattecote broke pinfold and said that he led away a horse and was therefore attached.* [John's horse had strayed and been put in the village pound ('pinfold') but John had broken in and taken his horse away and hence was arrested, or 'attached'.]

1396: *William Geffray and John Thomas sought of Thomas Shourte on a plea of trespass separately, who is attached for one ox and is distrained.* [Thomas was not only arrested but his ox was seized and held to ensure that he paid his fine.]

1413: *William Ellis and the bailiff in mercy because they did not produce John Westlake on the complaint of Thomas Sergey in a plea of debt and let them be distrained.* [Here the bailiff is in trouble for not doing his job. The court ordered that goods of his be seized to force him to pay his fine.]

Breaking into the pound, 1396.

1413: A bad year for the Witheridge bailiff – he was fined on 38 occasions for not doing his job, his fines for the year totalling 5s. and 7d., a big sum at that time.

1443: *Henry Denys executing the will of Matilda Yeaminstor sought of Roger Hayward in a plea of debt, who did not come and the bailiff did not distrain him, therefore in mercy, let him be distrained.* [This was another poor year for the bailiff, who often failed to get the accused into court, even though he had the power to 'distrain' them (to force them by seizing their belongings). In this instance, Henry was Matilda's executor and found that Roger owed her money. Roger did not turn up and the bailiff was at fault because he failed to compel him to do so.]

1443: The clerk of the parish, Robert Baker, was also in bother. The court ordered that he be arrested after William Coll and John Salter accused him of trespass.

1555: *Wutherygge Turn of our Lord the King and our Lady the Queen of their Duchy of Lancaster held there the 15th day of October the year above name. The tithing man* [the head of the borough] *came and presented all things well... The bailiff came there and presented that William Crosse assaulted Stephen Diener, and that Walter Symons sold wine and that Thomas Grenyslade sold cider and they are in mercy... The free tenants came there and presented all things well.* [Being 'in mercy' meant they were guilty and liable. William and Thomas were fined 3d. each but Walter's wine-selling offence was considered more serious so his fine was 6d. The free tenants paid rent only and were not liable for other services. Among the 15 names listed are several familiar even in 2003: Gibbings, Vicary, Ware, Jordan, Hodge, Mogridge, Symons, Downey and Hooper.]

1561: *The bailiff came there and presented that Ralph Hernaman, Richard Forde and Thomas Downey tapped cider by false measure. They are in mercy.* [They were guilty and fined 2d. each.]

The Revd Castlehow unearthed these lists. They are included here because after over 400 years a number of the names are still commonplace, either as family names (Wall, Stevens, Thorne, Oxenham, Vicary, Crooke, Southwood, Partridge) or as house or farm names (Grendon, Thorne, Ford, Mill, Cobley, Lashbrook). A neighbouring parish appears in the form of Agneta Thelbrygge (Thelbridge) although the is no mention of a Witheridge. It is strange that in spite of all the efforts of the worldwide Witheridge Family History Society, it has never been able to place any in the parish itself, although there is a Witheridge family in the South West today.

Plovers Barrows, West Street. This cruck house dates from the fifteenth or sixteenth century.

Inside Plovers Barrows, West Street.

THE PROTESTATION RETURN FOR WITHERIDGE, 1641

On 21 April 1641 the House of Commons passed a Bill for the Attainder of the Earl of Strafford, a friend of King Charles. There were rumours in London that the King might try to use the Army to overawe the Commons; he had already attempted to occupy the Tower of London. On 3 May John Pym told the House that it should remind the King that he must maintain

1543 Lay Subsidy Roll

Leonard S...	Thomas Melhuyshe	William Tanner
John Upcott	Andrew Gybyns	John Dodderyg
Robert Uppynton	Thomas Nycoll	Richard Wall
Walter Towke	John Grendn	Richard Stevyns
John Ware	Hugh Melhuyse	George C...
Richard Thorn	Richard Wear	Richard Ford
Roger Chastey	John Lot...	John Downe
Thomas Thorne	Marye Gover	Richard Tanner
John Hoyge	John Glasse	Ralph Po...
Richard Thomas	John Bremelcomb	Willymot Orchard
Laurence Vikery	Julian Adams	Robert Smalrygge
Walter Crugge	Thomas Radford	Agneta Thelbrygge
George Condy	Martin Condy	Thomasine Condy
Agneta Condy	William, H. Ren	John C...
William Oxenham	Thomas Drab	Thomas Myll
John Pateryg	John Callanie	John Smyth
John Hoyge	William Vikery?	Philip Coddyston
Robert Down	Mathew Bremelcomb	John Upcott
Thomasina Crown	John Herton	John ...
John ...	John Cro...	Richard Cro...
John ...yerd	William Hoyge	John Pare
... Bremelcomb	Richard ...	Elizabeth ...
John Downe de ...	Hugh Downe	Thomas Tanner

Lay Subsidy Roll Henry VIII

John Mersh pro bonus suis		10s.	0d.	John Dodderidge	do	10s.	0d.
Thomas Melhuish	do	12s.	6d.	Thomas Rockes ?		10s.	0d.
Thomas Tanner	do	10s.	0d.	Richard Wall		10s.	0d.
William Tanner	do	10s.	0d.	John Upcott		10s.	0d.

1591 Lay Subsidy Roll 34 Eliz Terrarum Tax

Thomas Melhuish gen	£12.16s.	Laurence Zelleman	20s.
Wm Walle	40s.	John Vicary	40s.
Jn Crooke	£3.4d.	John Cobley	40s.
Chris Southwood	20s.16d.	Wm Cokerham	20s.
Leonard Holle	40s.	Jn Trixie	20s.
Jn Crudge	20s.	Hugo Thomas	40s.
Jn Chilladon	20s.	John Hopper	20s.
Jn Cade	20s.	Rich Partridge	40s.
George Tanner	20s.	Thos Nott	
Thos Notte	20s.	Wm Frost	
Jas Stofforde ?	£3	Alexander Marrish (Norrish) ?	
Leonard Partridge	£3	D Uppington	

BONORUM

James Broughton	Jn Gibbins	Eliz Uppington wid
Philip Bowden	Jas Hamley	George Tanner
William Mayre	George Chilcotte	Thomas ...ersen
Rob Upcott	Philip Southwell	Wm Lellande ?
Jn Rowe	Rich Thomas	Robert Laishbrooke
Johan Radford wid	Joha Lillande ?	Johan Tanner
Thomas Gryndon	Thomas Uppington	

---

the law. Consequently, a committee of ten members drew up a Protestation, signed by all the present members of the House of Lords. Its main points were to defend the reformed Protestant religion and:

... maintain and defend His Majesty's Royal Person, Honour and Estate, as well as the Powers and Privileges of Parliament and the lawful Rights and Liberties of the subjects and every person that maketh this Protestation.

On 6 May a Bill was introduced that obliged all Englishmen to sign the Protestation. The Lords rejected it but the Commons won the day, so in January 1642 copies were sent to county sheriffs with a letter of instruction. Sheriffs were reminded of the serious situation caused, a few days before, by the King's attempt to arrest five MPs. Every male of 18 years and up was to be urged to accept the Protestation. Names of those accepting, and of those refusing, were noted and full returns made to Parliament.

For Witheridge 141 names were recorded by the same hand(s) – possibly the vicar and his clerk. The following nine signed their names themselves: William Tyler, vicar; James Thomas, constable; Christopher Partridge, constable; Richard Thomas, churchwarden; John Bidgood, churchwarden; Richard Burne, overseer; Richard Cockeram, overseer; Edward Phillips, overseer; William Parkhouse, overseer. No refusals were recorded. In August 1642 the Civil War began.

A rough estimate of the size of Witheridge's population in 1642 can be made by multiplying the number of names by four; this gives a population of 600. Among the names in the list of Witheridge men are a number that are still in use today, such as Beare, Bidgood and Blackmore, Cockeram and Crooke. The Grindon/Grendon family took their name from the farms of that name. Greenslade has been one of the most commonly occurring names for over 340 years. There have been recent Heards and Hills, and the Hodges gave their name to Hodges Tenement, which was pulled down to make room for the Mitre. The Lashbrooke name is still attached to a house in North Street, while the Melhuishes were prominent as vicars, landowners and founders of the Church School. Nott, Parker and Partridge are familiar to us and the Shortridges were also vicars and landowners. Southwood, Sowden and Thomas have made their mark, as have Tucker, Western and Whitfield.

THE PROTESTATION RETURN FOR DEVON, 1641

Some men did not sign the Protestation themselves:

(Westerne, John, Westerne, John and Westerne, Thomas). Richard Maunder being sick took and acknowledged the protestation the same day and year at home in his bed before Andrew Hosegood, constable and John Waterman, churchwarden. George Waterman being sick and within the compass of this order did acknowledge the protestation in the presence of Andrew Hosegood, constable and John Waterman, churchwarden.

Others signed it themselves: John Radford, parson; Andrew Hosegoode, constable; John Waterman, churchwarden; John Maunder, overseer.

Protestation Return, Witheridge Parish

Atkins, Thomas	Averie, Robert gent.	Baron, Mark
Battin, John	Beare, Roger	Bidgood, George
Blackmore, Gregory	Blackmore, William	Bounser, Alexander
Browne, Edward	Cade, James	Canne, Robert
Chilcott, Andrew	Chilcott, James	Chilcott, John
Chilcott, Richard	Chilcott, William	Cobley, William
Cockeran, George	Cockerham, Henry	Cockeram, John
Cockeram, Laurence	Cockeram, William	Crocker, Robert
Crooke, John	Crooke, William	Didgett, George
Donkins, Christopher	Dove, William	Downey, William
Downishe, Thomas	Dyer, Stephen	Ellis, Richard
Ford, Lewis	Garnesey, John	Gater, John
Gater, Robert	Gater, Thomas	Gibbons, William
Gosse, Samuel	Gosse, William	Grantland, Peter
Gregorie, Richard	Grindon, John	Grindon, Thomas
Grindon, William	Grinslade, Abraham	Grinslade, Alexander
Grinslade, Gilbert	Grinslade, Hugh	Grinslade, John
Grinslade, Lewis	Grinslade, Nathaniel	Grinslade, Robert
Grinslade, Thomas	Hagley, George	Hanger, Richard
Heard, Hugh	Heard, Hugh	Hill, John
Hill, Thomas	Hodge, Jerman	Hodge, John
Hodge, Philip	Hodge, Thomas	Hodge, William
Holmes, John	Kelland, Thomas	Lashbrooke, Robert
Mapery, Elias	Mapery, John	Melhuish, Hugh gent.
Melhuish, Robert gent.	Melhuish, Thomas gent	Milton, John
Molland, Robert	Molland, Thomas	More, Walter
Morrishe, John	Norton, Robert	Nott, James
Nott, John	Nott, Philip	Oake, Matthew
Oxeland, Humphrey	Parker, Robert	Patridge [sic], John
Partridge, Peter	Paule, Richard	Perrie, John
Phillippes, Giles	Pine, Giles	Plaice, Robert
Radford, John	Radford, Lewis	Radford, Richard
Radford, Stephen	Richards, John	Rod, Robert
Samson, John	Shilladon, Richard	Short, Thomas
Shorte, George	Shorte, Henry	Shortridge, Richard gent.
Skinner, George	Skinner, John	Small, William senr
Small, William junr	Southwood, Thomas	Sowden, Philip
Sowdon, Augustine	Stempson, George	Stemson, George junr
Stemston, John	Thomas, Andrew	Thomas, Hugh
Thomas, Nicholas	Thomas, Philip	Thomas, Philip
Thresher, Joseph	Thresher, Mark	Thresher, Thomas
Toake, William	Tolley, John	Tolley, Matthew
Tolley, Roger	Tracy, David	Tracy, Hugh
Tracy, Walter	Trix, Philip	Tucker, John
Upcott, Hugh	Upcott, Thomas	Vicarie, Alexander
Vicarie, William	Vicary, John	Wall, John
Waterman, William	Westerne, Richard	Whitfield, John

The above names were all written in the same hand, whereas the following nine were signatures.

William Tyler, vicar	James Thomas, constable	Christopher Partridge, constable
Richard Thomas, churchwarden	John Bidgood, churchwarden	Richard Burne, overseer
Richard Cockeram, overseer	Edward Phillips, overseer	William Parkhouse, overseer

Church Property

Although kept in the Devon Record Office with Terriers, the following document is actually a hand-over between churchwardens.

Witheridge: This Bill indented by John Holland and Nicolas Thomas, churchwarden in the ? Year of the reign of our most ? Sovereign lord King James 1613 of all the bookes and implements pertaining to the church ? Witheridge and delivered by and from John Partridge and William Tanner, churchwardens, for ? ?

Item a bibell booke 2 communion bookes 1 booke of Jewell* and Harding 2 bookes of homilies 1 booke for the fifth of August**
Item 2 surplesses 1 covering for the table and a tablecloth 1 cloth for ye pulpit
Item 1 pawle 1 communion cup of silver with a cover 1 quart of pewter
Item 1 chest with 3 lockes and kaies and 2 other chest for the keeping of our bookes and surplesses.
Money given to the poor forever by Hugh Attwill clerk 30s., Hugh Ellworthie 15s., Thomas Cruwys 20s.

*Bishop Jewell was Bishop of Salisbury in Elizabeth's reign.
**No explanation of this from the Record Office.

To the right Worll Mr Doctor Goche, Chancellor of the Diocess of Exon.
Whereas John Bidgood of Witheridge, is summoned to apeere at your Consistory, by reason of a presentment exhibited against him by one Thomas Farrant of Washford, these are to certify your Worshippe that wee whose names are subscribed doe beeleeve that hee is presented rat... out of spleene and malice, than of just deserte.
Wherefore wee request your Worshippe (if you please) to dismisse him your Court soe will wee rest your Worshipps to bee commanded.

Witheridge – this 3rd day of May 1625.

Hugh Tollie	*John Partridge*
John Tollie	*Vincent Uppington*
John Parkhouse senr	*Thomas Thresher*
William Garnesey	*Thomas Gator*
James Thomas	*John Crooke*
William Tylor Cler	*John Greenslade*
Robert ...brooke	*Nicholas Thomas*
Richarde Burne	*George Mortymer*
John Haines	*Robert Melhuishe*
John Morrice	*William March*
Richard Radford	*John Hodge*
Hugh Mare	*Robert Bond*
Richard Chapman	

Hugh Stephens and Phillip Hodg – Churchwardens, the last yeer past
John Parkhous junr and John Sampson – Churchwardens

I Gyles Pyne of Wotheridge doe acknowledge and confesse myselfe to bee faulty in Ancinge the Churyard of Witheridge in the County of Devon by cartinge of Dungge into it for which I was presented at the last visitation of the Lord Bishopp of Exon the 24th of March 1624.

Christopher Wall	*Thomas Typper*
John Vicary	*Gyles Pyne*

THE CIVIL WAR

There was a taste of North Devon's Parliamentarian sympathies before the Civil War began. In the summer of 1640, 600 North Devon men had been unwillingly conscripted to join a Royal Army being formed to march north against the Scots. On 11 July a company passed through Tiverton on its way to Wellington, where it spent the night. The following day was a Sunday and some of the men noticed that one of their officers, a Lieutenant Evers, had not attended church. They at once suspected him of being a Catholic and angrily broke into his house, dragged him out and murdered him in the street. The men deserted and made their way back to their homes in North Devon, boasting of what they had done. Eventually a number of them were questioned or sought in connection with this crime. It has been established that nine came from Bishops Nympton and South Molton, while the remaining 12 came from the nearby parishes of Landkey, Chawleigh, West Anstey, Chittlehampton, Bishops Tawton, Oakford, Rackenford, Swimbridge and Witheridge.

In the light of this it is not surprising that, when two years later the Earl of Bath came to South Molton and attempted to publish the Royal Commission of Array (another form of conscription) he met opposition. A threatening crowd of 1,000 people quickly gathered and sent him and his supporters packing. South Molton's hostility continued into 1644 and 1645. Much of the rural areas felt the same. Mark Stoyle has written:

... what evidence that does survive suggests that the countrymen were every bit as Parliamentarian as their urban neighbours. There is evidence that in 1643 the inhabitants of many local parishes failed to attend the Royalist posse. The five communities that produced the largest number of defaulters included Bishops Nympton and Witheridge. In January 1646 the Constables of Cheldon, Kings Nympton, Worlington and Thelbridge were all noted as being 'ill-affected to His majesty's service'. It is likely that Witheridge was not far behind.

As the war and its effects swung through North Devon and back again, villages found themselves at the mercy of uncontrolled bands of horsemen on both sides. Cattle, sheep, poultry and crops were seized and the communities were left terrified. It is not surprising that a Witheridge inhabitant tried to hide his money until the troubles were over. What happened next is described by William Chapple in his response for Witheridge to the Milles Inquiry of the 1750s, a questionnaire sent to all Devon parishes:

There was a remarkable instance of the effects of a Damp in a well here in 1646. It seems the then troubles which rendered property precarious had induced one Walter Moore to hide a Bag of Money in this Well, which he fastened to a Pump-tree therein; after his death some Persons, having information of hid treasure, opened the pit and one of them went down in search thereof, but, staying longer than expected, was followed by another, and he for the same reason by a third; none returning, a fourth person (one Thomas Molland) was let down by a rope, who, falling off the ladder, was drawn up half dead and with difficulty recovered. And after having left the well sometime open for the air, they got up the dead bodies of the other three, as well as ye money that they went in quest of, which, they privately divided amongst themselves.

Three men died after treasure was found in a well, 1646.

The Parish Register (which I have seen) mentions the burial of these three persons in one day (viz. John Greenslade, Robert Greenslade, and John Whitfield) and it was from thence that I knew the year when it happened, which however is not material, as the whole can only serve to caution people against endangering their lives in such circumstances.

By 1645 there was growing discontent against roving undisciplined groups, from either side, whose only purposes seemed to be theft and destruction. This led to the creation of bands of Clubmen, dedicated to defending their local parishes from marauders, whether Royalist or Parliamentarian. Clubmen were active in the Barnstaple and South Molton areas, particularly against Royalist thugs, nominally commanded by Lord Goring. So badly did these marauders behave that in Molland Squire Courtney, a one-time supporter of the Crown became leader of the Molland Clubmen. Events so near at hand may well have had an effect on Witheridge.

In 1643 John Radford became vicar of Witheridge, on the presentation of Robert Melhuish. For some reason he was presented again the following year, when he also became vicar of Puddington. He had been vicar of Thelbridge since 1632. In 1650 Robert Melhuish presented Hugh Shortrudge. We are not told what happened to Radford.

Up to the 1640s the Witheridge registers averaged about 25 entries a year. However, the Civil War seems to have had some effect, as entries became rather erratic: in 1642–43 the churchwardens failed to sign them; there are only seven entries for 1644–45; there are two baptisms in September 1645 followed by the signatures of the wardens, one of which has been erased; there are no further entries until September 1646, from which date there are eight entries; there is no warden's signatures at the end of March 1647.

Rates for Reparation

A rate made for the reparation of the Parish Church of Witheridge in Devon, the eleventh day of May, Anno Domini 1682. Exeter Dioc. [Registry copied by Mr G.A.T. Fursdon.]

	£.s.d.
John Mills for Chipp walls	2d.
The occupier of East Horehill	1d.
John Cudde for Elsworthy	5d.
Mary Cockram for Malson	3d.
John Veysey for West Pilemoore	5d.
John Tristrum for East Pilmoore	3d.
Robert Avery gent for Stretchdon	1s.9d.
Matthew Tollye for Westcott	1s.10d.
John Graunt for Philip Nott for parte of Mill Toune	1½.
The occupier of the other part of Mill Toune	1½.
Laurence Davey Esq, for two parts of Heale	1s.7d.
Francis Radford for Yeatheridge	1s.10d.
James Partridge and Joane for Stirton and ...lete	1s.9d.
Robert Avery for Rensford	1s.6d.
George Maunder for Upcott	1s.5d.
Thomas Elsworthy for eight acres	1d.
John Heard for Moreparke	1½d.
Benjamin Bidgood for Woodlington	1s.0d.
Thomas Veale for part of do	3d.
John Hind... for moy of Minchin	7½d.
The occupier for the other parts of Minchin	7½d.
Mary Grant for Buttson	6d.
Andrew Thomas for moyetie of Westway	5½d.
William Thomas for moyetie of Westway	5½d.
Henry Quicke for moyetie of Eastway	5½d.
Thomas Partridge for other moy of do	5½d.
George Maunder for West Upcott	7d.
Peter Hole for part of Marchweeke	10d.
Thomas Elworthy for Shillison	4d.
Agnes Partridge for part of Hele	3d.
Peter Hole for part of Marchweek	3d.
John Chollice for parte of Hill	1½d.
Thomas Pridham for Northmoore	1½d.

Elizabeth Tolley for Stockeparke	2d.
Christopher Partridge for Berrie Cleave	1½d.
The occupier of Rondon	4d.
Lewes Nott for Foxton	9½d.
Richard Elsworthy for Downey	9½d.
Edmund Gridmore for West Hostone	1s.0d.
The occupier of East Hostone	10d.
The occupier of Hole	10d.
John Parkhouse senr for Yeo	10d.
Thomas Walter for Bythem	10d.
Richard Cockram for Southcombe	9d.
Jonathon Holmes for Lashbrooke house and ground	½d.
The occupier of Venbridge	1½
John Simpson for Lateland	9d.
Thomas Burne for Durt Ground	4d.
Andrew Thomas for Fridayes Close	6d.
William Greenslade for moy of Hodges	3d.
Richard Thomas for do	3d.
George Moore for Broome House	2d.
John Parkhouse senr for Trucies Green and Durt Close	2d.
John Parkhouse senr for Vixen Meadow	4d.
Richard Greenslade for ye Barton Ground	8d.
Richard Thomas for Witheridge Mill	8d.
John May for Ford	2d.
Richard Moore for Fords	2d.
Williams Stephens for his tenement in toune	3d.
John Muxerie for Woodparke	2d.
John May for Whitteridge Cannaton	2d.
Richard Parkhouse for Bonds	2d.
John Parkhouse senr for ye dounes	1½d.
John Vicarie for his house and ground	½d.
John Touke for Southwoods	2d.
Charitie Greenslade for Penford	1d.
Thomas Molland for Shippinghay	1d.
Thomas Atkins for Grabpark	1d.
Richard Partridge for Ellis	1½d.
Henry Quicke for Netherlittleburne	1d.
John Warren and Edward Bodley for Guters	1½d.
Mary Thresher for Little Burne	1d.
Thomas Moore for Hoopers	1½d.
William Cockram for Ditches	1½d.
John Parkhouse for Bendell and ye broune close	2½d.
Thomas Commins for Gunhole	½d.
Alexander Vicary for his house and ground	½d.

TOTAL: 3s.16s.7d.

The names of those who have subscribed their hands to the Rate above written:

Robert Avery	James Partridge
John Warren	George Maunder
Nicholas Crooke	Andrew Thomas
John Parkhouse	James Thomas
Henry Cockram	Richard Grinslade
Edward Bodley	

Excerpts from an Estate Book, 1714–19

In the North Deveon Registry Office are notes for the years 1714–19 and some for the years of the 1670s and 1680s. Clues place them firmly in Witheridge, and a reference to the writer receiving rent for the Vicarage ground confirms the author as Samuel Shebbear, vicar of Witheridge 1672–1717. In 1673 Samuel married Elizabeth, daughter of Thomas Melhuish of Northam. Their son John was born in Witheridge in October 1679 and followed him as vicar from 1717 to 1742, where he used Samuel's note-book for a couple of years. John married Gertrude Melhuish of Northam and it must have been their son, Sam, who went to Mr Southcombe's school in 1715. The Melhuishes were the patrons of the living of Witheridge from 1643 to 1793.

The red cow went to bull May 23rd 1718.

Sam went to Mr Southcombe's school August 17th being Wednesday 1715.

Mr Cole of Ashbeare [Francis Cole was tenant of Essebeare].
Received March 6th 1715, 6lbs of yarn   6s.6d.
For spinning 2 pounds quarter and half yarn   4d.

April 14th 1716 – An Account of Nich Mellishes serge (Melhuish)
For the chain   14s.
For weaving   9s.4d.
2lbs of wool   6s.8d.
For dressing   2s.

Allowed for Disbursement about Ananias Moore's house in glass, reed, mendind, Midsommer 1717. [Ananias Moore was a blacksmith and grandfather of the Hugh Moore, details of whose will appears on page 40 of this book.]

Received quarter rents from Christmas the butcher £1.5s., the smith 12s.6d., 1714.

Allowed May 27th 1718 to Mr Francis Cole for a hundred and a half of reed for Nich Bullhead's house.

July 3rd 1719 received from Hugh Ditchett £1.7s.6d. [We learn later that Hugh was a miller. He may have given his name to today's house called Ditchetts].

1718 Expended in setting the fields 2s.5d.

18/8/1716 Received of Mr Francis Cole the sum of 26s. in full for six years High rent for East Esse-beare to the use of my master Andrew Davy Esq, by me James Hunt. [High rents were small sums that relieved the tenant of duties to the lord of the manor].

December 28th 1715 Bought of Alexander Air (Ayr?) two cheeses 25lbs weight seven farthings a pound.

My wife and daughter went to Exon June 5th 1716 (Exeter).

James Follet for the vicaridge ground 1716–18 paid rent and was paid for barley and oats.

March 5th 1718/19 Hugh Ditchett Miller to leave next Lady Day.

The names of those that pay me pigs and geese every Michelmas
James Pook of Knowstone: a pig
John Redler
John Delbridge of Molland

There is a page of short-term loans; such a thing was not uncommon in estate accounts. A selection follows on the opposite page:

Lent Nich Melluish 5s. Oct 7ᵗʰ 1715 which he is to pay Nov 1ˢᵗ
Tom Lock's wife 5s. Oct 22ⁿᵈ 1715
Henry Loch ten shillings, which he promised to Saturday, which will be June 16ᵗʰ 1716
Henry Lock half a guinea and half a crown which he is to pay in a fortnight's time
Jeffrey Lock Oct 29ᵗʰ 1716. The sum of twenty shillings to be paid in a fortnight's time, for which he gave me his note.
Lent by my wife to John Brownscombe August 17ᵗʰ 1717 £4.
Lent by my wife April 19ᵗʰ 1718 to the wife of old Henry Lock the miller 8s. Witness Mary Turner.

THE PARISH ARMOUR

The following entry appears in a Witheridge estate notebook for 22 June 1716. We do not know who wrote it.

Paid George Elworthy (Head of our fifty) the sum of fourteen shillings and seven pence for my share according to the poor rate towards a new stock and cleansing the musket, a new baggonett, a new cartridge box, a new scabbard and cleansing the sword, and a new belt.

The musket and sword must have been part of the parish armour and was the responsibility of the parish constable. Muskets and swords were typical of such equipment, which could also have included a pike, stockings, hats, coats and body armour. For centuries there was no regular or standing Army in England. If one was needed, it had to be specially raised. The method of doing this filtered down through counties, hundreds and parishes, all of which were organised to provide a militia when called upon. It was the constable's job to see that when the call came, it was answered. He was also responsible for ensuring the parish arms were in good repair. He had general tasks to maintain law and order, and to see that the parish butts were kept in good order for shooting practice. Our Butts Close tells us where the local butts were once located.

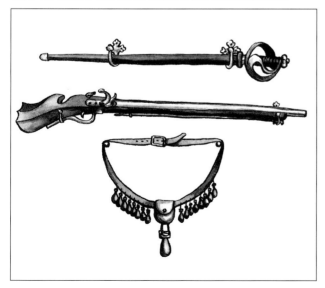

Part of the parish armour, 1715.

Why Witheridge's arms needed costly repair work in 1716 is a mystery. The wars with the French had ended in 1712 and the Jacobite rebellion in 1715 had not threatened the South West by land. However, in 1715 Parliament had called out the militia, and it is possible that Witheridge men were among those called upon. The word 'cleansing' in the above entry suggests that the musket and sword may well have been used.

George Elworthy is referred to as 'Head of our fifty'. This may mean that the contingent from Witheridge hundred numbered 50.

WITHERIDGE CHURCH, VICARAGE & GLEBE
As laid out in the terrier of 1726.

In the Devon Record Office in Exeter are a number of terriers for churches in Devon. These are statements of a church's possessions. Glebe ground is usually the main content, but some terriers contain descriptions of vicarages, church silver, vestments, books, etc. Witheridge has four terriers, dated 1601, 1679, 1683 and 1726. That of 1679 has been transcribed. The information that follows has been taken from that of 1726. A proportion of the document is taken up with detailed descriptions of 'fences' (hedges) and who was responsible for them. The document is damaged down the right-hand side and across the middle; it appears to have been torn in two at one time.

The Vicarage was built partly with stone and partly with mud (cob), daubed over on the outside with a white lime and sand mix 'commonly called Rough'. It was covered with thatch and consisted of the following rooms, starting downstairs: (1) a stone-paved porch with walls and 'top' white lime and plaster; (2) the entrance was paved with small stones (cobbles) with white plaster except between it and the hall, which was of timber (the screens passage); (3) a kitchen on the east side of the entrance paved with cobbles, with white plaster walls and ceiling; (4) a little house adjoining the kitchen on the north, 'commonly called the washhouse' paved with cobbles and at the top open to the thatch; (5) on the west side of the entrance a hall with a lime-ash floor, white-plastered walls and an oak-plank ceiling; (6) on the west of the hall was a small passage leading to a parlour, staircase and cellar, with a lime-ash floor and white-plastered walls; (7) the south side of the passage was floored with oak planks; (8) the cellar to the north of the passage was cobbled with white-plastered walls and ceiling; (9) west of the passage was the best stair-case with 'wainscot and ballister', the walls and ceiling were plastered; (10) above stairs: a chamber above the parlour, one chamber above the hall, two chambers and a closet above the kitchen and entrance and a closet commonly called 'the Minister's ...'. From this description it is possible to surmise that the building was a Devon longhouse, which appears to have been around 40ft long before the parlour was added.

Together with a yard... Kitchen... Before the Hall and parlour separated from the courtledge by a stonewall about 4 feet in height and all three encompassed by a mud wall thatched... Belonging to the Vicar except a small part or parcel thereof... Adjoining the garden of Richard Greenslade, which is to be repaired by the said Richard Greenslade... To the north of the Dwelling is situated what is called the Back Courtledge enclosed on all sides partly with outhouses and partly with a mud wall about ten feet high... This courtledge is above three parts paved with small stones and in it are the following outhouses viz 1st a pump house containing one bay of building... 2nd one bay of building, 3rd a cyder cellar two bays of building, 4th a stable two bays of building with hay loft over it, 5th a cow house one bay of building, and 6th an hogstay [pigsty] one bay of building, all these with mud walls and thatched.

This totals eight 'bays of building', which suggests a range not less than 120ft long. On the west there was the outer courtledge, enclosed on the east by the back courtledge cowhouse and on the west by the western wall of the garden. This outer courtledge included a 'linney' and a cowhouse. Also on the west was the 'Vicarage Barn' and the churchyard wall. The premises were bounded on the south by 'a cottage house of Richard Greenslade'.

The glebe fields are listed as Home Meadow, Bell Close, Sentry, Throat Meadow, Middle Sentry, Lower Sentry, and The Cleve – in all about 24 acres. The 20 acres at Fulford, mentioned in the 1679 terrier, are not included here.

The damaged middle section of the terrier seems to include much description of field boundaries and of the tithes and cropping. The document then goes on to deal with matters within the church as follows:

The Bible folio, three books of common prayer in folio, History of Martyrs 3 volumes in folio, Book of homilies folio, a Pulpit cloath and cushion Green velvet trim with green silk fringe, two surplices for the Minister and Master of Arts hood Cambridge, a silver chalice with a cover markt: W.T. [or W.J.] I.M. 1682 weighing about one pound and two ounces averdupois, one silver paton or salver weighing about 7ozs averdupois, one pewter flagon, two wooden boxes to gather the offerings

in, a white knapkin to cover the consecrated elements, one white linen cloath to cover the Communion Table, two other communion carpets, one scarlet cloath trimmed with gold lace... The other cloath trimmed with green silk and fringe, in the vestry one round table, two coffers, one with three Locks and Keys to keep the Register and Parish Records in, kept one by the Vicar the others by the churchwardens separately, the other coffer had only one Locke and Key kept by the Parish clerk... One Bier, two Bier and Hearse Cloaths, in the Tower five bells of large size and a Parish Clock.

The terrier notes that the churchyard bounds were repaired by the churchwardens, as was the church except the chancel, which was repaired by 'the Impropriator'. Duties are listed as follows:

Clerk   office of clerk   £4
*   keeping the clock   10s.*
*   washing the surplice and communion linen*
Sexton and Dog Whipper, for sweeping the church and
keeping out the dogs   10s. yearly

This document was signed by Richard Shortrudge, John Radford, John Elworthy, William Greenslade, Francis Cole, Edward Snow, Robert Thorne, plus 12 others whose signatures are damaged.

WILLIAM CHAPPLE

William Chapple was born in Witheridge on 14 January 1718, and baptised four days later in the church at Witheridge. His parents, William Chapple and Mary Sowden, had been married in the same church on 5 February 1717. The name Sowden (or Souden) appears in the parish registers throughout the 1600s and back to 1595. The Chapples (or Chaples) were more recent arrivals. The first mention of them is on 3 August 1657, when Edward Chapple came to Witheridge, married Ann Hopkins, and stayed. Their son William was baptised on 21 April 1663. It is very likely that this was our William's grandfather.

At the time of William's birth, the Chapples were tenants of a small farm, which William later referred to as 'Stukely's Lower West Yeo alias New House'. In 1840 it was called Stucklys and had 47 acres of meadow and arable land plus a house and buildings. The foundations of these can still be seen in the field immediately south of the southern boundary of West Yeo. Across the Little Dart valley with Witheridge on its ridge, is the three-tier church tower. The Chapples would have been able to see a two-tier tower with a wooden spire, weather-vane and cross, as their son in later life would remember it in the sketch he did for the Milles Inquiry.

William's father was Parish Clerk, but he fell on hard times and the family was reduced to poverty. In spite of this he made every effort to teach his son all he could, since he could not pay for an education.

A Teacher's Licence, 1729

To the Right Revd Father in God Stephen by Divine Providence Lord Bishop of Exon.

We the Minister Church wardens and Chief inhabitants of the Parish of Witheridge in the County of Devon do hereby certifie Your Lordship that the barer hereof John Pulsford late of the Hamlet of Sandford in the Parish of Crediton hath the space of four months last past resided in our town and Parish of Withridge in quality of teacher of Reading writing and Arithmetick during which time he hath behaved himself peaceable and soberly and given due attendance on the servis of this Church of England and for ought we know or have heard holdeth nothing Contrary to the Articles of Doctrine of the same, and is well affected to his present Majesty King George and the established Government and farther do hope and believe with due submission to Your Lordship's better judgement that he is a person qualified for and deserving of the licence he now petitions viz to teach to Read, write and Arithmetick, in the town and Parish of Witheridge none other beside him at present teaching, or that we know of having Lawful Licence for the same, witness our hands the 6th day of March in the year of our Lord God 1728–9.
John Shebbeare, Vicar of Witheridge.
Robert Bidgood and John Grant, Wardens.

John Thomas	Robert Tanner	John Radford	George Bodley
Thomas Greenslade	John Elworthy	Andrew Elworthy	Henry Stevens
William Commis			

Fiat Licent SE

[The Bishop of Exeter accepted the Witheridge petition and granted (*Fiat Licent*) a licence to John Pulsford to teach reading, writing and arithmetic, dated 6 March 1729, after his four-month trial period.]

After his death his son paid tribute to him in verse, including these lines:

His labouring hand procured his daily bread,
His pious care his children taught and fed,
Earnest to guide their steps by virtue's rules,
Plain sense supplied the learning of the schools.

William was quick to learn and at a young age he was appointed secretary to the vicar of Witheridge, John Shebbeare. He was determined to improve his knowledge, so when he was sent to Exeter on the vicar's business, he spent his savings on a Latin grammar book, a dictionary and other books. His dictionary served him well, for he began to contribute riddles and word puzzles to a publication called *The Lady's Diary*. These attracted the attention of Revd Bligh, the Silverton parson, and they became acquainted. Before long Mr Bligh recommended him to his wife's uncle, an Exeter surveyor named John Richards, who in 1738 took him on as his clerk. This was an important step, for John Richards was about to play a prominent part in the building of the Devon and Exeter Hospital in Southernhay, Exeter, and William's life was to change.

In 1741 Dr Alured Clark, Dean of Exeter, decided to found a public hospital in the city. Subscribers were sought and found; they included Sir William Courtenay, who would later play an important role in William's career. On 23 July Dean Clark called an inaugural meeting to discuss trustees, a site, specification, management and finance. A site in

A view of the church and church house from the west, c.1800. In 1568 the building of the tower was begun, thanks to a legacy of Joan Melhuish. The spire was taken down around 1835. It was a feature in the landscape; a field on the parish border with Templeton was called Spire Close, because of the view.

The Devon and Exeter Hospital.

Southernhay was provided. On the morning of 27 August 1741 plans for the new hospital were approved and the same afternoon the foundation-stone was laid.

In his book *A History of the Exeter Hospitals*, P.M.G. Russell tells us that Mr John Richards, a prominent builder and subscriber, proposed plans for the hospital and offered the services of a Clerk of the Works without fee. His generous offer was accepted. Russell adds:

A further word should be said about the architect of the hospital, John Richards. He was born in the remote village of Mariansleigh in North Devon and educated at a grammar school. He was then apprenticed to a joiner, Abraham Voysey, in the parish of St Thomas near Exeter, whose widow he later married. As Professor Hoskins points out, all the Georgian buildings up to this date were designed by builders, and the hospital was no exception. It is an astonishing thought that the original hospital with its handsome frontage and elegant board room was the creation of a builder with no formal training in architecture, and working against time because of the atmosphere of enthusiasm and urgency surrounding the project.

The hospital was opened on 1 January 1743, 16 months after work began.

John Richards delegated the task of Clerk of the Works to William Chapple, who about that time married John's niece. In the building accounts for 1741–43 there are a number of references to 'William Chapple the clerk' and 'the clerk Chapple'. Various sums of money are mentioned: On 26 October 1742 'Mr Richards and Chapple were reimbursed to the tune of £193.16s.'

The hospital trustees were so satisfied with William's work that they appointed him secretary to the hospital, a post he held for 38 years. We do not know the date of his appointment but on 1 September 1748 records reveal him as 'the Secretary', receiving his half-year's wages of £5. There are a few mentions of him in J.D. Harris' *History of Devon and Exeter Hospital*. For example, in October 1771 'Mr William

Chapple was voted £2.12s.6d. for compiling the Register of Presidents and Vice-Presidents and others from 1741 to 1772.' In April 1775 'the General Court of Governors added ten pounds to the Secretary's salary, making 25 pounds a year.' Near the end of his life he was made an honorary governor.

Mrs R. Day, the chair in 2003 of the North and East Devon Health Authority pointed out that:

... the exterior of the eighteenth-century building is now almost exactly as it was after the modifications effected soon after 1743; William Chapple would have little difficulty in recognising his work today. This is quite a testimony to the quality of eighteenth-century builders.

In 1755 his father died and William put up a tablet in Witheridge church with 16 lines of verse on it in tribute to him. Four lines have already been quoted; a further six lines follow:

His steady honesty still kept its ground,
Unshaken, whether fortune smil'd or frown'd
Lover of peace, sincere, religious, just,
Guiltless of fraud and faithful to his trust.
This much his son with modesty may say;
This tribute to a father's memory pay.

Sir William Courtenay Bt had been associated with the hospital from the start and was, for the year 1743, chairman of the court of governors. He would therefore have been aware of William Chapple's abilities, and so it is perhaps not surprising that, at some date after William became hospital secretary he was appointed to undertake the stewardship of the Courtenays' Devon estates. He is said to have filled this post for 20 years with 'an integrity equal to his abilities'. His responsibilities were considerable. At that time the Courtenay estates were spread throughout Devon. In addition to Powderham, Kenton, Exminster and Starcross, there was land at North Bovey, Wolborough, Malborough, Okehampton, Tavistock, Whitchurch, Holsworthy, Braunton and Honiton. It is unclear exactly when William took up these duties, but as the top part of a servants list shows, he was in post by 1749.

When the First Viscount Courtenay died on 16 May 1762, his heir was a minor, and the Court of Chancery and his late father's executors had a major task to perform. William Chapple was appointed receiver by the court and agent by the executors. Separate accounts had to be kept until July 1764, when the Court of Chancery ordered the accounts to be amalgamated. William's duties in this matter continued until the summer of 1767, when the accounts were approved and responsibilities handed over to the Second Viscount on his coming of age. The final totals of these accounts show that £74,008.10s.2½d. had been received and £70,510.3s.9½d. had been paid out. The estate still owed £4,123.17s.8d. and was owed by 'arrears from the Irish Tenants' £12,862.3s.10½d. William had a clerk to help him, Charles Scott, but it is worth remembering that in these years (1762–67) this work was performed in addition to his ongoing stewardship work for the Devon properties. William was involved from time to time in the personal supervision of building work. In the spring of 1761 he was reimbursed for the money he had to spend while staying at Mary Bussell's house at Starcross 'during the erecting of the Quay and other buildings.'

It is clear from an account book entry of 6 December 1761 that William's annual salary was £26.5s., but additional to this a range of expenses incurred by him were met, as the following example from 31 December 1761 shows. Extra expenses at the time of Lady Frances Courtenay's death were claimed by William and met:

... preparations for the Funeral obliging me to be the greatest part of that time in Exeter and to have people almost continually at my house to consult and transact Business relating thereto.

The 'extra' included:

Meat, Drinke, Firing and Candle expended according to the last Account my Wife and I can make from our Memorandum therefore over and above our own common expenses.

He set the figure at £2.12s.6d., which he said was 'much less than it would be had the necessary transactions in Town on this Occasion been at any Public House'.

That his duties ranged from major to minor can be seen from these examples:

Dec 31st 1761 gave the Clerk of the Post Office at Exeter his usual Christmas gift 5s.
March 2nd 1762 Paid Jane Borne to the use of Powderham Ringers for ringing Sir William's birthday.
Dec 24th 1762 Distributed at Christmas Eve as usual among the poor people of Powderham and Kenton £3.

Eventually serious illness forced his resignation, but the Courtenay family thought highly enough of him to settle on him:

... a handsome Annuity, with Survivorship to his wife and daughter, as a Recompense for his Fidelity and Attention, and a Mark of Esteem for so long and faithful Service.

In addition to his hospital work and activities for the Courtenay family, William took a great interest in antiquarian matters, as well as Hebrew, Latin and other languages. In 1746 he published his Exmoor Vocabulary under the name Devoniensis in *The Gentleman's Magazine*. In the 1750s he completed the

Witheridge return to the Milles Inquiry, probably because the vicar of Witheridge had failed to do so. It gives a useful picture of the parish, although he had been away from it for many years and his knowledge was incomplete.

In 1772 William began to work on his *Review of Risdon's Survey of Devon*, but this was not published until after his death. The subscribers to this work included the vicar, the Revd Thomas Melhuish, Henry Stevens, William Spry and John Partridge, all of Witheridge. In 1778 the *Exeter Flying Post* carried an advertisement for an octavo volume with six engraved plates, costing 4s., entitled *Sciatherica Antiqua Restaurata* by 'William Chapple of Exeter'. This contained the results of his study of a cromlech on Shilstone Farm near Drewsteignton, Dartmoor. His text covered aspects such as possible 'Astronomic Construction', links with 'the Druids... the Romanized Britons and Pagan Saxona', with 'Topographical, Etymological' and other observations.

After a long and painful illness William Chapple died at Exeter on 1 September 1781. In its next issue the *Exeter Flying Post* published this obituary:

On Saturday last died at Exeter after a long illness in the 63rd year of his age, Mr Wm Chapple, who for upwards of 40 years had been Secretary to the Devon and Exeter Hospital, and from its foundation had discharged the duties of his office with that regularity and precision which in great measure contributed to the acknowledged excellence of its present establishment – to which institutions therefore he may be considered as having been a most considerable benefactor, and in which light he was considered by the Governors, who lately unanimously voted him an honorary Governor and standing committee-man, as the most honourable mark of their esteem for his long and faithful services and unwearied assiduity. He possessed the strongest natural abilities which, by the most unremitted attention from his youth enabled him to overcome all obstacles in the attainment of that depth of knowledge in mathematics, chronology, antiquity, history and the dead languages, as well as learning in general, in which he had few equals, so that his death may be esteemed a public and irretrievable loss. His knowledge in the sacred text, and criticism on the most ancient versions of it, established his faith on the most solid basis, and he died, as he had always professed and lived a sincere and pious Christian.

In a late addition to his will, signed and dated on 22 July 1781, he left to Witheridge church a prayer book that had previously belonged to the Royal Chapel at Windsor. The book had passed to Dr Keppel, Bishop of Exeter, from whose executors he had purchased it. It was to be 'some token of my regard for the place where I drew my first breath.' It is sad to record that a later vicar gave the prayer book to one of his churchwardens, and that there is now no trace of William Chapple's memorial to his father.

On 15 November the *Exeter Flying Post* printed a notice of the sale of more than 300 volumes of the library 'of the late Mr William Chapple'. As a lad he had spent his savings on books and his love of books had lasted him a lifetime.

A road in Witheridge has been named after William Chapple to commemorate his life and work. Hopefully these notes will help the parish to remember him, not only for his inclusion in the *Dictionary of National Biography*, but also for being a man who, with the help of his father and by his own efforts, made his mark in Devon but did not forget the place where he was born.

WITHERIDGE IN THE MID-EIGHTEENTH CENTURY

In 1747 Dean Milles of Exeter decided to carry out a survey of all Devon parishes, covering every aspect of each in detail. He decided to rely on local clergy to complete the questionnaires that he distributed. The response was uneven. Some replied promptly, some were slow, while others failed to reply at all. He got no answer from Witheridge, so he turned to an acquaintance of his in Exeter, a man who was known and respected and on whom he could rely. This, of course, was William Chapple. Although he had left Witheridge some years earlier he agreed to do his best to answer the questions. Sometimes he has to admit that his memory has let him down, but his reply is all we have for a description of Witheridge in the 1750s.

The parish that he describes includes the outliers of Little Witheridge, Yeatheridge and a block of land enclosed with Thelbridge; all of this was reallocated during the reorganisation of parish boundaries at the end of the nineteenth century. William Chapple estimates 80 to 100 dwellings in 'the town of Witheridge' itself, with 500–600 inhabitants. He reckons to add another 600 from outside the town, giving a total of 1,100–1,200 people. He tells us that he himself kept the registers for some years, and estimated that 12 baptisms took place per year, with the same number of burials. He refers to the:

Manor and Borough of Witheridge, the present Lord whereof is Coulston Fellowes of Eggesford Esq, in whose Court-Leet here the Portreeve and other officers of the Borough are appointed and sworn.

He adds the manor of Witheridge Cannington, in the possession of the Melhuish family. 'The borough', he says:

... enjoys the common privileges of the Duchy of Lancaster, viz Exemption of Toll and Customs of Markets and Fairs etc... A Duchy Court is kept up here, beside the Manor and Hundred Court.

The church he describes as 'built with stone and covered with shingle, the walls roughcast, the battlements leaded.' The sketch he includes is:

... though done from memory pretty correct with respect to the proportion and all other circumstances (I have known it from a child). The tower is very big about in proportion to its height, which I think is about 70 feet, besides the spire, which with the stem of the weathercock is at least 20 if not quite 30 feet. It is (as usual) at the west end of the church. The church at the east is lower and not battlemented, on the north side whereof is a convenient vestry, the entrance whereto is opposite the chancel door.

The church is handsomely decorated within, has an antique stone pulpit with niches where are the crucifixion, the image of ye blessed virgin, Mary Magdalene, St Peter and St Paul, but their heads were cut off by the Oliverian Reformers. It has two rows of pillars, an handsome font and is pretty well sealed. A gothick screen separates it from ye chancel, which is much deformed by the high pews or closets lately erected there. It also wants an altarpiece. Fonts for holy water appear in 2 or 3 places and on the south side of the porch. A staircase to the rood loft between the church and chancel yet remains, but the rood loft itself (where an organ might conveniently be placed) is disfigured by the partition, which comes half way down from the roof... There is not a monument in the church, only plain grave stones. There are 2 or 3 coats of arms in one window but I have forgot what they are, probably they were done since the restoration, for the Saints Militant in ye civil wars appear to have made such havoc here that I can scarce think we have escaped them.. I had forgot that there were some coats of arms painted in 1727 on the spandals of the arches of the screen between the church and chancel, viz the Bishop of Exeter's arms, the Melhuishes (Patrons of the place), the Shebbeares (one of whose family was then Vicar), and the Shortrudges – before that time the Stucley Arms was there, but then obliterated to make room for another.

He goes on to say that:

... here were anciently three Chappels, dedicated to St Margaret, St Peter and St Paul, some traces of which still remain at Myll, Bradford and West-Yeo in this parish; the last-mentioned was turned into an oxhouse and since to a dwelling house and other two are quite demolished, having nothing to perpetuate their memory but the names of the fields adjoining where they stood, viz Chappel-Hill at Myll, and Chappel-Meadow at Bradford. These Chappels very probably occasioned the division of the parish in to 4 quarters now called the town quarter, the east quarter, the south quarter and the west quarter. The church is situated in the town quarter, Bradford Chapel in the east, Myll Chappel in the south, and West-Yeo in the west.

William Chapple has nothing to offer on the subjects of abbeys, almshouses, ancient stones, crosses, castles, etc. He has heard of Berry Castle but 'never saw it'. The only 'Gentleman's seat' that he remembers is Bradford, now in the possession of the Shortrudges. To questions about recent improvements to the parish he says:

These have chiefly been in taking in and tilling the coarse moory and fursey grounds, of which large quantities have been consumed to tillage within my memory. They first beat and burn (or Devonshire, as some call it) and then manure it with lime and dung.

He claims that there are no bridges or roads worth mentioning. 'Bullocks and sheep and other things usual in a country fair or market' are sold at Witheridge market.

He has little to report on the landscape except to say that the hills are gentle and that:

... the town itself is flat and level, but has a very steep descent every way round except to the eastward. In the north and east there are diverse coarse moors abounding with short furse and having some quagmires, the soil clay... The south and west parts are generally of a better kind of soil.

As to value:

... meadow ground round the town I have know let for £3 an acre, but in other parts 30 or 40 shillings may suffice. Moor from two pence to five pence or even less.
Manuring is by eight hogsheads of lime or 160 to 200 loads of dung to an acre. 'They chiefly sow wheat, barley and oats, scare any rye, though this is frequently sown in ye wet moor ground about 70 or 80 years ago.'

He says that a variety of apples were planted and that the best cider was made of the 'Tythe apples, being a mixture of all sorts.' He suggests a parish annual cider production of at least 100 to 150 hogsheads, and that the quality was 'tolerably good', and 'rather rough than sweet'. He values it between 10s. and 20s. 'at the pounds mouth', according to season.

Questions were asked about trees and woodlands, and William is concerned at the shortage of timber trees in the parish, the majority being coppice. He complains that the statute which requires that at each coppice felling 12 young saplings per acre be left to grow up, is largely ignored, 'as in most other places in ye county.' He urges greater penalties. Oak, he says is most common in coppices and old hedges. Elm does not thrive; ash is sometimes planted and there is much birch and willow. When asked about plants he refers to the celandine with which 'swallows are said to cure the blindness of their young.'

He has nothing to say about wells and has forgotten the names of the streams. The Dart 'is ye only one to be called a river' and there is 'the stone bridge at Drayford being in ye road from Exeter to South

Moulton'; the river there is fordable in summer. He recalls no floods. He praises the air in Witheridge, being sharp and dry, and says 'people are in general pretty healthy here, and some live to a good age, a sign of an wholesome air.' He can think of two or three people who lived to the age of 95 or 96.

They were commonly esteemed robust and heretofore would often challenge their neighbours to a wrestling or football match, but they cannot afford so many days of diversion as heretofore, and their activity and liveliness is I think somewhat dimmed even since my remembrance.

He has nothing on history, except a remark that 'it seems to have been too much out of the route of Fairfax and his rebels to have had any remarkable share in these intestine broils.' This reference to the Civil War of the 1640s rather contradicts his description of the vandalised pulpit.

William Chapple ends his answers to the questionnaire with an apology for his shortcomings.

GRIST MILLS

Devon was not a county known for its windmills. In most parts there was ample water-power for grist mills. In his book *Windmills of Devon* Walter Minchinton states that 'the 56 possible windmills in

Witheridge windmill, 1757.

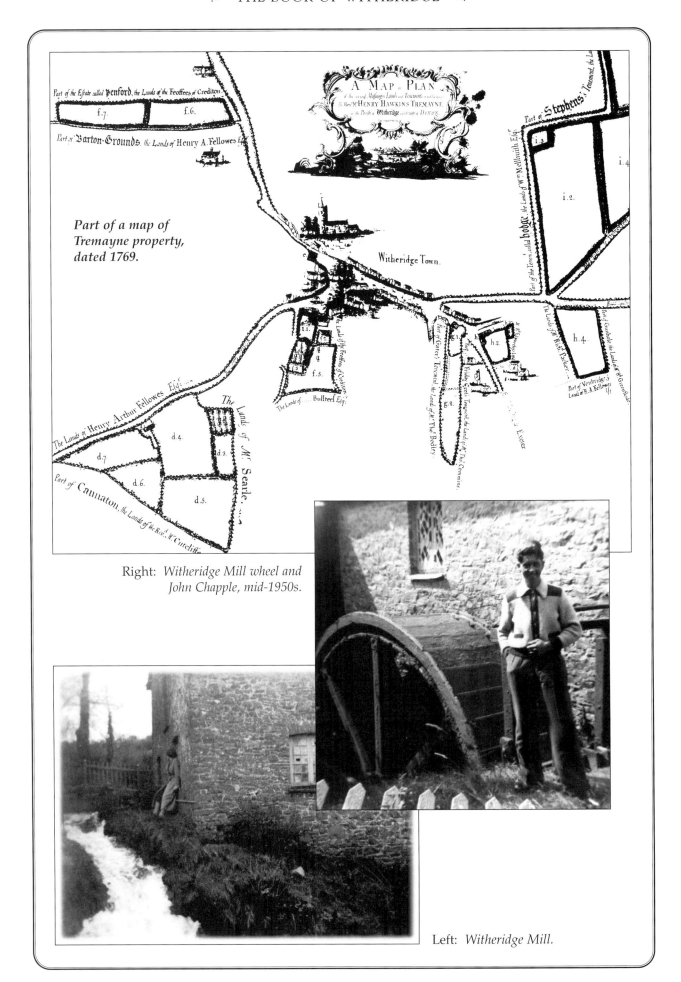

Part of a map of
Tremayne property,
dated 1769.

Right: *Witheridge Mill wheel and
John Chapple, mid-1950s.*

Left: *Witheridge Mill.*

Devon must be compared with the certain existence of 13 tide mills and over 600 water-mills.' The earliest windmill mentioned was in Woodbury in 1296 and Cruwys Morchard had one in 1561. Donne's 1765 map of Devon shows only four – Abbotsham, Rackenford, Holsworthy and Witheridge. Donne may have missed a few, and more may have been built in the late-eighteenth and early-nineteenth centuries, before wind power gave way to water and steam. Most were built of masonry, some with a straight tower, and some tapering. The average windmill was 30ft high with three storeys. It was said that with a brisk wind a windmill could grind 12 bushels in an hour.

The Witheridge windmill was situated across the road from Woodington Farm, on the road to Puddington; the Tithe Map of 1837 recorded a Windmill Field there. This is in one of the original outlying parts of the parish, reallocated in the 1880s. The site is puzzling, for the old Westway and Stourton mills on the River Dalch were much closer. The 1841 census shows the mill occupied, not by a miller, but by a labourer, Richard Phillips, and his family. It may have stopped working long before that, as it does not appear in the Land Tax returns of 1780–1830, whereas the other mills in the parish do.

In a 1692 rate for the reparation of the Parish Church of Witheridge William Govier paid 6d. for 'Dreford Mill'. Donne's map shows Drayford Mill, as does the Tithe Map. In 1811 William White paid a 5d. farthing rate towards the repair of Drayford Bridge. In 1841 John White was miller there, with his 15-year-old son John, also described as 'miller'. In 1851 it was George Phillips, with his wife Ann and three children. He came there in 1846 or 1847. By 1878 George had died and his widow was miller. In 1891 their daughter Jane had taken over, with her 14-year-old son William, as miller's assistant, and her miller uncle, Thomas Stoneman. The Stonemans continued as millers there until the end of the mill's working life in the 1930s. Loveday Venner (née Stoneman) remembers her father Richard's decision to close the mill, and how on the final day of working he asked her mother to start the mechanism for the last grinding.

Rather less is known about Bradford Mill. There is a lease of Bradford Tracy Mill in 1579 from John Snow to John Crooke, and a reference in 1726 to 'a new unfinished mill beside the River Dart at Bradford Bridge in Bradford Tracy Manor.' Donne has it on the map and it is on the Tithe Map. William Crooke was miller in 1841, 1857 and 1870. In 1893 it was Henry Blackford and in 1902, 1919 and 1930 it was William Roberts. His grandchildren, William and Pamela, recall that towards the end of the 1930s there was a very severe winter, during which the leat froze solid and no grinding could be done. Soon after closure came. The leat continued to be popular with unofficial fishermen, as eels were plentiful.

Witheridge Mill is not on Donne's map, but is in the Land Tax returns. In 1780 the miller was James Davey, and the owner was Henry Arthur Fellowes; members of this family later became Earls of Portsmouth. In 1820 William Bodly was there, as he was in 1841. By the end of the nineteenth century Amos Maire was miller. He was succeeded by his sons, and Charlie Maire was in charge when it closed in the 1950s.

THE POOR IN THE 1700S

In every parish overseers of the poor had a duty to care for the poor. There was no help from outside. Parishes raised their own rate and looked after their own. Here are some examples from Witheridge from the 1750s.

Paid William Hodge in need	*1s.6d.*
Paid for 2 wastcoats for his children	*6s.8d.*
Mary Warren several times in need	*4s.*
For a coat for her and making	*4s.8d.*
For a under wastcoat for her	*2s3d.*
For a pair of shoes for her	*2s.8d.*
For a shroud for her	*2s.8d.*
For lying her forth and affidavit	*3s.*
For a coffin for her	*5s.6d.*
For making the grave and ringing the bell	*2s.*
Paid for her in all	*£1.6s.9d.*

The Devon and Exeter Hospital (the 'Royal' came later) opened in 1743. It was possible for parishes to subscribe to the new hospital and so become entitled to send patients there. Witheridge was one of the first to subscribe. This may have been partly due to the fact that the hospital's secretary was Witheridge man, William Chapple. In 1757 the parish was caring for Susannah Milford, and when she became ill they sent her on horseback to the new hospital in Exeter (Exon was the old word). Ambrose Burrow's wife went with her to care for her on the way.

Paid Susannah Milford at several times in need	*8s.*
Paid for cloathes for her and making when sent to ye hospital	*£1.3s.8d.*
Paid for a change for her	*2s.7d.*
Paid for a coat and cloak for her and making	*7s.*
Paid for a horse to carry her to Exon	*1s.*
Paid Ambrose Burrows wife for keeping her and going to Exon	*2s.6d.*
Paid for a pair of shoes for her	*3s.3d.*
Paid for her in all	*£2.9s.10d.*

Later in the accounts we find that John Veysey was paid 5s. 'for carrying Sarah Cornelius to Exon'. Some of the poor were helped on an annual basis:

Paid Grace Downey 50 weeks at 1s.3d. per week
£3.2s.6d.
Paid Richard Chilcott 50 weeks at 1s. per week £2.10s.
Paid Parkhouses child 50 weeks at 1s.6d. per week
£3.15s.

Paid for a change for her	*1s.*
Paid for a coat and apron for her	*2s.9d.*
Paid for Bechoram, Serge and Canvas for her	*1s.4d.*
Paid Mrs Coles for keeping Collards boy 37	
weeks at 6d. per week	*18s.6d.*

Parishes generally did not help those from outside their boundaries, but there were exceptions, as an undated entry reveals two poor sailors were paid 1s.

A WILL OF 1794

Hugh Moore was baptised in Witheridge on 5 November 1717. He was the youngest son of Ananias and Susanna Moore. Ananias was a blacksmith; both this name and trade ran like a thread through the eighteenth century, although Hugh himself became a cordwainer or bootmaker. Hugh's brother Ananias was indeed a blacksmith; he died in 1789, leaving 'all that dwelling house and appurtenances... In Witheridge' to Hugh. In turn, Hugh left it to his own son, Thomas. Hugh's other son Ananias was aged 50 when his father died; he received the large sum of £30, but had little time to enjoy it, for within three months of his father's passing he too was dead.

Hugh must have been a successful man, for in addition to Ananias' £30, he left £10 each to his grandsons – Thomas, Robert, Hugh and Ananias. Thomas got the anvil and coal trough and the residue of the estate as he carried on the family's smithy tradition. However, he was obliged to meet all claims and was the sole executor. Meanwhile Robert received 'the large chest that stands in my room'. Hugh got a 'silver table spoon with a yellow head', and Ananias 'my silver cup'.

Boys were much more favoured than girls, for Hugh's granddaughter Mary received only two guineas, while his other two granddaughters (not even named) received one-and-a-half guineas each.

Hugh Moore's signature at the bottom right of the will, next to the seal, was shaky, but shakiness could be from lack of patience as well as ill health. The will was signed on 5 November 1794, and Hugh lived until May 1797, only six months short of his 80th birthday.

WITHERIDGE LAND TAX RETURNS, 1780–1832

An Act authorising a tax on land was passed in 1692, and assessments were made. Regular imposition of the tax began in 1697. A quota was fixed for each county and local assessors allotted amounts to each parish and then to each taxpayer. From 1772 all occupiers of land were included. At that time the normal levy was 4s. in the pound. The returns reveal the owners and occupiers of land, the name of the site and the tax payable. It was land and not the buildings on it that was taxed.

It is at once clear that Witheridge was a parish of tenants. Of the 113 properties listed, only nine were occupied by their owners. The largest landowner was Revd Mr Melhuish, with 20 properties. He also paid Land Tax for the 'Shief', in other words tithes. There is nothing to suggest that he lived in Witheridge. As vicar he would have appointed a curate to carry out his duties. The next largest landowner was Henry Arthur Fellowes, with 12 properties. Members of his family were Earls of Portsmouth, whose large local estate was based on Eggesford. He was also an absentee. Henry Hawkins Tremayne had seven properties and he lived at Heligan, in Cornwall. His family had acquired Witheridge land through marriage with the Dart family of Dart Raffe. Other major owners included Sir Thomas Ackland, Bt... of Killerton, John Chichester of Arlington, the Revd Mr Cutcliffe of Damage Barton, Mortehoe and Richard Copplestone of Colebrooke – all of whom were absentee. Their holdings totalled 50. In the remaining 54 was a curiosity; Penford and Shippenhay, in the town quarter, belonged to the 'Poor of Crediton'. In other words, they formed part of the endowment of Crediton Charities for the Poor.

It was a time of sharp social distinction, of which the Witheridge Officer of Excise seems to have been well aware. Top of his social list was a baronet, Sir Thomas Ackland, followed by a knight, Sir Stafford Northcote. Next up came nine who were labelled 'Esquire', including such names as Tremayne, Copplestone, Fellowes, Speke, Chichester. There were nine misters (Mr), among whom the Officer of Excise, Mr Thomas, included himself. William Pennycott, gent., was the only one given that title, and Captain Partridge was the only naval officer. Finally, there must have been something special about 'Madam' Shortrudge.

Until the 1880s Witheridge was blessed or cursed with three outlying parts of the parish, separated from the main bulk of land by sections of other parishes. These outliers were included in the Southern Quarter and played an important role; their Land Tax total of £50.14s.8d. was nearly a quarter of the parish total of £228.6s.1d. Farms such as Stourton, Hele Barton, Westcott Mill and Yeatheridge were certainly on a par with the likes of Dart (Dart Raffe), West Essebeare (Newhouse), Pilliven and Hilltown.

Town Quarter properties, in or near the village itself, present some identification problems. Some retain their names even in 2003, including Lakelands, Muxeries, Gunhole, Lashbrooke, 'ffords' (Fords Folly), Ditchetts, Penfords and Vixen Meadow. However, it is not clear where other properties were located, including The Malthouse, The Bellhouse, The Great House (in spite of its name it was rated very low), Gaters, Borns, Hoopers, Pearsses, Vicaries, Fridays Cross. Hodges was two tenements now occupied by the Mitre, and the Congregational

Chapel was built on part of Diers. Application of personal names to property was obviously commonplace; some name changes occurred with occupancy or ownership, but others were remarkably durable; for example, Trixies, in Drayford, lasted for centuries, and the name Tracy Green, listed in 1780, remains at the time of writing although the cottages burnt down in 1947 and were not replaced.

By 1832, the last year the records are available to us, there had been a few changes, mainly in the Town Quarter. 'Brick House' was mentioned for the first time, and it is tempting to identify this with the house in West Street. One Robert Joseph Coster owned and occupied 'Part of Sevenses'. At that time Ebringtons Row consisted of seven dwellings, so there may be a link here. 'Slewpark' and 'Gallens' were also listed for the first time in 1832. It is curious that four members of the Burgess family, Robert, John, William and Francis, individually owned and occupied four houses, each rated at 7½d. The lowest rated, however, was a house occupied by Alexander Adams, who paid 6d. At the other end of the scale West Yeo paid £8.8s.

WITHERIDGE HUNDRED

As assessment and certificate made the 31st day of May 1780 by Robert Throne, William Lake, James Partridge and Samuel Wilcocks, appointed assessors for the Parish aforesaid of the money raised by virtue of an Act of Parliament and made in the twentieth year of his present Majesty's reign intituled an act for granting an aid to his Majesty by a Land Tax to be raised in Great Britain at the rate of four shillings in the pound for the service of the year 1780.

East Quarter

Proprietor of Lands	Occupiers	Tenements	Money Payable
Sir T. Ackland Bt & Revd Mr Melhuish	Abraham Anstey	Bradford & Leete	£10.2s.1½d.
Revd Mr Melhuish	John Burgess	Bradford Mill	12s.0d.
Revd Mr Melhuish	Mr Richard Cooke	Pilleven & Downland	£4.19s.0d.
Revd Mr Melhuish	Sarah Smale	Higher Hilltown	£2.8s.0d.
Revd Mr Melhuish		Middle Hilltown	£2.8s.0d.
Revd Mr Melhuish	Richard Churchhouse	West Pilleven	£1.4s.0d.
Revd Mr Melhuish	Richard Milford	Ffords	£1.10s.0d.
Sir T. Ackland Bt & Revd Mr Melhuish	John Tanner	Northcombe	£2.14s.0d.
John Denham	Thomas Kerslake	Lower Hilltown	£5.4s.0d.
Richard Greenslade	Richard Greenslade	Berry Mead & Dart Downes	£1.4s.0d.
Sir T. Ackland Bt & Thomas Greenslade	Thos Greenslade	Higher Dart, Piley Ground & East Newland	£3.18s.0d.
William Lyddon Esq.	William Heywood	Lower Dart	£2.8s.0d.
William Lyddon Esq.	William Heywood	Upcott Squire	£1.10s.0d.
William Lyddon Esq.	William Heywood	Piley Moore & Close	£18s.0d.
Clergy of South Molton	John Thorne	Fforedown & Rosemoor	£2.2s.0d.
Wm Pennycott Gent.	Robert Thorne	Elworthy	£1.4s.0d.
Mr Robert Ayre & Mr Thomas Addicott	Thomas Addicott	West Newland	£1.16s.0d.
Mr Robert Ayre & Mr Thomas Ayre	Mr Robert Ayre & Mr Thomas Ayre	Moieties of Wilson	£4.16s.0d.
Sir T. Ackland Bt & Wm Lyddon Esq.	John Courtney	Down	£3.0s.0d.
Revd Mr John Cutcliffe	Widow Thorne	Heavers	£3.12s.0d.
Mr Thos Tanner	John Davey	Malson & part of Dart Down	£1.16s.0d.
William Cockram	William Cockram	Whodehill	6s.0d.
Total			**£60.9s.1½d.**

West Quarter

Proprietor of Lands	Occupiers	Tenements	Money Payable
Revd Mr Melhuish	Revd Mr Melhuish	For the Shief	£7.4 s.0d.
Henry Hawkins Tremain Esq.	George Thorne	Dart	£5.8s.0d.

Sir Thomas Ackland Bart	Mr George Luxton	West Essebeare	£5.14 s.0d.
Madam Shortrudge	Mr Francis Cole	East Essebeare	£6.0s.0d.
Richard Copplestone Esq.	Mr Thomas Elworthy	West Yeo	£8.8s.0d.
George Speke Esq. & Richard Copplestone Esq.	William Adams	Higher & Lower Adworthy	£2.8s.0d.
Revd Mr Melhuish	William Venn	South Grendon	£3.6s.0d.
Revd Mr Melhuish & Wm Lyddon Esq.	Jacob Cobley	Wheadon	£2.2s.0d.
Richard Copplestone Esq.	Ann Smale	Hellinghayes	£1.10 s.0d.
Henry Arthur Fellowes Esq.	Robert Veysey	Mays, Cobleys, Warrens	£2.8s.0d.
Henry Arthur Fellowes Esq.	James Partridge	Stucleys in Drayford	£2.14s.0d.
Henry Arthur Fellowes Esq.	James Partridge	Trixes	18s.0d.
Henry Arthur Fellowes Esq.	Catherine Brownstone	Studleys Tenement	£1.16s.0
Henry Arthur Fellowes Esq.	John Foxford	Drayford Mills	£1.4 s.0
George Speke Esq. & H.A. Fellowes Esq.	Richard Gibbings & John Foxford	Stockham & Haves	£2.5s.0
Henry H. Tremaine Esq.	Thomas Wilcocks	Rowden	£1.16s.0
Henry H. Tremaine Esq.	Thos Fisher	Cockhay	18s.0d.
Revd Mr John Cutcliff	Mr George Bodley & Mr Edward Bodley	Combe	£5.8s.0
George Buck Esq.	John Price	Three ?	18s.0d.
George Buck Esq.	Thomas Cole	Milltown ?	12s.0d.
Henry Arthur Fellowes Esq.	Thomas Vicary	Thos Pearses House & Garden	6s.0d.
Total			**£63.3s.0d.**

South Quarter

Proprietor of Lands	Occupiers	Tenements	Money Payable
Capt. Partridge & William Bowden	Capt. Partridge	Tidlakes	12s.0d.
Capt. Partridge	Capt Partridge	Stourton	£4.16s.0d.
Capt. Partridge	William Thomas	Barton of Hele	£5.8s.8d.
Sir Thomas Ackland Bt & Mrs Cleeve	Mrs Cleeve	Westcott	£4.16s.0d.
Sir Stafford Northcott	Mrs Cleeve	Stockpark	12s.0d.
John Chichester Esq.	Richard Elworthy	Mill	£4.16s.0d.
John Chichester Esq.	John Hedgeman	Henesford	£3.9s.0d.
John Chichester Esq.	Thomas Bennett	Batson	£1.10s.0d.
John Chichester Esq.	George Venner	Eastway	£2.8s.0d.
Mary Down & Grace Melhuish	Thomas Bennett	Berry Cleave	9s.0d.
William Bidgood	Frances Bidgood	Heals	12s.0d.
Mr John Radford	Mr John Radford	Yeatheridge	£4.4s.0d.
Samuel Wilcocks	Samuel Wilcocks	Westway	£2.8s.0d.
Mr Robert Ayre & Mr Thomas Drake	John Elworthy	Higher and Lower Upcott & 8 Acres	£4.16s.0d.
John Bidgood	John Bidgood	Woodington and Moorpaths	£2.14s.0d.
John Elworthy	William Elworthy	East & West Minchine	£3.0s.0d.
Arthur Venn	Arthur Venn	Marchweek & Moorparks	£2.2s.0d.
Mr Robert Ayre & Mr Thomas Drake	John Vent	Shilladon	£1.10s.0d.
Capt. Partridge	William Greenway	Tuckers Tenement	12s.0d.
Total			**£50.14s.8d.**

Town Quarter

Proprietor of Lands	Occupiers	Tenements	Money Payable
Henry Arthur Fellowes Esq.	H.A. Fellowes Esq.	For the growth of ye wood	12s.0d.
Revd Mr Melhuish		Vicar	£6.0s.0d.
Revd Mr Melhuish	Mr Blake & John Burgess	Hodges	£1.10s.0d.
Henry Arthur Parkhouse	Richard Downey	Lakelands	£1.16s.0d.
Henry Arthur Parkhouse	Mr Andrew Elworthy	Hole	£1.16s.0d.
Henry Arthur Parkhouse	Mr Andrew Elworthy	? The Down	£2.2s..0d
Bultail Esq., Mr Chapple & Wm Greenslade	Mr Elworthy & Mr Cole	? and Broomclose	6s.0d.
Henry Stenham	Walter Tidbeald	Venbridge	18s.0d.
H.A. Fellowes Esq. & Henry Stephens	Walter Tidbeald	Vixen Meadow and Ffords	£1.10s.0d.
H.A. Fellowes Esq. & Henry Stephens	Walter Tidbeald	Muxeries and Barton Ground	£2.8s.0d.
Henry Stephens	Walter Tidbeald	Grabpark	6s.0d.
John Hooper	Robert Snowdon	Cross Park	6s.0d.
Thos Melhuish Comins	Thos Melhuish Comins	Broomcloses	9s.0d.
Wm Smale & Thos Melhuish Comins	Wm Comins & Samuel Foxford	For their part of Ffrydays Cross	15s.0d.
Richard Parker	Richard Parker	For Lashbrook	6s.0d.
H.A. Fellowes Esq.	Wm Lake	Southcombe	£1.16s.0d.
Revd Mr Melhuish	John Commins	Foxdon	£1.16s.0d.
H.A. Fellowes Esq.	Richard Hodge	East Whorestone	£1.0s.0d.
H.A. Fellowes Esq.	D. Bodley, J. James & Robert Stooke	West Whorestone	£2.0s.0d.
H.H. Tremaine Esq. & H.A. Fellowes Esq.	Samuel Wilcocks	Tracys Green, Hoopers & Vicaries	£1.16s.0d.
Revd Mr Melhuish	Samuel Wilcocks	Town Park	6s.0d.
H.A. Fellowes Esq.	Robert Norrish	Rondon	18s.0d.
Mr C. Chapple	Thomas Walker	Bythen	£1.16s.0d
?	Margery Greenslade	Stephenses	£1.4s.0d.
H.H. Tremaine Esq.	William Lake	Borns	18s.0d.
Revd Mr Melhuish	Mr William Sory	Witheridge Cannington	18s.0d.
Mr Morrish	Thomas Western	Ffords	6s.0d.
Poor of Crediton	Mr James Cole	Shippenhay	2s.0d.
Revd Mr Melhuish	William Comins	? Barnfors ?	6s.0d.
Revd Mr Melhuish	Mr Thomas Elworthy	?	6s.0d.
H.H. Tremain Esq.	Robert Sowden	Stodham	6s.0d.
Mr Yard	John Ford	Gunhole	6s.0d.
Richard Elworthy	Richard Elworthy	Bonds & Diers	12s.0d.
H.A. Fellowes Esq.	James Davey	Witheridge Mill	£1.16s.0d.
Thomas Bodley	Joan Bodley	Gaters	12s.0d.
Edward Bodley	Edward Bodley	Ditchetts	6s.0d.
Revd Mr Melhuish	William Veysey	Downhays	£1.4s.0d.
H.H. Tremaine Esq.	John Moor & John Burgess	Broomhouse	12s.0d
Poor of Crediton	John Hill	Penford	6s.0d.
H.H. Tremaine Esq.	George Spencer	Southwoods	12s.0d
H.A. Fellowes Esq.	John Burgess	The Great House & Garden	4s.3d.
Revd Mr Melhuish	Walter Tidbeald	The Bellhouse	4s.3d.
Thos Gunn	Thos Gunn	For his houses	2s.2d.
William Comins	Thos Melhuish Comins	The Malthouse	2s.6d.

| H.A. Fellowes Esq. | Frances Cole | His houses | 2s.2d. |
| Mr Thomas Officer of Excise | | for his Sallery | £10.0s.0s. |

Total   **£54.1s.4d.**

SUM TOTAL   **£228.6s.1d.**

James Partridge, Robert Thorne, William Lake, Samuel Wilcocks – Assessors.

June ye 19th 1780 Allowed by us John Cruwys, J.B. Karslake, John Southcombe.

THE CHURCH & POOR HOUSES IN THE EARLY-NINETEENTH CENTURY

The earliest churchwardens' accounts that we have begin in 1817. The following information is from these times and should be read whilst also considering the picture of the church and the poor houses that shows the church spire *(see page 33)*.

The year 1817 saw the installation of a gallery at the back of the church for the musicians and singers. Subscriptions in that year brought in £26, but the final bill from a local carpenter, John Western, came to £77.12s. The same year new strings for the violin cost 7s.6d. Having the poor houses swept cost 1s. and 'keeping the yard, hedges and cutting of weed' cost another 1s. 'Drawing the clock' cost a further 10s. Lime was brought from Watchet in Somerset at £4.6s.8d., and a letter from London cost 1s., as in those days the recipient paid for the letter, not the sender.

In 1818 a cello and bow were purchased, to accompany the violin, at the heavy price of 6s.6d. There are references to buying 'reeds', and it is known that the church owned a clarinet. Books were also bought for the singers.

The poor houses needed to be re-thatched regularly; on one occasion the reed and spars cost £3.9s., and the work cost £3.4s. The church made regular payments to masons, carpenters and glaziers.

In 1828 new railings and gates cost £28.8s. In 1830 the churchyard was troubled by moles, so the church spent 10d. getting rid of them. In 1831 there is record of 'staking and minding trees in the yard 6d.' This may mean that the oldest tree in the churchyard is over 170 years old. In 1836 a new tower clock was bought and installed for £30.3s. At the end of the 1830s disaster struck: the wooden spire was hit by lightning and destroyed. Rather than replace it, a third masonry tier was added to the tower. This involved a lot of expense over the next few years:

1840–41 Paid Mr Thomas towards the repairs of the tower £150
1841–42 Paid Mr Bassett for fresh hanging the bells £25.5s.
1842–43 Paid Thomas Western mason his bill £51.5s.6d.
1842–43 Paid John Brawn Carpenter his bill £47.17s.4d.

The vicar watches the tower extension through a telescope, c.1830.

Chapter 3

THE VICTORIAN AGE

Drayford Bridge

This is part of a document of 1811, levying a special rate on a list of properties in Thelbridge, East Worlington, Woolfardisworthy and Drayford, for the repair of Drayford and East Worlington bridges. The Drayford properties charged were:

Thomas Partridge for part of Stuckleys	*1s.3.*	*three farthings*
John Vicary for part of Stuckleys	*10d.*	
Thomas Partridge for Trixes	*4d.*	*one farthing*
William Nichols for Warrens	*4d.*	*one farthing*
William Nichols for Mays and Cobleys	*6d.*	*one farthing*
Susan Carnall for part of Stockham	*6d.*	*halfpenny*
William White for Drayford Mills	*5d.*	*one farthing*
	4s.4d.	*one farthing*

Thos Partridge and Wm Bennett – Tythingmen
October ye 16th 1811
Allowed by us J.B. Karslake and ?

Repairs to Drayford Bridge, 1811.

[Tithingmen were Parish Officers appointed by the manor court to carry out a range of responsibilities. Those included in the above list were only responsible for Drayford Bridge, together with the occupant of Rock in the parish of East Worlington.]

WITHERIDGE CHARITIES

The oldest charity was the £1 a year given by 'John Gaydon, Vicar of this Parish'. Gaydon was vicar from 1587 to 1620. His pound was later added to those forming the 'Poor's money'.

By his will of 19 February 1670, Humphrey Brooke gave for the poor of the parish of Witheridge a yearly rent charge of 60s.; 20s. from Edgerley in Cruwys Morchard; and 40s. from West Bradley in Tiverton. At an unknown date Richard Greenslade gave 5s. from Gunhole.

In 1715 Hugh Shortrudge left £100, the income from which was distributed among five poor men and five poor widows of the parish of Witheridge.

An unnamed person left £5, the interest from which was to be laid out in two copies of 'The Whole Duty of Man' by the vicar and churchwardens. Various other sums were added to this, including £3 from Mrs Joan Spry, for the poor of the parish. The total sum was called 'the Poor's money' and consisted of 13 individual donations.

In 1799 Richard Melhuish gave £500 of stock to endow a school for 40 children residing in the parish. In 1801 he added £200 and in 1804 he assigned the school a house and garden.

In 1845 John Partridge left £100 to be invested for the poor of the parish, to which was added £10 from the family of Thomas Comins.

In 1870 the Revd John Peter Benson, vicar of Witheridge, gave £300 to be invested for the maintenance of the church, the walls, fences, gates and paths of the churchyard, although nothing was to go to the bells, organ or lighting. This charity was augmented by £43 from Revd J.P.M. Benson. In 1919 the will of Elizabeth Benson added £80 to this same fund. In 1912 she had set up a Church nursing charity with £20.

THE CONGREGATIONAL CHAPEL & SCHOOL

In 1838 a plot of ground, part of a field called Dyers:

... was conveyed on trust to permit a chapel to be built

thereon to be used as a place of worship by the Congregation or Society of Protestant Dissenters of the Congregational Denomination called Independents.

In 1845 'a piece of land upon which a school was then being erected, situated and late part of Tracy Green at Witheridge' was conveyed on trust for a school to be called The Witheridge Independent Chapel Day School. Following this, in 1848, a piece of land of about a quarter of an acre 'part of a close called Dyers, bounded partly by the Independent Chapel' was obtained for use as a burial-ground.

In 1854 a further piece of Dyers, with a house and private access from the highway, was obtained to act as a parsonage house, and in 1859 the rest of Dyers was acquired.

In 1861 John Lake's will provided £200 to be invested for the poor and sick members of the chapel. In 1877, 1884 and 1900 legacies came to the chapel from Revd J. Smith, Sarah Davey and Thomas Elworthy Adams. In 1898 the original independent-school building was condemned as inadequate for educational purposes by the education authorities, and replaced by a new school, built on a piece of land known as Slew Park, adjacent to the chapel.

In 1899 John Bragg created a charity to provide

The Congregational Church. In 1814 a group of dissenting Christians met for worship at Robert Turner's house in Tracy Green. Around 1819 a Congregational Church Sunday school was established for 30 children. The first minister, the Revd O'Neill, came in 1837; his first service was taken in Mr Henry Davey's carpentry shop in The Square, attended by a large crowd. Fundraising began and in 1839 a plot of ground in Dyer's Field was obtained. The chapel that we see today was opened in 1839. Its success brought the addition of a gallery for 100 in 1855. In 1845 the first Chapel (British) School (now the Church Rooms) was built following a generous contribution from Mr John Lake, whose bounty also covered the master's salary and money towards the school fees of the poorer children. The new school (now the surgery) was built in 1898, any debt being cleared by the following year. Mr Lake also gave land for a burial-ground and manse, for which he also paid. In 1859 the candles in the chapel were replaced by oil-lamps and in 1931 electric lights were installed. The chapel celebrated its 150th anniversary in 1989.

an annual sum of £5 for the deserving poor of Witheridge, plus a dozen blankets and five shirts. The land on which this charge was laid was 'Southwood's', consisting of the several fields or closes of land called Garden, Fooks First Field, Fooks Second Field and Fooks Third Field, numbered respectively on the Tithe Apportionment of the Parish of Witheridge 643, 644, 645, 646 and containing in the whole by admeasurements 9 acres, 1 rod, 37 perches. (Over the years the name 'Fooks' has become 'Tooks'.)

THE TWO SCHOOLS IN WITHERIDGE

The first reference that we have to schooling in Witheridge is a petition dated 6 March 1728, sent from the parish to the Bishop of Exeter for a licence for John Pulsford to teach 'to read, write and arithmetic in the town and parish of Witheridge.' The petitioners were the vicar John Shebbear, the churchwardens Robert Bidgood and John Grant, eight 'chief inhabitants' whose names have a familiar ring in 2003: Tanner, Thomas, Radford, Bodley, Greenslade, Elworthy, Stevens, and Comins. John Pulsford had already been teaching in Witheridge for four trial months and the petitioner believed him to be competent, 'peaceable and sober'. The bishop granted the licence.

The next reference to schooling was in 1799 when Richard Melhuish founded a school and endowed it. At this time there were less than 40 endowed village schools in Devon. The Melhuishes had had a long connection with Witheridge. In 1425 a Richard Melhuish collected tithes for the vicar, in 1581 a Thomas Melhuish owned Dart Raffe Farm and was patron of the living, and another Thomas Melhuish was vicar from 1745–93. In the 1790s a Richard Melhuish lived at Bradford, and was a churchwarden and patron of the living. His new purpose was to keep a daily school for teaching 40 of the poorest children resident in the parish to read, spell and say their catechism. If spelling included writing, then Witheridge's school was one of the 19 per cent of Devon schools teaching these two subjects. Around 60 per cent of them just taught reading.

Richard Melhuish's endowment of £500 invested in 3 per cent Consols proved not to be enough.

The National School became Mole Valley Farmers Engineering Division.

In 1801 he added a further £200 and in 1804 he made over to the trustees a house and garden for the school and master for the sum of 5s., on a 1,000-year lease, with an annual rental of 2s. The precise location of these premises is unclear. The trustees were the vicar and churchwardens, and the owner of the Bradford estate. At this time the Melhuishes owned it, to be succeeded by the Bensons.

There is little detail of the school's early years. The headmaster's salary was £14 a year, and in 1833 a mistress was taken on at £6 a year. Books and bibles were bought, and in the 1830s knitting was included in the curriculum, partly to generate funds – in 1841 it accounted for 15 per cent of the school's income.

In 1845 the British (Chapel) School was built (now the Church Rooms). It was only the sixth such school in Devon at that time. The Church was quick to respond, so in 1846 the National (Church) School and headmaster's house were erected with help from the National Society by way of grants, textbooks and standards of teaching. The British Society had performed the same function for Nonconformist schools. In the space of 12 months church and chapel families were provided with schools that had the capacity to teach all the children in the village and surrounds.

At this time it was not unusual for children to leave school before they were aged 14. As the century moved on, the authorities increased their vigilance and child employment dwindled. The census of 1851 paints a picture of mid-century Witheridge. At that time 26 children between the ages of 11 and 14 were in work or tied to an apprenticeship. There may well have been more, for it was common for farmers to enter their children of this age group as 'at home', where they no doubt worked in the house or on the farm. The three youngest at work in 1851 were aged 11. They were Ann Thorn, a servant, Philip Thorne (not a relative), who was an agricultural labourer, and William Crook, apprentice to a cordwainer (boot- and shoemaker). Of the 26, a dozen were described as servant, house servant or farm servant, while 14-year-old William Hodge was a mill servant. As well as William Crook there were three other young apprentices – William Western aged 12, plus Joseph White and Henry Dinner, both aged 14. Some of the youngsters seem to have bypassed the apprenticeship stage and gone directly into a trade. Sarah Cockram (aged 12) was a dressmaker, Lucy Francis (14) was a glover and Mary Ann Cockram (14) was a milliner. The 12-year-old William Cruydge was entered as an errand boy, and William Paul (12) was already an agricultural labourer. Three children were aged 11, seven were 12, three were 13, and 13 were 14 years old. Half a century later the picture would be very different.

The British School, 1845–96

Delighted as chapel families must have been with their own school, certain difficulties had to be faced.

Firstly, there was no land at all other than that on which the school stood, so the village square had to serve as a playground. Local residents objected and were rebuked by Mr Rogers, the head, who told them that boys were boys and had to get rid of 'their superfluous spirits' somewhere. Secondly, the building was difficult to heat, as there was no stove upstairs until the 1880s. Certainly the school's log-book recorded on one occasion that 'it is a hard matter for the children to hold their pens and pencils at all, and the ink is frozen in the inkwells.' There were times when the children were sent outside to run about in the wintry weather in order to get warm enough to come back inside and continue with their lessons. Thirdly, as there was only one teacher in the early years and the school was on two floors (infants and Standards One and Two were upstairs, while Standards Three, Four, Five and Six were downstairs) his task was exceedingly difficult. It took a stern warning from Her Majesty's Inspector (HMI) to stir the managers into appointing an assistant teacher, which was just as well, as by the 1880s the school roll had reached 90.

Little is known about the early years, as the school log does not begin until 1872. From that point on there were five head teachers in 25 years, and a wide range of methods were used. W.H. Rogers (known for his poetry and his press reports in verse) believed in the involvement of parents and managers, not only in visiting the school but also in helping with tests and exams. One Mrs Coles was impressed by the discipline, because on arriving at the school she heard no noise. She assumed the pupils were on holiday, but they were hard at work. A Mr Comins examined the first and second classes in dictation, composition and transcription. Mr Partridge and Mr Maunder visited on behalf of the Thelbridge ratepayers and expressed their satisfaction. Mr Rogers seems to have been a lively teacher, full of ideas, and he introduced English history in rhyme and gave lectures on physiology, taxes and blood transfusions. He began annual school visits to Creedy Park, Sandford. He started quizzes and offered prizes, and he was praised by HMI and by a former pupil in

The original British School, now the Church Rooms.

America who attributed his success to the training he had received at the school.

Mr Rogers' successor, Mr Stokes, introduced magic lantern shows in order to raise funds for books, and was also praised by HMI (who often criticised the premises). Sadly Mr Stokes' log dwindled to a list of those who got the cane – on two occasions 12 pupils were caned on a single day. He was quickly succeeded by Mr Saunders, who made sparing use of the cane and who was better placed than his predecessors in that his wife was an assistant teacher. He was also aided by a 14-year-old girl who acted as a monitor. After 18 months HMI wrote 'the efficiency of the school is so high that I feel justified in classing it as excellent.' However, HMI was scornful of the local way of speaking; and wrote 'Composition is particularly difficult in this district owing to the false concords constantly used in the speech of the peasantry.' After five years Mr Saunders left; the log provides no explanation.

In 1890 Mr and Mrs Jones took over and recorded 39 boys, 37 girls and 28 infants on the register, a total of 104. HMI's criticism that the infants lacked desks, pictures and a room of their own, stirred the managers into providing desks. Managers also took the crucial step of accepting the 'Fee Grant', which replaced the old system of School Pence and made education free. This encouraged parents and gave more security to teachers who had formerly relied on School Pence to make up part of their salaries. Nevertheless, the log at this time was full of complaints at the restrictions of the school accommodation and of the authorities' failure to enforce attendance. Absence had been a problem for years and the reasons given varied – the local fair or menagerie, the Sunday-school anniversary tea, harvest, stone picking, the races, snow, scarlet fever and outings were some reasons given for why pupils stayed away from school.

The National School 1846–94

The part of the new school that was the teacher's house was very compact at 20ft by 20ft. However, the two classrooms, which could be used as one, measured 30ft by 20ft. It was said to have been designed for 200 pupils, perhaps on the assumption that the Chapel School would not be built. The average attendance of 60–70 pupils must have rattled about in such a space. The school cost £434.4s.11d., including £16 for lavatories. The bulk of the money was provided thus: £150 from the leasehold of the old property, £70 from the National Society and £177 from a Government grant. The school was expensive to heat and maintain, and endowment interest needed to be supplemented by School Pence, the scheme by which each child brought a penny to school each day.

The 1862 Act that required head teachers to keep log-books has left a great legacy; we are now able to glean the personality of the head, not simply give a straightforward picture of school life. Some heads laid emphasis on the weather, others on the recurring problem of absence. The more absences there were, the less School Pence came in and less money was available to be spent on books, materials or topping up salaries. In addition, if HMI was not pleased with the attendance or the teaching, the grant might be reduced. There was also the annual visit by the Diocesan Inspector, whose reports were invariably blandly approving. HMI, on the other hand, could and did sharply criticise managers for their failings.

The head in 1863 was John Mansfield, who was often irritated by the reasons for children's absences. In addition to those mentioned above for the British School, other excuses included: 'Rackenford Races', 'Worlington Revel', 'market day', 'gardening', 'weeding', 'Fossett's Circus', 'election day', 'Queen Victoria's Jubilee'. Formal holidays were three weeks at Christmas and midsummer and ten days at Easter. The attendance officer visited with little effect. Some parents were unhelpful; one mother sent a message to say that if 9.30a.m. was not early enough for her children to come to school then she would not send them until dinner time. Parents could also play one school off against the other. One family of five youngsters were withdrawn for being punished for lateness and sent to the British School. The following year they were back, only to be switched again after a few months.

Mr Mansfield's log showed that he and the vicar were satisfied with the running of the school, but HMI was more critical. In 1865 a letter from Whitehall stated that:

Their Lordships of the Treasury have had some hesitation in allowing an unreduced grant to the school, on account of the deficiencies in the instruction pointed out by HMI.

It seems odd to us today that there was no intervening authority between the school and Whitehall. After a particularly critical report Mr Mansfield stopped keeping a daily log and in 1872 the grant was reduced by a tenth, the first of many such reductions. In 1879 HMI said the pupils' skills in arithmetic and spelling were discreditable, geography was almost nil and needlework poor. The managers were told that they should take a more active and intelligent interest in the school and to exercise some control over the system of instruction and financial management. When John Mansfield died in 1881 HMI came close to rejoicing, as he wrote 'the death of Mr Mansfield is a favourable opportunity to put things on a different footing.'

His successor, Henry Westacott, quickly earned high praise from HMI, as 'the premises are much improved... the work is remarkably good', but the attendance was 'irregular'. Indeed in 1883 Mr Westacott wrote in the log:

I have great difficulty in making the children come punctually to school; when the school opens at 9, not more than one third are early; the rest stroll in between 9 o'clock and a quarter to 10.

If late children were punished, their parents promptly removed them to the other school. Presumably rivalry between the schools prevented the heads getting together and agreeing a common policy on punishment for lateness. In 1885 he received an unusual instruction from a parent. The mother of a boy who suffered from fits ordered Mr Westacott not to teach him arithmetic, as she was sure this was the cause of the fits.

In 1885, after four years, Mr Westacott left, following the Diocesan Inspector's report on his 'neglect of duty'. No details were given. His successor's stay was even more brief and disastrous. Mr Broadridge lasted only ten months and when he left the log recorded: 'Things in great confusion, there being no register or timetable', and the roll had fallen from 50 to 28.

Mr Henry P. Cornish followed, who was made of sterner stuff. He shrewdly involved the managers, getting them to visit regularly, at the same time drawing their attention to the shortage of teaching materials, and to the need for repairs to the building. By 1890 the roll had risen to 71, but Mr Cornish's task as the only teacher for infants and six standards of education would seem to have been too great for one person. However, HMI's recommendation of an extra teacher was ignored. Soon there were 89 pupils on the roll and the managers grudgingly provided one very young monitor. By 1891 HMI had had enough and forced the managers to appoint Miss Jessie Ford as an assistant mistress. There was an immediate improvement, although the class of 26 infants desperately needed physical separation from the older children.

In 1893 School Pence was abolished, to the relief of the parents who had to pay it, teachers who had to collect it, and managers who relied on it to balance their budgets. As at the British School, it was replaced by 'Fee Grant' from the Government. In the same year HMI was scathing; the arithmetic was poor, dictation was defective, the general work was below standard and there was still no gallery where the infants could be taught separately from the rest of the school. Mr Cornish added his own comments to this report, describing it as unintelligible and ignoring all the good work done in his seven years as head. A month later he resigned. The supply teacher who temporarily replaced him accused the managers of meanness in failing to provide such basics as slates, pencils and books.

So by the mid-1890s each school had had unhelpful managers, frequent changes of head and poor reports. The time had come for some continuity and major changes. By the end of the century, changes had been put in place that led to new premises and a headship of 25 years for one school, and to greatly expanded premises and a headship of 36 years for the other.

WITHERIDGE & THE TURNPIKE ROADS

Risdon, writing of the roads in Devon in the 1630s, described them as 'painful for man and horse'. So bad were they in North Devon that even carts were a rarity. The packhorse was the main means of transport. Sheldon, writing in his *From Trackway to Turnpike*, stated that in the early-eighteenth century the coming of wheeled traffic made slower progress in Devon than in most of southern England. In those days parishes were responsible for the roads that ran through them. If it was a main road then clearly the parish's resources were likely to be inadequate for the task. Sheldon said that 'the roads around Tiverton by 1758 were so bad that the parishes could not keep them operational.' By then, however, the 'turnpike' idea had caught on. A Turnpike Trust in an area could be set up by an Act of Parliament. This made trustees responsible for certain roads, allowed them to raise money for road improvement, and permitted them to charge the users of such roads. Devon and Cornwall were slow to adopt this idea, but in the West between 1751 and 1772 there was a boom and 50 new Acts were passed for Devon and Cornwall. In the Witheridge area a turnpike road was established for South Molton to Tiverton via Rackenford, and another for South Molton to Exeter via Alswear, Meshaw Moor, Drayford, Thelbridge Cross, Kennerleigh and Crediton. Witheridge therefore missed out, which may have contributed to its failure to become a borough. However, Witheridge names occur among the trustees, such as Partridge, Cooke, Shortrudge and Melhuish.

A good idea though the turnpike was, Vancouver in *Agriculture of Devon 1808* accused Devon's roads of being narrower than they should have been, badly maintained, worn by lime carts, and 'broken into so many holes and unevenness as to endanger the knees of the horse and the neck of the rider.' They could not therefore have done the newly introduced coaches much good either; the route from Barnstaple to South Molton, Rackenford and Tiverton was a through route to London. Turnpikes needed a shot in the arm and they got it from an unexpected source, namely the railway. North Devon in the 1830s woke up sharply to the fact that the railway would run from London to Bristol and on to Exeter. It was vital that North Devon improved its roads in order to be connected to the railway. Tiverton helped with a new turnpike that linked the town with Nomansland, Thelbridge, Chawleigh and the new Exeter–Barnstaple turnpike at Eggesford. It was better still for Witheridge when in 1837 the trustees of South Molton Turnpikes proposed an Act for a number of roads from that town, including a direct road through Witheridge connecting with the other at Westway Cross. This Act was passed in 1839.

The new road entered Witheridge parish at the point where West Yeo Bridge crosses the Adworthy Brook. An old road plunged straight down and straight up again but 1830s thinking preferred a more gentle descent and climb, to make it easier for the horse-drawn vehicles that had largely replaced pack-horses. The road then curved and ran level to Dart Cross, whence it sliced straight through the fields of Dart Raffe and West Yeo before dropping down to cross the river on a causeway and a new bridge over the Little Dart River. The bridge engineer, G.A. Boyce, has his name on it. The bridge was high above the water and the road ran diagonally up the steep slope on the other side to the village. Just past the old road to Witheridge Mill was, on the left, a toll-house, known as Witheridge Town Toll Gate.

The Act of Parliament laid down in minute detail the specifications for the road, including the 20ft width, the camber, the drainage, the hedge banks on either side and their planting, as well as the provision of pavements where the road passed through the village itself. Investment money was needed in order to purchase land and to acquire and knock down buildings in the village. It is clear from what eventually happened that not enough money was raised to meet all the conditions. Where the road passed the churchyard the church houses were bought and demolished. The Act did not require the trustees to buy and knock down the houses on the other side of the road, so no pavement was built and the width of the road is below standard. Similarly, there was no requirement to knock down the buildings at Trafalgar Square so the pavement is seriously deficient on both sides of the road.

Coach proprietors were quick to cash in on the new road, and in the early 1840s Mr Marsh's 'Emerald' coach left the Golden Lion in Barnstaple daily at 8a.m., picked up in South Molton and Witheridge and reached Tiverton station in time for the 12.40p.m. express train for Taunton, Bristol and Chippenham, which reached Paddington at 5.25p.m. *White's Directory* for 1850 shows coaches leaving South Molton three times daily to connect with trains for Bristol and London. To attract the coaching trade the proprietors of the Angel Hotel rebuilt their thatched premises in the form it retains in 2003, and the Benson family knocked down most of Hodge's Tenement and built Aston House (later the Mitre). This was opened as a coaching inn but the Angel had stolen a march on them and it closed, not to reopen as such for another 120 years. The Bensons used it for many years as a Vicarage after the original parsonage house burnt down.

The tolls for passing through each toll-gate were set out in the Act of Parliament. For each horse drawing a stagecoach or wagon the charge was 8d., unless the fellies of the wheels were less than 6in. in

The toll-house opposite the National School, c.1920.

width, in which case the fee was 1s. (the narrower the wheels the more the surface could be cut up). Any vehicle drawn by 'steam, gas or machinery' paid 2s. Droves of oxen or other cattle were charged at 1s.3d. for 20, and sheep at 7½d. Return journeys within 24 hours were free. Needless to say attempts were made to avoid payment. At Thornham's toll-gate a friendly farmer of East Worlington would allow a flock of sheep to be driven through his fields, so avoiding the gate, and horse riders were known to spur their horses on to jump the toll-gate to escape payment.

By the 1870s it was clear that the system was not working. Investors were not being paid interest, the value of their capital was declining and the turnpikes were not being well managed or maintained. Together with many others, the Trust was wound up on 1 May 1882, and investors received a token sum when roads became a county responsibility. The Witheridge Town Toll Gate was sold for £20 to the vicar, who repaired it, added a bedroom and rented it out for 1s. a week. Part of the front wall can still be identified, near the lower iron gates of the churchyard. Cannington's toll-house, at the top of the village, was bought by George Cutcliffe for £25; only its garden can be seen today.

That Mr Boyce and his workmen did a good job 190 years ago is proven by the fact that the line and width of the road are as they were left in 1840; only the tarmac surface is relatively new. West Yeo Bridge and New Bridge are structurally sound, although the latter has taken a few knocks over the years. Mr Boyce could not have foreseen the coming of the motor vehicle or the huge increase in weight and amount of traffic. As far as Witheridge is concerned, only the road east out of the village has had to be straightened and widened.

WITHERIDGE UNION SOCIETY

One day in 1849 the chairman of the Witheridge Union Society, Mr H. Davey, was visiting Thorverton, where he had been told that a member of the Society, William Elworthy, had been seen selling shoes on three occasions at a time when he was drawing sickness benefit from the Society, of which he was a member. Naturally, working while drawing sickness benefit was against the rules. The doctor who signed Mr Elworthy's sickness certificate had meant to indicate that he was incapable of hard labouring work, but the Society's rules said that any work done must invalidate benefit. The Society cancelled Mr Elworthy's membership and claimed the money already paid him. Mr Elworthy denied any wrongdoing. However, the Society's lawyers advised that money could only be reclaimed from members and, as Mr Elworthy was no longer a member, no money could be reclaimed. The case went to the magistrate's court, who rejected both the Society's claim, and Mr Elworthy's counterclaim against it. Even the Registrar of Friendly Societies could not help the Society, and each side ended up meeting their own costs. A year later Mr Elworthy took the Society to court for damages and lost. This case shows how far the Witheridge Union Society was prepared to go to recover lost money.

For centuries the village poor were the responsibility of the overseers if they could not work because of age or sickness. Medicines, a room in the poor house, a re-thatched roof, a repaired floor, clothes, and at the end a decent laying out and burial – all this came from the parish rates paid by those whose property required them to do so.

A farm worker.

Parishes looked after their own; people from elsewhere who became a burden were sent back to their home parishes.

By the end of the eighteenth century a new system was in place whereby working men (and only men) could make a weekly contribution to a fund, on which they could draw in time of sickness and which at the end would contribute towards a decent funeral. This new system meant that men were entitled to draw from a fund to which they had themselves contributed and were no longer at the mercy of the Parish Officers. Such a fund was legally registered and managed by the contributors themselves and by the vicar or lord of the manor. The members were responsible for dealing with fraudulent claims, for seeing that the finances were properly managed and that the rules were obeyed. Each year two stewards were appointed to check on claims and no member could refuse this task without being fined.

In the early days of 'Union Societies', or 'Friendly Societies' as they were sometimes called, many failed because they lacked the actuarial skills needed to establish the proper relationship between age at joining, weekly subscription rates and extent of benefits. If the rate was too low, there might not be enough money for benefits; too high, and there might not be enough members to make the Society viable. If benefits were set too high and too many members joined in their forties and fifties there might not be enough money to meet eventual claims. Acts of Parliament in 1819 and 1829 established guidance and rules to help societies avoid these pitfalls.

The Witheridge Union Society was formed on 19 June 1839 and a set of 35 rules were adopted. Among the points covered were the classes of membership. At the start there were only two classes of membership: class one was for tradesmen earning not less than 10s. a week, and class two was for farm workers earning not less than 7s. a week. In 1867 a group of members called a special meeting; they included Joseph Churchill (saddler and landlord of the Bell Inn), William Crook (miller at Bradford), James Dinner (wheelwright) and William Western (boot- and shoemaker). As a result an extra class of membership was added, namely 'tradesmen, mechanics or yeomen earning not less than 15 shillings per week', another sign of success. At the start the subscription was 1s. per four weeks for class one, and 8d. per four weeks for class two. 'Month Nights' were held in the Club Room for subs to be paid. Stewards, elected by members, were fined if they missed such a night – their most important task was to check that claims were genuine. Stewards were elected annually from among the members, and any member refusing the duty was fined. The Society was indeed run by the members for the members. Once a steward had verified that a sickness claim was genuine, then if confined to bed 10s. per week was payable, or if capable of walking then 5s. per week. Once payment began stewards had to visit each claimant 'at uncertain times' to prevent fraud. When a member died £8 was paid towards his funeral expenses, raised not from subscriptions but from a levy on all members. An extraordinary feature of the Witheridge Union Society was that, instead of banking a year's surplus against a possible future run on funds due to an epidemic (as most societies did) the bulk of Witheridge's annual surplus was distributed to members. It is not surprising therefore that the Society became popular and drew its membership from a wide area.

How It Worked

In 1843 a member, John Barnes, was ejected from the Society 'for drinking in a Public House at West Morchard Fair being under sick pay at the time.' Another was excluded for being more than four months in arrears with his subscriptions. By May

1844 there were 171 members, of whom 156 attended the annual dinner, which had become a feature of the Society. In the same year Mr G.H. Pullen was appointed as treasurer, a post he held for 47 years. He was succeeded by his son for a further 22 years. G.H. Pullen was a Witheridge grocer and tea-blender who had, in 1840, built the eight houses of Pullens Row that are still standing in 2003. In 1845 Samuel Foxford was expelled for applying for a medical certificate and going to work on the same day. A rule insisted that new members must be aged between 20 and 25, but that after the age of 67 paying members would have their monthly subs returned to them, provided they had received no sick pay in that year (retirement ages were at this time a thing of the future).

In 1846 Joseph Tucker became clerk to the Society, and eventually the *South Molton Gazette* reported that in 43 years of membership he had never drawn a penny of sick pay. The annual dinner was put out to tender, and in 1849 the tenderers were W. Rippen (the Commercial Inn) at 1s.4d. per head, Mr J. Brawn (the Angel Hotel) at 1s.2d., Mr R. Churchill (the Bell Inn) at 1s.4d., and a non-landlord Mr W. Bulled whose price of 1s.1d. won the day; he presumably would have hired a marquee. Later history suggests that the Black Dog Inn would have been too small, and the Mitre's short career as a pub had already come to an end.

By 1854 the Society had already been troubled by fraudulent claims for burial money. Two safeguards were introduced: there had to be a medical certificate confirming death was not attributed to 'Poison, violence or criminal neglect', or a coroner had to certify that the dead man 'had not been deprived of his life by means of any person beneficially interested in obtaining Burial Money from any Society.' This seems to suggest that it was not unknown for next of kin to hasten a member's end to get their hands on the burial money.

In 1858 it was decided to commission a flag 'to be made of silk, red with a Union Jack in the corner, made of blue and white.' This would be carried in the well-established 29 May procession. By 1869 it is clear that members could transfer from one class to another, and that membership from outside Witheridge was increasing. Places of residence included Birmingham, Torquay, Weston-super-Mare and London – clearly members who had left Witheridge still valued the benefits. One unlucky member had gone further afield, for William Vickery sent his claim for sick pay from America, but it was refused on the grounds that his medical certificate had not been received within the specified time limits. In view of the time taken for his letter to cross the Atlantic, this ruling seems harsh. Another member also ventured overseas: in 1881 the War Office told the Society that one of their members, George Docket of the Second Battalion the Foot Regiment, had died in Kandahar in the second Afghan War.

Expansion

Attendance at the annual dinner rose from 170 in 1853 to 240 in 1855. In turn, this rose to 270 in 1859, 300 in 1863, 440 in 1884, and over 500 in 1886. By 1890 it had reached its peak of 'about 1,000'. The existing committee structure could not cope with these numbers and an 'Extra Committee' was created, with one representative each from no less than 25 parishes in the area, from Brompton Regis in the north to Tiverton in the east, Crediton in the south and George Nympton in the west.

After meeting for years in Mr Davey's house in The Square, they moved two doors along to 'Mr Churchill's'. He had been landlord of the Bell Inn when it and the whole row along the north side of The Square had burned down in 1886, to be rebuilt in the style still evident in 2003.

Expansion brought a touch of pride and defiance to the Society, for in 1881 the decision was taken to inform the registrar of Friendly Societies that it was no longer deemed necessary to complete the five-yearly valuation required by law. For this, however, the Society was brought to heel and in 1883 it did send in its valuation. It had already defied the registrar by refusing to deposit the required bond in 1875 with trustees as security for the money of which their treasurer had charge. This defiance lasted eight years before a bond was finally deposited in 1883. Even then it was at fault for the Society could give the registrar no reason why large sums remained in the treasurer's hands without being invested for the Society's benefit. Two more years passed before the rules were changed to allow spare funds to be invested in the Post Office Savings Bank. It is doubtful whether the registrar ever approved of the Witheridge Union Society's policy of distributing to members on 29 May each year nearly all the year's surplus funds, but perhaps the law tied his hands in this matter.

The Club Walk

Like many similar societies Witheridge's annual celebration included what became known as the Club Walk. This took place on 29 May and took the form of a procession around the village. In the 1840s there were strict rules; members had to walk two by two and in the order that their names were listed on the roll. A band took part in the march – in the years when Witheridge had no band of its own one was usually hired from South Molton. The route seldom varied. A start would be made outside the Club Room (near today's newsagent) before the procession crossed The Square, rounded the Pound House and passed up West Street to Trafalgar Square. From there it went to what was described as 'the head of the village', which was probably the Congregational Chapel. From there the procession returned past the

Mitre to the church. Reports suggest that there were times when the course was covered twice. A banner was acquired in 1858, which was carried high at the front of the procession. As the years went by, the two-by-two formation was abandoned for something less formal, although fines could be imposed if behaviour became disorderly.

As for the dinner on the day, from 1883 a marquee was hired, as the inns could not accommodate the numbers. In 1892 Mr George Cutcliffe of Coombe gave the Society its own marquee. A favourite site for this seems to have been Mr Selley's Field (now the sports field). It was, of course, impossible to have a dinner without speeches, so the chairman and the clergy of all three dominations usually obliged. Sometimes they would be joined by the local MP and one year the local member, George Lambert, took time off from his ministerial duties as Civil Lord of the Admiralty to come down and address the gathering. Another function of the dinner was to elect the committee and extra committee for the following year.

By the 1880s, the celebrations of 29 May in Witheridge had become a major attraction for the surrounding area, and hundreds of people came to enjoy the roundabouts, shows, shooting galleries, swings and coconut shies. A good deal of cider was drunk but a suggestion in the *South Molton Gazette* of June 1886 that the day ended in 'drunkenness and excess' was indignantly denied the following week by the chairman and all the ministers of religion.

The Last Years

In the 1890s commercial insurance companies began to make their presence felt, particularly with their lump-sum payments on death, which guaranteed a good deal more to widows and children than the simple funeral expenses offered by societies. One effect was the reduction in membership of the Witheridge Union Society. From a peak of about 1,100 in 1892, it fell to 719 in 1904 – a drop of 381 in 12 years. It was ominous that in 1904 £348 was paid out in sick pay, the same figure as in 1892, although membership had fallen by a third. In 1904 £210 was paid out in dividends, leaving so little in balances that a special meeting had to be called to deal with the problem. A sudden epidemic could have crippled the Society, and in any case the Friendly Societies Act of 1896 had called on societies to keep balances in hand for emergencies. The Witheridge Union Society had ignored this advice for eight years. It was also perhaps unaware that medical science was helping to prolong life, leading to more sick claims in old age. In addition the national birth rate was declining with the effect of reducing the number of young workers who might be expected to join societies. This was not all. In 1908 National Old Age Pensions were introduced and the National

Insurance Acts of 1911 and 1920 gave people health and unemployment insurance.

By 1900 there were nearly 24,000 societies in the UK, with about 4,250,000 members; the two largest, The Oddfellows and the Foresters, each had over 700,000 members. The 1911 Act allowed societies to serve as the channels for the National Insurance Scheme, and in 1913 the Witheridge Society was given these responsibilities. In the same year the Society's funds were placed in Fox Fowler's bank in Witheridge. In 1914 membership was down to 540, with only 180 at the dinner. In 1917 funds were so tight that a new rule restricted the total amount of sick pay a member could draw in one year, and allowed permanently disabled members to benefit for a maximum of eight years only. By 1918 only Tiverton, Oakford and Morchard Bishop were represented on the extra committee. Annual dinners had not taken place during the First World War, and although discussions took place in 1920 regarding this tradition's revival the event was not held again.

In April 1922 what must have been long dreaded came to pass. There was not enough money to meet claims. In May members were called on to pay an extra levy, and again in December. In 1923 sick pay rates were reduced, but a further levy had to be called in for January 1924. Members could not be expected to pay levies as well as subscriptions, and they could not continue in a Society with no future, nor could a Society continue with a dwindling membership. On 18 March 1924 it was resolved to dissolve the Society. Assets were realised and divided among the remaining members. In April the marquee was sold to the Horticultural Society for £22. The final AGM was held on 29 May 1924.

For 85 years the Society had played a major role in the life of Witheridge; it had been the members themselves and their involvement in the management of their own Society that had given it strength. It had lasted until a combination of commercial and national insurance made it redundant.

Societies such as this were overwhelmingly democratic, with the vast bulk of the movement in the hands of working people themselves. The members made the rules and saw that they were kept; the members set the rates to be fair to all and finally the members saw to it that 29 May and the Club Walk was a highlight of the year.

WITHERIDGE UNION FRIENDLY SOCIETY

Below is a summary of the report of the annual festival
in May 1892, from the *South Molton Gazette*.

The members of the Society held their annual festival on Monday. The Society extended over several parishes and the membership was about 1,100. At noon the town was paraded, the music being supplied by the Crediton Volunteer Band under the conductorship of Mr Benellick. Divine Service was held at the Church of St John the Baptist, the sacred edifice being crowded. The dinner was held in a large marquee in a field lent by Mr Hill Partridge. Mr Whitfield provided a capital dinner; a number of toasts were drunk, beginning with 'The Queen'. Archdeacon Seymour spoke and hoped the club would continue to be successful. The chairman proposed 'The Lord Lieutenant and Magistrates of the County'. He was glad that Mr Cutcliffe resided in their midst, and they could not wish for a better magistrate than he had proved himself to be. He had shown the greatest interest in the club, and the large and expensive tent in which they were met had been presented to them for their benefit. Whenever Mr Cutcliffe made a promise they were sure it would be fulfilled. In rising to respond Mr Cutcliffe was greeted with loud cheers. The chairman told the gathering that their club was a progressive and prosperous one; this could be testified by the balance sheet. Over £616 had been expended in sick pay during the last year. Mr J. Greenslade was then elected the new secretary. Mr Pullen junr was re-elected treasurer. Mr Pullen, in returning thanks, said he was the third generation of his family to hold the treasurership. Parish committees were elected for Witheridge, East and West Worlington, Morchard Bishop, Cruwys Morchard, Puddington, Templeton, Rackenford, Washford Pyne, Thelbridge, Meshaw/Rose Ash, Sandford, Oakford, Tiverton, Kings Nympton, Poughill, Woolfardisworthy, Chulmleigh, Knowstone, Stoodleigh, Crediton, Bampton, George Nympton, Cadbury, Withleigh and South Molton.

During the afternoon and evening the Crediton Volunteer Band and the Witheridge Brass Band under the conductorship of Mr S. Hill played through the town and gave selections of music in The Square. Roundabouts, shows, shooting galleries and swings occupied the greater portion of The Square, and during the evening many hundreds of people visited Witheridge from the adjoining parishes.

TITHE MAP & APPORTIONMENT

Once the nineteenth century was under way, it became clear that the system whereby the incumbent of a parish received annually a tenth of all produce of the land was difficult to collect, abused, inaccurate and unsatisfactory. It was decided that a simple money payment, charged upon each farm and tenement, would avoid argument and bitterness and would be easier to collect. In 1836 Tithe Commissioners were appointed to survey the parishes of England, recording owners, occupiers, names of holdings, names and crops of fields, and to assess the sums to be paid. The results are the Tithe Maps and Apportionments that we

have today. There were three sets for each parish. One copy of Witheridge's remains; it is in the County Record Office in Exeter, and is dated 20 October 1837.

The document offers some statistics; the total acreage of the parish (including outliers) was 9,048 acres, 1 rod and 33 perches. Of this total only 7,634 acres were cultivated and thus liable for assessment. There were 3,844 acres of arable land, 3,550 acres of meadow and pasture, 131 acres of woods and 109 acres of orchards. This leaves the relatively large amount of 1,414 acres of uncultivated ground. Witheridge Moor must have accounted for a good part of this, together with areas such as West Yeo Moor and Dart Raffe Moor. The total payable from the parish was £710, of which half went to the vicar, and half to the patron of the living, whose responsibility it was to provide a vicar and vicarage, and to maintain the chancel of the church.

There are buildings on the Tithe Map that no longer exist. East Yeo farmhouse burnt down in the 1930s and was never rebuilt; Trixes Cottages at Drayford were cleared away in the 1960s. A few heaps of nettle-grown rubble are all that is left of Stuckleys Newhouse, the birthplace of William Chapple. Broomhouse, the small farm near Venbridge, is long gone, but remembered in the name of a new development. In addition there are farmhouses that no longer serve their farmland, such as Newhouse, Hole and South Combe.

The Apportionment sometimes provides us with fresh information. Our windmill beyond Stretchdown (now Thelbridge) is recalled in the Apportionment by Mill Farm and Windmill Field. The curious property name in Drayford of 'Mays, Cobleys and Warrens' makes sense only when we realise that this was three separate pieces of land brought together under the single ownership of William Nicholls.

The largest landowners in 1837 were the vicar, the Revd William Prockter Thomas, and the Hon. Newton Fellowes. Prockter Thomas was successor to the Melhuishes and predecessor of the Bensons, major families in Witheridge's history. The vicar owned nearly 1,150 acres, including the 350 acres of Bradford Barton. Fellowes (later Earl of Portsmouth) owned almost as much and several other thousand acres in the area, including Eggesford, but this part of his Devon estate was sold in the early 1900s.

The Apportionment lists fields by their names. Fields have always had names; workers had to know in which field they must work, and the farmer's family needed to know where he would be if needed. The notes below give an idea of the diversity of Witheridge field names in 1837. Many of these names are still in use in 2003. Fields were usually named for their nature or for what was in them:

Pigs Close
Furze Park
Oxen Park,
Thistle Close
Dry Meadow
Potato Plot
Rookery Orchard
Daisey Land
Willow Plot
Poor Field
Stoney Field
Linney Close
Hare Bottom

Strawberry Orchard
Coney Park ('coney' = rabbit)
Broom Close
Ragg ('ragg' = rough stone)
Cleave (steep ground)
Ham (flat land by river)
Tansey Close
Crabtree Close (crabapple tree)
Win Close Moor ('whin' = berry)
Sanctuary (part of the Glebe)
Colley Park ('colley' = blackbird)
Barren Nap ('nap' = hill)
Mowhay

Summer Leers ('leary' = empty or hungry)
Gutring Field (with a drainage channel close by)
Gratton (where geese grazed the stubble after harvest)
Lime Close (lime may have once been burnt there).

Fields named in relation to other features:

Mill Close
Barns Close
Signpost Field
Quarry Hill

Windmill Field
Higher Backside
Weir Close
Pond Meadow

Hither, Middle and Yonder Broadclose
Horestone ('horeston' = boundary stone)
Bury Meadow (has the outline of an ancient earthwork).

Fields named for their size, shape or orientation:

Long Park
Five Acres
Three Corner Piece

North Hill
Big Field

Quillet (long and narrow like a quill).

Fields named after people may record a tenant, a worker, or an event that happened to an individual, which stuck in people's minds. Fook's Field was at one time tenanted by someone of that name:

Fulford's
Andrew's Mead

Rendall's
Robert's Spot

Here are a few of the puzzles:

Cripping Close (might refer to cripping or clipping dirty wool ends of sheep).
Higher and Lower Shillings (possibly high-value fields).
Charmsrey (an easily managed field – a charm to work).
Lower Stubby Close (where tree stubs had been left, or where stubble had been long left)
Dog Garden
White Piece (possibly a thin soil field that burnt white in a dry summer)
Rumsery
Lower Grape Close

THE 1841 CENSUS

The 1841 census can give us a picture of the occupations of the people of Witheridge town at that time. The list is followed by some interpretative comments extrapolated from the census.

33 servants	8 carpenters
4 dressmakers	3 milliners
2 thatchers	2 builders
2 surgeons	1 officer of excise
1 watchmaker	1 stonecutter
1 lacemaker	1 scrivener
7 shoemakers	69 agricultural labourers
4 sawyers	3 blacksmiths
2 hawkers	2 butchers
1 glazier	1 tailor
1 joiner	1 tinker
1 postman	1 gatekeeper
9 masons	4 wheelwrights
3 carriers	3 innkeepers
2 sweeps	2 coopers
1 cotton spinner	1 maltster
1 saddler	1 lace mender
1 attorney at law	

The attorney would have needed the scrivener (writer) to write out legal documents for him.

The three innkeepers ran the Angel Hotel and the Black Dog Inn, plus either the Bell Inn or the Hare and Hounds.

Four dressmakers and only one tailor suggests a difference of opinion between men and women over the importance of clothes.

The presence of the masons, carpenters, thatchers, builders, sawyers, the joiner, the glazier and the stonecutter reveals the local resources for building.

The three carriers mark the need of contact with places such as Tiverton, South Molton and Exeter. Their successors were prominent in the transport expansion 80 years later.

The presence of the gatekeeper shows that one of the two new turnpike gates and toll-houses was in being.

The maltster may have made malt or dealt in it.

The new national postal service began in 1840, hence the postman.

Coopers would always be in demand to make and repair barrels.

The schoolmasters were Thomas Comins (aged 50) and William Cann (24). The Comins family were leading church people, so Thomas was probably head of the old National School before the new one was built in 1846. William may have been assistant to Thomas, or possibly head of the original British (Chapel) School before the new school was built in 1845.

By 1841 Heathcoats Tiverton factory had been making machine lace for 20 years, but the decision of

Queen Victoria to have handmade lace on her wedding dress made such lace fashionable.

The number of agricultural workers in the town itself seems high at 69, bearing in mind the need for them to get to work by foot. However, there were three farms in the town, and another 20 within half an hour's walk. Few farms included farm-workers' cottages on their land.

The 1841 census uses the term 'Witheridge Town' in reference to what we know as the village. This may be because Witheridge's borough status had not long decayed and local pride was still in evidence. The term was to have a long life, for in the early years of the twentieth century there was at least one resident who used the expression 'going up town', when she was talking of going up to Witheridge.

ARTICLES TAKEN FROM THE *SOUTH MOLTON & TIVERTON GAZETTES*

25 May 1858
A Foolish Prank.
A few days ago, as the post woman was returning from Witheridge to Rackenford, she was obstructed on her way at Dart River by some fellow unknown who pushed her headlong into the water. The police were informed of the matter and were quickly on the spot, but the mischievous scamp had walked off, and has not since been seen or heard of.

1 June 1858
Witheridge. A Hoax,
The post woman, who was reported in our last as having been ill-used and thrown into the water, is an impostor, no such outrage having been committed. This is not the first imposition, we hear, she has practised upon the public.

17 March 1863
Witheridge.
The worthy rector of this parish, not being troubled with scruples in respect of Lent, headed the subscription list to provide the means for a general holiday. A tea was provided in the National Schoolroom, of which about 500 of all classes partook – old and young, rich and poor, all sitting down in harmony together. In the evening there was dancing in The Square to the strains of the Witheridge Band.

15 October 1864
Witheridge. The Ploughing & Agricultural Association.
The anniversary match and festival of this association took place here on Thursday last. The crack Devonshire ploughman Henry Griffith won the first prize for plough-ing. The judges were Mr Cobley and Mr Potter of Thorverton, and Mr Roberts of Tiverton. The dinner was served in the National Schoolroom by Mr Reed of The Angel Inn. Lord Portsmouth presided and was supported by the Revd Mr Karslake of Meshaw, and

Melhuish Comins Esq. of Witheridge. A large number of yeomen and others were present. The plough used by the victorious Griffin was one of Hornsby's of which Mr Thomas Hawkes, the enterprising implement maker of Tiverton is the agent. Mr Hawkes also had a general purpose plough here which was greatly admired and attracted much attention for the superior work it made. Mr Wright's plough was also much admired, and took the prize, it being left to the umpires to decide, who had not had time to test the respective merits of the two ploughs.

18 September 1866
Mary Kent was 'walking post' between Rackenford and Witheridge twice a day for 14 years, making 17 miles per day, or 102 miles per week, besides the village and roadside delivery. She resigned this office three years since. This is considered by able practitioners as a very healthy locality.

21 December 1869
South Molton Petty Sessions.
George Cruwys, of Witheridge, summoned his master, Mr John Webber, of Minchion Farm, Witheridge, for a sum of 14 shillings and 3 pence amount due for wages. [Webber claimed that Cruwys had been injured 'larking about', but his fellow servant Thomas Bristol said Webber wanted to get rid of Cruwys.] The justice made an order in Cruwys' favour for 13 shillings and ten pence half penny and costs.

Thomas Bristol summoned William Bulled, of Witheridge Farm, for an assault on the above-named George Cruwys on the 1st October last. [Bulled and Cruwys were picking blackberries and got into a scuffle, which involved throwing apples and grap-pling for a 'spar' in the course of which Cruwys got hit on the head.] After lecturing both parties, the bench dismissed the case, believing there was no intention of committing an assault.

27 February 1872
Witheridge. Think of the Poor.
On Monday a good substantial tea was provided for about one hundred and fifty of the poor by Host Mead, Commercial Hotel. The Ploughing Match Committee supplied the requisite funds, and the whole affair was in every respect a success.

26 March 1872
The Fruit of Strikes.
On Thursday a meeting was held by the smiths of North Devon at The Bell Inn, for the purpose of deciding what alterations should be made in the price of their work, these alterations being compulsory owing to the dear-ness of iron and coal. The following gentlemen were present: Messrs W. Greenslade, Baker, W. Dinner, G. Greenslade, Clegg, Pope, Venn, Western, E. Holmes, H. Greenslade and Southcote. After much discussion the following was decided: standard price for shoeing

6d., removing 2d. Secondly, owing to the great rise in the price of coal and iron, we find it necessary to charge for the future twenty per cent more for smith's work in general than we have hitherto done. Several letters were read from gentlemen who were unavoidably absent, stating they should abide by the decision of the meeting.

25 June 1872

About four o'clock on Wednesday morning the lightning set fire to the thatched house of Mr Selley, large cattle dealer and butcher. About £500 worth of wool was burnt and damaged, and the house and the one adjoining in the occupation of Misses Comins (draper and grocers) were destroyed. Men belonging to Ginett's Circus, which had been performing in the surrounding neighbourhood, rendered assistance, removing a number of sheep carcasses ready for market, furniture, etc. Getting upon one another's shoulders they rescued Mrs Selley from her bedroom. She secured her cash box, Mr Selley being absent at Challacombe. Eight sheep and four lambs in a field were killed by lightning. There is no fire engine within ten miles of the town.

20 August 1872

A Dismal Wedding.

On Monday last some lady visitors, not many miles from here, hearing it was probable a grand wedding would take place in the Parish Church, repaired there to behold the bridegroom lead the third lady of his choice to the altar, and to hear him once more promise to love and to cherish till death etc. Snugly ensconcing themselves in one of the pews, they awaited the coming of the bridegroom, who, on his arrival, assumed great importance as a parochial officer and gave them peremptory notice to quit the sacred edifice. The ladies left, and the doors were fastened during the ceremony. A correspondent asks whether this arbitrary act was legal. The ringers, dissatisfied with their actual receipts on a former occasion, did not appear on the scene.

Mrs Selley was rescued from a fire. She managed to save her cash box from the blaze.

10 December 1872

Accident.

A few days ago Messrs Hill, Burrows and Benson were returning from South Molton in their dogcart, when about three miles on the road their steed became fractious and finally landed himself on a gate and the drivers in the road. He soon succeeded in scattering the bars of the gate. After this feat he displayed great agility in smashing the lamps, the front of the trap, and breaking the shafts. Fortunately the gentlemen and Bucephalus escaped uninjured.

18 March 1873

Railway Wanted.

On Thursday last a public meeting was held at The Angel Hotel to consider what steps had better be taken to procure railway accommodation for this locality. It has been ascertained that most of the principal owners will give their land if a line is cut from Tiverton. After a brief discussion it was decided to have a second meeting next Fair day (April 17th). A committee was formed for Witheridge, Thelbridge, Worlington and Rackenford. The motto is to be 'Union is Strength'.

22 April 1873

The Railway.

On Thursday a meeting was held in the schoolroom to consider what steps should be taken to connect the town with the railway system of the country. The Revd Hosegood presided. Among those present were: Messrs T. Comins, J. Partridge, G. Smyth, J. Troake, G. Ayre, T. Strong, Jas Partridge, J. Selley, Cocks, Ayre junr, Lake Mildon, etc. The proceedings lasted but a very short time but they were of a hopeful character. Four plans are suggested. One is to make a line from Eggesford to Witheridge through the valley of the Dart; another is to get a line from here to Tiverton; a third from here to Lapford; and the fourth plan is to get it made towards Cheriton Fitzpaine and so on to Crediton. It is thought that the second plan would be the most suited to the convenience and requirements of the locality, the trade being done here chiefly with the London markets, and a line to Tiverton will give direct communication with the main line. As most of this land would have to be purchased it would make it an expensive undertaking, and therefore the proposal to make the rail to Eggesford is more popular, as Lord Portsmouth and Sir G. Stucley have offered to give all the land necessary for the work. Mr Comins suggested at the meeting that they should get the land surveyed, as the cost of this would be only £40, which they could raise among themselves. On the other hand it was urged that a committee should be appointed to walk over the land between this and Eggesford and report. Eventually this was agreed to and the following were appointed: Messrs J. Selley, John Troake, G. Smyth, Lake and Cocks. They are to report to another meeting two months hence.

26 October 1875

On Thursday the Cricket Club held their last Social Meeting for the season. The object was to present the highest scorer (Mr John Partridge) with a bat. This was done by Captain Comins, who gave with it a very encouraging speech. Mr Partridge, in responding said that cricket was a game he was exceedingly fond of, and whilst in the town he should do his utmost to support the Club. The Captain had said that he (Mr Partridge) had done well for the season but if he did not do better still another year it certainly should not be his fault.

30 January 1877

Pay Day.

A few days ago Mr J. Leach, manure agent, invited his customers to the Thelbridge Inn, where a capital dinner awaited them. About 60 sat down and about £2000 was paid. After the cloth was removed the evening was devoted to speechifying and singing. At the close the health of Mr John Leach was proposed, when many complimentary things were said respecting his business qualities and fair dealings. In responding Mr Leach gave the company this advice:

> You like a good crop of barley and wheat
> You like good roots for cattle to eat
> You like for your cash an article pure
> Then let me supply you with Langdale's manure.

8 June 1880

The Proposed Railway.

A short time ago the promoters of the scheme waited upon the Directors of the South West Railway and urged them to take the matter into consideration. After a little discussion two of these gentlemen offered to survey the proposed route for £50. Letters were sent to the resident gentry and to those whose land would be affected by the line. Answers soon came in bearing congratulations and cheques. The notes from the Earl of Portsmouth and Sir Stafford Northcote were most encouraging. The sum is subscribed and the route will be surveyed during this present month, the surveyors starting from Witheridge.

24 August 1880

Witheridge CC v Tiverton CC.

This match was played on the Tiverton ground on Wednesday last, under circumstances which, for the credit of cricket, it is gratifying to think are of rare

occurrence; for it was difficult to avoid the conclusion that the 'tail' of the Witheridge team by a series of systematic delays managed to get 'time' called whilst their last man was still putting his pads on. Perhaps it may be only charitable to suppose that intervals of sometimes ten minutes duration between the incoming batsmen were due to ignorance, and not intended as a flagrant violation of MCC rules, which it is needless to say proscribe two minutes grace only. In this instance time regulations were applied exclusively to drawing the stumps, for by a very rigid observance in this particular, what would certainly have been an honest defeat was converted into a dubious draw.

15 March 1881

South Molton Rural Sanitary Authority.

The general drainage of villages has been attended to, and in some cases rendered fairly efficient and the closet accommodation has been much improved; most of the old cesspits, the fruitful source of serious water contamination, have been done away with, and earth closets substituted. In Dr Body's opinion the pail system with ashes is best adapted for rural districts, as judging by his experience, the ordinary earth closets not being properly attended to by the cottagers, soon become a great nuisance.

4 July 1882

Witheridge Fair.

The Midsummer Fair was held here on Thursday last, and there was a good attendance of buyers and dealers. The supply of stock was larger than that of previous years. Messrs Ayre, auctioneers of Tiverton and Crediton, held an auction as usual, at which they succeeded in disposing of 30 bullocks and a few lots of sheep and horses, all of which realised very good prices. Quotations: cows and calves £15 to £17.10s.; barreners £12 to £14.10s.; pair steer yearlings £15 to £19; heifer yearlings £7 to £10; fat lambs 30s.6d. to 35s. Mr Hannaford also disposed of a goodly number of horses, cattle and sheep at fair prices.

11 September 1883

Glass Ball Shooting Match.

A shooting match at glass balls, was held on Monday, and a large number availed themselves of the opportunity of showing their skills as sportsmen. The first prize was won by Mr Hill Partridge, the second by Mr T.P. Watkins, the third by Mr J.M. Partridge. Some sweepstakes were afterwards shot for, and were principally carried off by the above gentlemen. A public dinner was provided by Mr Baker at The Angel Hotel, and a merry evening was spent, which resulted in the appointment of a similar meeting in the middle of October next.

26 February 1884

Exciting Chase.

Squire Tremlett's harriers on Monday started a fox at New Buildings, Sandford, and ran it at a smart pace towards

A hunt in 1884 found the fox under a gooseberry bush at Lashbrook.

Witheridge. There it found its way to Stourton Coppice, from thence to Lakelands, then to the great excitement of the inhabitants Reynard paid a visit to Ebringtons Row, in the town, from thence to Lashbrookes [sic] garden, where he hid under a gooseberry bush. Being closely followed by the hounds and a number of people, the fox returned to Ebringtons Row, where it was killed and his brush cut off as a trophy of the chase.

27 February 1886
Destructive Fire at Witheridge.

On Monday night a disastrous fire occurred at Witheridge. The scene of the conflagration was a block of four houses adjoining the churchyard, three of which are owned and occupied respectively by Mr Joseph Churchill, saddler, Mr J. Dinner, wheelwright, and Mr W. Way, carpenter. The fourth belongs to Mr Trawin, who vacated it some weeks since. The whole property had thatched roofs. Fire was discovered shortly after seven in the chimney of the unoccupied house, and before steps could be taken to extinguish it, it had gained a firm hold and seriously threatened to envelope the whole block. A telegram was despatched to Tiverton, the nearest town with a fire engine, and the West of England Fire Brigade, in charge of Mr John Grater, proceeded to the spot, arriving there shortly before ten. By this time the fire had played great havoc with the buildings, the roof of which had fallen in, and there being very little left on which the firemen could direct their efforts. Moreover, there was a scanty supply of water – only sufficient, it was estimated, to enable the engine to play

A block of houses burn, 1886.

on the flames for ten minutes. Consequently the firemen, after assuring themselves that there was no danger to the fire spreading to other property, deemed their services of no avail and returned home. It should be stated that the destroyed houses were isolated ones. Fortunately Messrs Churchill, Denner and Way were able to remove the bulk of their furniture and movables before the fire had made substantial headway. All the houses are insured – two in the Royal Farmers Office and one in the Caledonian Office and one in the West of England Office. The loss is therefore limited to a few things that could not be removed before the buildings were enveloped.

23 April 1887
A Witheridge Lunatic at Westminster Abbey.

At Westminster Police Court on Saturday, Lewis Burgess, otherwise Greenslade, a man who spoke with a strong American accent, was charged on remand before Mr Partridge with brawling in Westminster Abbey on Good Friday afternoon. The prisoner, as when first charged, was dressed in white knickerbockers and jacket, with a large heart-shaped cutting of red cloth on his breast. Prisoner at the conclusion of the service threw off an overcoat, which concealed his extraordinary attire, rose from his seat and shouted 'I am come as a judge; you can stay in hell and be ----'. As he spoke he flung in the air a number of printed bills, clearly productions of insanity. They were headed to 'asinine dunces', 'heathen Christians', 'ignorant infidels', etc, and in the lines that followed pious sentiments alternated with oaths, blasphemies and curses with scraps and phrases of scripture curiously intertwined. Inspector Peters of the A Division, said the prisoner was a native of Witheridge in North Devon, but had passed the greater part of his life in America. Last Christmas Day he was taken into custody for breaking into Witheridge Church, was certified mad and taken to the asylum at Exminster. He was released some little time after, his wife stating that she had taken a passage to America for him. The police said they had received a number of letters complaining of his conduct. Mr Partridge said he had a certificate from the surgeon of Holloway Gaol that the prisoner was insane, and he must order his removal to an asylum. A woman, said to be his wife, rushed forward with three little children and clung to him as he was led out of court, shouting that he had not been able to speak on his own behalf, that he was perfectly sane, and that he had been condemned to a legal death without proper trial. The police conveyed him to the workhouse as a lunatic.

11 June 1887
A Confiding Tom-Tit.

At Bythen Farm, Witheridge, a tom-tit thinking the farmer, Mr Adams, to be a kind-hearted man, has taken the liberty of building its nest in the letter-box erected in the lane. There she has laid her eggs whilst the letters have daily dropped on her back, and there she has sat whilst the

Blue tits nest in the letter-box at Bythen, 1887.

owner has unlocked the box, taken the letters from off her back and again locked her up in her secure little nest. Now she may be seen with her little brood peeping from underneath the envelopes with their mouths wide open, as much as to say 'thank you for our lodgings, and as you cannot make a very high price for your corn, you may as well supply us with our food too'.

VESTRY MINUTES IN THE NINETEENTH CENTURY

In 1846 the Vestry was the chief governing body in the parish. It consisted of ratepayers, who were summoned by a notice pinned to the church door. As the years went by the number of ratepayers increased, and by 1860 the church vestry could not contain them. After that date they continued to meet at the vestry itself, but immediately adjourned to the schoolroom for their meeting. Their responsibilities included the appointment of the churchwardens, the overseers of the poor, and the waywardens. The latter cared for all the roads in the parish that were not owned by Turnpike Trusts. The Vestry also checked the accounts of these bodies and fixed the rates. Some of their work comes across in this selection.

8 August 1846: *Thomas Comins, Clerk, and James Vickery, Surveyor of the Highway, summoned a meeting to discuss rebuilding Witheridge Mill Bridge.*

21 August 1846: *The Vestry authorise Messrs Baker, White, James Partridge, Thorne, Adams and Bragg, to replace the bridge at less than £50.*

28 January 1847: *It was resolved that the beam of the old bridge at Witheridge now lying in the orchard of William Bodley be given to him in compensation for the damage done him by the public path passing through his orchard whilst the new bridge was building, and that the Waywardens be authorised to sell the other beam of the same to Mr Wm Thorne on the valuation of John Brawn.*

24 April 1848: *The Minister nominated Mr White of Coombe Farm and the parishioners unanimously elected Mr William Thorne to be Churchwardens for the ensuing year.*

1 July 1848: *It was resolved that the sum of four pounds be granted to the Assistant Waywarden for the purpose of putting the southern half of Drayford Bridge in thorough repair.*

9 September 1848: *It was resolved that Messrs Adams, John Cole and John Baker be constituted a committee for... enquiring the probable expense of the appointment of a policeman – also whether any (and if any, which) of the adjacent parishes will be disposed to assist.*

7 October 1848: *The Vestry resolved to render the highway passable over Monkey Moor and Newhouse Moor.*

24 February 1849: *The Vestry resolved that Messrs Henry Davey, John Dinner and Joseph Dinner be recommended to the Justices to be appointed by them Constables of this parish for the ensuing year.*

16 March 1849: *Overseers of the Poor, Wm Smale, Henry Brailey, John Cole, Wm Bater, Abel Blake, George Phillips. Waywardens Samuel Tucker, Wm Burgess, Wm Cruwys, Wm Putt. Assessors of Land and Assessed Tax, John Moore, Wm Anstey.*

20 June 1852: *Resolved that William Commins be requested to take an opinion of a Barrister at Law on the doubtful points of law involved in the removal of Mary Groves, a pauper, from St Sidwells in Exeter to this parish.*

3 December 1853: *The South Molton Board of Guardians require a parish appointment of a local Board of Health.*

29 December 1853: *The Vestry appoints the Churchwardens, the Overseers, and Messrs Carter and Haley to constitute a Board of Health.* [Mr Haley was the village surgeon.]

12 June 1863: *The High Constables of the Hundred of Witheridge having received notice that the inhabitants of the Hundred were indicted at the last Quarter Sessions for not repairing Cove Bridge in Stoodleigh, you are requested to meet the said High Constables at Witheridge on the 15th of June 1863 at 12 o'clock to determine what steps shall be taken in the matter.*

13 June 1863: *The Vestry resolve to pay £11.3s.3d. and a farthing into The National Provincial Bank for the purposes of Cove Bridge.*

DRAYFORD – A HISTORICAL NOTE

There were Stone-Age people on the ridge by West Yeo 6,000 years ago, but all they left were traces of the flints that they used. The first known mention of Drayford comes in AD1086, in the Domesday Book, in which it is listed as a manor. At that time it was spelt 'Draheford', and the name is said to be made up of two Old English words – ford and dray, the latter possibly meaning drag or carry, but the experts do not agree. In 1086 there were seven families in Drayford; they had cattle and sheep, and there were meadows, pasture and woods. By 1555 it belonged to the Stucleys of Affeton. They sold it in 1632 to the Chichesters of Eggesford. The deed of that year contains the first reference to Drayford Mill, and to a tenement occupied by Philip Trix, whose name persisted down the years in Trixes Wood and Trixes Cottages. The parish registers for Witheridge have several references to the Trix family, and to William and Elizabeth Godswell, who may have given their name to Godswells (or else their ancestors may have taken their name from 'God's Well'). In 1836 the manor belonged to the Fellowes family, Earls of Portsmouth. At that date Drayford Mill had 7 acres, Trixes Tenement 13 acres, Stuckeys 46 acres, and Godswells 75 acres.

In 1759 the road from South Molton was created a turnpike, and called 'The Great Road to Exeter'. The local toll-house was at Thornham Chapel Cross. In spite of being on a main road the old packhorse bridge at Drayford was not replaced, and wheeled traffic had to use the ford beside it until the new bridge was built in 1914.

In 1850 the *Directory of Devon* shows Drayford as having a blacksmith, a butcher, three carpenters, a tailor, and a boot- and shoemaker. However, 80 years before that Drayford was home to other fine craftsmen. William Bradford made long-case clocks from 1760 to 1808, after which time he and his son, also William, moved to Tiverton. Their sign remained on the wall of one of Trixes Cottages until the 1960s.

Agriculture had always been a major source of employment in Drayford, although cloth making and milling also played their part. Of significance was the development in the 1920s of Coombe Quarry by Archibald Nott, together with an aerial ropeway to the processing plant on the main road near New Bridge.

As the twentieth century continued things changed: the mill ceased working, the shop closed, Mill Quarry opened up, and for a time became a filling station for petrol. Trixes Cottages were

Flood at Drayford, 1909. The footbridge on the left over the Adworthy Brook is nearly submerged.

demolished and replaced by a house, and other new dwellings were built. A Japanese potter took over the mill, a few yards away from where another craft specialist had made his clocks a century and a half before. New businesses had their origin in Drayford, and history moved on.

Drayford Mill

When the manor of Drayford was sold in 1632 by Scipio Stucley to Sir Edward Chichester, the schedule of properties in Drayford itself consisted of four tenements, two cottages, a house and the mill, which is described as a 'Tuck Mill'. It was not therefore used for grinding corn, but for driving a wheel studded with wooden hammers used in pounding cloth. Previously, woven cloth had to be pounded or 'tucked' by being trodden in troughs, but by the early 1500s some water-mills had been converted to play their part in the cloth industry, which was well established in North Devon. The cloth trade did not thrive forever, and by the early-nineteenth century many mills were being reconverted to grind corn. Drayford Mill may have changed at that time.

The miller in 1632 was Hugh Moore, but no other name has been traced for the next 180 years. However, there is a document dated 1811, which lists the properties charged a special rate for the repair of Drayford and Worlington Bridges. Drayford Mill was one of these and the miller was William White. The next reference is the schedule to the 1840 Tithe Map, which reveals the mill had 7 acres of ground, and John Moss was the miller. The 1851 census shows that he was followed by George Phillips, who came to Drayford in 1845, when he was 27. His family ran the mill until the arrival of the Stonemans in the 1890s. In 1871 George was still there, and the land had grown to 15 acres. Before the next census George died, for in 1881 his widow Anne was miller, assisted by her daughter Jane as 'dairyman', and by her brother Thomas Stoneman, also a miller. Ten years later there is no mention of Anne, and Jane is now miller, with her 14-year-old son William as 'Assistant Miller'. Thomas Stoneman was still present at this time.

By 1889 the old mill house attached to the barn had been demolished and the present house built. This allowed for a second wheel to be attached to the east side of the barn, and the mill leat to be divided so that both wheels could be used. Loveday Venner remembers no barn wheel or barn leat, and thinks that this was covered in with the spoil when Mill Quarry was opened up. She is sure, however, that the barn machinery was still in use, linked to that in the mill itself.

By the turn of the century Richard Stoneman was miller, followed by his son, also Richard. The mill ceased work some time during the 1930s.

Drayford in Victorian Times

The Tithe Map of 1840 shows a few differences from the OS map of 1889. In 1840 the mill house was attached to the barn to form an L shape. Hillside, Godswells and Stucleys were much the same, but there were several farm buildings across the road from Hillside. Across the Worlington road by Rock was a cottage. In the schedule that accompanies the Tithe Map the Hon. Newton Fellowes (lord of the manor of Drayford and, later, Earl of Portsmouth) was shown as owning Godswell (75 acres, occupied by Robert Middleton), 'Stuckleys' (47 acres, occupied by John Vicary) and four dwellings under the common heading of 'Rock'. The main house had with it 11 fields and an orchard, totalling 54 acres.

The census of 1861 gives a picture of the population of Drayford. It totalled 83 people, of whom 23 occupied the cottages called Rock. In one of them a 33-year-old widow, Charlotte Middleton, kept a shop. In another was a stonemason, William Milton, and seven members of his family, including his older sons Thomas (aged 16, stonemason) and Samuel (13, mason's labourer). In a third cottage was a family of six Kivells and a widow Conibear, who was a dress-maker. In the fourth cottage lived the eight members of the Reed family (including two farm workers and a dressmaker). The remaining population of Drayford was 60, among whom were a thatcher (William Knight), a blacksmith (John Greenslade), a seamstress (Jane Moss), a carpenter (William Moss), a butcher (William Clapp) and several farm workers.

By 1871 family names in Drayford included Tucker, Greenslade, Down, Moss, Reed, Chudley, Avis, Edworthy, Knight, Drew, Davey and Kivell. The Phillips family were at the mill, and Thomas Venner shared Godswells with the Webber and Bennett families.

In 1891 the Phillips family still occupied the mill, along with Thomas Stoneman. The Venners were on their own at Godswell; Thomas was a thatcher, as was his son William, and his son Thomas (aged 15) was a thatcher's assistant. Chudley, Lewis, Way, Gard, Sloman and Tanner were all Drayford families at this time. Stuckeys is not mentioned by name. In 1891 miller, thatcher and farm worker were the only trades quoted.

Down the road to Drayford, beyond Coombe Ball and short of the mill there lies on the left Coombe Quarry. For many years this had, on an ad hoc basis, provided stone for local buildings, including that for Drayford Bridge in 1914. However, in the early 1920s it was bought by Archibald Nott. Business expanded and a number of permanent jobs were created. Crushed stone was then much in demand for road maintenance and improvement. Laden lorries could not use Drayford Bridge, so they were obliged to use Coombe Ball and Have's Hill. Nott's heavy steam lorries soon cut the roads so badly that the County Council threatened to end his contracts unless he repaired them. Archie Nott was not a man to be threatened, so he refused. However, he came up with a clever alternative. He built an aerial ropeway from the quarry to the main Witheridge–South Molton road, where he set up a new crushing plant. This worked well. It also gave rise to a local legend: one day the unpopular quarry manager decided, against company rules, to take a ride in one of the buckets. When he was halfway along it is said that an unknown pair of hands put the machinery out of gear and left him suspended above the Little Dart River! By the end of the 1930s the ropeway had been sold to Scotts of Bampton, and the 'depot' as it was called, stopped work. The Second World War brought a new lease of life to the quarry for when, in 1943, Winkleigh Aerodrome was built hundreds of lorry loads of stone came from Coombe. So heavy was the traffic that a one-way system applied; laden trucks went up Coombe Ball, and returned empty down Have's Hill. The quarry closed some years later, and in spite of one or two attempts to reopen it, the site has remained closed.

The Building of Drayford Bridge
Information has been taken from contemporary issues of the South Molton Gazette.

By 1900 the old narrow bridge at Drayford had served its purpose for centuries. It is marked on Donne's map of Devon in 1765 and is likely to have existed long before that. It lies at the junction of the parishes of Witheridge and East Worlington, and is on the most direct route from South Molton to Exeter, known in those days as 'The Great Road to Exeter'. It became a turnpike road in 1759, but nothing was done to widen the bridge, and most wheeled traffic had to use the ford beside it. At the start of the twentieth century steam and internal combustion engines were changing transport, and there were those who thought Drayford should have a modern bridge, particularly since a new one had just been built at West Worlington. There were others who saw motor vehicles as merely a passing fashion, and believed that anything on two wheels should continue to use the ford.

At a meeting of the South Molton Rural District Council on 15 November 1913 a letter was read from the County Council asking for a meeting about Drayford Bridge. Councillor Thorne was sarcastic:

Some years ago the County Council talked of spending £1600 on this bridge, but nobody would have anything to do with it. If that was too much then, why spend £2000 now? The water is no higher than it was before. They had a new surveyor and they want a fantastical bridge. We could build one cheaper.

The District Council rejected the County Council's

plan as it made no arrangement to deal with the water of the Adworthy Brook, which flowed across the road at the bottom of the village. Eventually the County Council agreed to deal with the brook and the river, and to restrict the bridge width to 12ft as the District Council requested. It also offered £1,000 towards the cost on condition that the District Council built it. As it was a County Council road this annoyed local councillors. On being asked what traffic was to do while the bridge was being built, the County Council had replied, 'traffic must go some other way', and one local councillor had suggested 'taking it across in an aeroplane'.

In March 1914 the District Council was told that it would have to build the bridge and that it would not get any County Council money until the work was completed. The District Councillors were furious and refused, demanding that the County Council pay the grant by instalments on receipt of surveyor's certificates of completion of stages of work. The County Council agreed on 4 April 1914. Plans were accepted on 20 May and the agreement was signed in June. The lowest of three tenders was accepted, the figure of £1,212.3s.8d. submitted by Messrs Fothergill Bros, Exeter. The District Council had tried to buy Coombe Quarry but without success, and the owner, Mr G. Cutcliffe of Coombe House, agreed to sell 450 yards of stone for the bridge at 6d. a yard.

The final agreement was signed on 4 July and it was expected that the bridge would be quickly built. An inscribed stone was made ready (to be seen on the downstream parapet). It reads:

DEVON COUNTY COUNCIL	SOUTH MOLTON R D COUNCIL
CHAIRMAN	CHAIRMAN
EARL FORTESCUE	HARRY SMYTH ESQ
1914	
CONTRACTOR	SURVEYOR
FOTHERGILL BROS LTD	MESSRS GARDNER & SONS
18 CASTLE STREET	CHITTLEHAMPTON
EXETER	DEVON

However, the outbreak of war in the first week of August threw their plans into disarray. By the autumn, 12 of Fothergill's men had left on military service, and wartime rail congestion was blamed for the London and South Western Railway's delays in delivering materials. Nevertheless, by 20 March 1915 the work was complete and the contractor's final account was paid, with a saving on the contract price of £100 due to the discovery of a bed of rock requiring less concrete.

On 3 April the *South Molton Gazette* reported:

New Bridge at Drayford – Opening Ceremony.
On Monday 29th March 1915 a new bridge, erected over the river at Drayford, between Witheridge and Worlington was formally opened by Mrs Sanders, wife of Mr James Sanders, County Councillor and JP of South Molton, in the presence of a large gathering. The new bridge is a handsome structure of stone, with brick arches and coigns of Dartmoor granite. Begun last July the work was carried out by Messrs Fothergill Bros of Exeter, and in spite of the delay by men leaving their work to join the Colours, the Contract was completed within a month of the specified time... A procession marshalled by Acting Superintendent Newberry passed over the bridge, and, removing an ornamental rope, Mrs Sanders formally declared it open to the public. The structure was 'christened' by dashing a bottle of champagne against the centre of one of the parapet walls. School children who took part in the procession led in singing the National Anthem. Cheers were give for the King and also for Mrs Sanders. Photographs of the ceremony were taken by Messrs Chandler & Co. of Exeter. As the school children left they were presented with oranges. A large company was afterwards entertained to luncheon at Town Farm, the residence of Mr Smyth, Chairman of the Rural District Council'.

MEMORIES OF MR W. PYNE OF LITTLEBOURNE, WITHERIDGE
Recalled in 16 June 1977.

At the time Drayford Bridge was built Bill Pyne lived in the poor house in West Worlington and went to school in East Worlington. He recalled the opening of the bridge, as all the schoolchildren were given an orange in celebration. There was some opposition to the destruction of the old narrow packhorse bridge led by the vicar, who believed the old one should have been left and the new one built alongside. The vicar refused to attend the opening ceremony, and it was believed that for some time afterwards he shut his eyes when he rode past the bridge.

Bill Pyne remembered this rhyme:

Down to Drayford amongst the trees
Barley bread and vinnied cheese
Rashers of bacon tough as a thong
That's how Drayford people lived along.

He could offer no explanation of the old local joke about 'Drayford Docks', although he had heard people talk about 'the Drayford playboat going up to Creacombe'.

Drayford in Days Gone Past

By Cedric Tudball, 1995.

Dray-vord, een days gone pass, my gel,
Sakes alive, I was only a cheel!
Dray-vore to the vire and yet yersul
An I'll takee down Coombe Ball heel.

Coombe Cottages lied on the right
Then six gun shot, more or less
You come to th'oak, top o' Coombe Lane,
Where the wild bees 'ad their ness.

Arter a beet, thars a sort of a nap
What valls away zuant – dear zaul
When auver yoo goes and watch yer veet,
You'm gwain down Coombe Ball.

Wan in fower or is it dree
I knawse tis master steep,
Cos yer veet they rins away we' ye
Wain upright you tries to keep.

Pass 'Notts Kwaw-ree' on the leff,
Zee if the rid vlags up the mass,
An if he is – 'old 'ard a beet,
That means they'm gwain to blast.

Purt near six deep into the stone
In pairs they've had to drill it,
Then vire the charge and ide thur aids
From tons of stone and shillet.

Corry-gated iron they 'ad, a
Faggot 'ood covered safe place
And under this they rinned an zot,
When 'Burrowite' blawed the vace.

But let us git on, down the rawd,
Right on, pass the meal,
And mine the pipe, what drained the pit
Oot across the vield.

And so us comes to Dray-vord
Where the Quane Mary, her was launched,
But the waters narra, and theres nort there,
Seps viels what the bullocks av paunched,

An vifty pole o' rhubard, wild
That lies 'ginst the conker trees,
An outa West Yeo, Thornham or Whirlin-tun
Youken taak whichever you please.

Or, if yoo likes, yoo can turn on yersel
An make yer way up auver 'Ave Hill
When yoo'll come to Thelbridge – luvlee church
Wi 'a bootiful six bell peal.

'St Davids Church' – so Passen zed
'Dunstone wallin, vull of charms
Bot Oh Dear Me – the pubs misnamed
Vor there idn't no Thelbridge Arms'.

'Tis the insti-toot of arms' he zed,
'Wi Royal Grants an Warrints Abroad',
An us what was as daft as 'andcarts
Stood and gawped at what he knawed.

Dray-vord in days gone pass,
Man could settle down and bide there.
'But maid, aise off me boots, mi'dear
An vetch me a jar o'zider'.

Bill started work with Nott's at Coombe Quarry in 1921. He believed Nott's began there in 1919, and that the reason for the installation of the aerial ropeway from the quarry to the depot on the A377 west of Newbridge was a disagreement between Archie Nott and the County Surveyor over the damage to the roads by the heavy lorries. The ropeway was run by a big Tangye engine installed by Frank Lawrence. An old man called George Ash lived in a caravan by the quarry gate and lit up the boiler each working morning to raise steam. Buckets were clipped to the wire ropes; these buckets had small wheels on them so that they could run on rails at the quarry end where they were filled up without stopping (the shute operator had to be very quick). Stone for the tar plant went up, as well as most of the road stone in the various grades. Up to 40 men were employed in the quarry at any one time. The stone went to the making of Winkleigh and Chivenor airfields in the Second World War. Some building stone was produced, and it was said that Messrs Dart and Francis took stone from Coombe Quarry to carry out some of the repair work to Exeter Cathedral after the wartime bomb damage.

In the 1920s the 6ft 3in. foreman was called Bill Welch with a stiff leg and a thirst – he was reputed to drink a bottle of scotch in the Angel between 1p.m. and 2p.m. Bill Welch didn't like Archie Nott's methods of payment – if a man's pile of cash was a penny short, he'd take a penny off the pile due to the next man. Bill persuaded Archie to engage a clerk. This was to be Bill Vernon, who at that time lived in South Molton and rode a motorbike, which earnt him the nickname 'leatherneck'. His office was in the Black Dog in Witheridge Square. When 'Kissing Kate' – also referred to as 'Old Partridge' – came down to the quarry to preach to the men, Bill Welch

Drayford in Days Gone Past
The non-Devonian version!

Dray-ford in days gone by, my girl.
Sakes alive, I was only a child!
Pull up to the fire and warm yourself,
And I'll take you down Coombe Ball Hill.

Coombe Cottages lay on the right,
Then, six gun shot more or less,
You'll come to the oak, top of Coombe Lane
Where the wild bees have their nest.

After a bit there's sort of a hill
Which falls away smoothly – dear soul,
When over you go and watch your feet,
You're going down Coombe Ball.

One in four, or is it three,
I know it's very steep,
Because your feet run away with you,
When upright you try to keep.

Past 'Nott's Quarry' on the left,
See if the red flag's up the mast,
And if it is – hold hard a bit,
That means they're going to blast.

Pretty near six deep into the stone
In pairs they've had to drill it,
Then fire the charge and hide their heads
From tons of stone and shillet.

Corrugated iron they had, a
Faggot of wood covered safe place,
And under this they ran and sat,
When 'Burrowite' blew the face.

But let us get on, down the road,
Right on past the Mill,
And mind the pipe that drained the pit
Out across the road.

And so we come to Dray-ford
Where the Queen Mary was launched,
But the water's narrow and there's nothing there
Except fields that the bullocks have paunched,

And fifty pole of rhubarb wild,
That lies against the conker trees,
And out to West Yeo, Thornham or Worlington
You can take whichever you please.

Or if you like you can turn on yourself
And make your way up over Have Hill,
When you'll come to Thelbridge – lovely church
With a beautiful six bell peal.

'St David's Church' so Parson said,
'Dunstone walling, full of charms –
But Oh Dear me – the pub's misnamed,
For there isn't no Thelbridge Arms'.

'It's the Institute of Arms', he said,
'With Royal Grants and Warrants Abroad',
And we who were daft as handcarts
Stood and gaped at what he knew.

Dray-ford in days gone past,
Man could settle down and bide there,
'But, maid, ease off my boots, my dear,
And fetch me a jar of cider'.

---

refused to allow her to preach during the hours of work. She was said to have got her nickname from her habit of kissing every woman she met and shaking hands with the men.

Hours of work were 7a.m. to 5p.m., except on Saturdays when work stopped at 4p.m. This was the case until the Union insisted work ceased at 1.pm. on Saturdays. There was a rate of 9½d. an hour, and if rain stopped work, the men did not get paid, but were not allowed to go home either. In bad weather a weekly wage might only come to 10s. or 11s.

The stock in the explosives magazine was checked monthly by the police. Stone goggles were issued, but nothing was done to protect the workers from the dust.

All drilling at the quarry in the 1920s was done by hand; one man turned the drill and two men did the striking. Later on, however, Holmans of Cambourne brought up a steam drill driven by a traction engine. This proved successful until the arrival of the compressed-air drill. Bill Baker, the blacksmith, used to sharpen the drills. At the quarry face two men worked together at loading a skip; the rate was 8 tons an hour. The skip was then pushed on rails down to the crusher. A day's work was hard, and if men came to work at 7.01a.m., then no work counted for wages until 7.30a.m. Once or twice men tried to organise themselves to obtain better conditions, but it was useless, as Archie Nott would not give way. In addition, the workers had little to gain by striking as there were plenty of unemployed men who would have been willing to be taken on in their place.

(Hannaford's 1920 sale catalogue of Coombe property makes clear that the quarry was in the occupation of Mr Nott on a lease for ten years from 29 September 1919. The purchase date is confirmed at 1920.)

HEALTH IN WITHERIDGE IN THE NINETEENTH CENTURY

In early-Victorian times the very young were greatly at risk. Nationally 50 per cent of all deaths were of children aged under five. Our figures were better – 31 per cent in the 1820s – but children were at the mercy of diarrhoea, whooping cough, croup, measles and smallpox. Measles was a killer at this time. In rural areas, however, there still persisted a general belief that 'fever' was forever in the air waiting to strike. Although age brought greater immunity, people were subjected to greater dangers at work, such as dust in bakeries, quarries, mills and barns, and mishaps with mill and barn equipment, work implements and horses. From about 1838 death rates for people over 14 began to improve, as a result of better diet, sanitation and medical care. The poor did not always benefit, as they had to weigh up the cost of treatment against the chance of a cure. In villages such as Witheridge women in childbirth or with sick children often preferred to rely on the knowledge of a local (although untrained) woman who in addition to helping at a birth would clean, help with the washing, feed the husband and care for other children. Medication came in gradually, but for a long time, people preferred their traditional methods. For example, there were those that preferred to take a sick child to a field in the early morning and lay it face down in the 'form' where a ewe had slept.

Witheridge had some advantages over towns, as it was not blighted in the same way by polluted water and sewage-ridden streets. In addition, there were less people, so conditions were not so cramped. In 1851 an average household in Barnstaple held between five and six persons, while Witheridge's figure was about four. An Act of 1834 put emphasis on work in workhouses and the chronically sick were already classified with the insane. Soon, however, these places were occupied by aged paupers; the last Witheridge infant to die in South Molton workhouse was in 1864. There were no cottage hospitals until the next century. Witheridge was lucky to have a few places in the Devon and Exeter Hospital since its building in 1841, primarily as a result of the role William Chapple played in its construction.

From 1850 to the end of the century there were always two medical men in Witheridge. In the 1860s these were Drs Llewellyn and Burrows. When they died the press wrote respectfully about Dr Burrows, but Dr Llewellyn got a warm tribute. His kindness to the poor was particularly stressed. These were followed by Drs Pollock and McArthur; the latter broke new ground in the winter of 1894 by giving a series of lectures on health, first aid and home nursing.

In 1872 the South Molton Board of Guardians became, in addition, the South Molton Sanitary Authority. Reports were requested to assess village drains, including those in Witheridge. In 1875 diphtheria was reported here, and in 1876 a local mother was taken to court for allowing her child with scarlatina to come into contact with others. In 1877 a case of smallpox was reported. The sufferer was a local man and his wife was summoned for 'exposing clothes in a public place without disinfecting them.' It was a far cry from earlier, more easy-going days.

Risks came not only from disease but also from accidents. For example, a man jumped from a rick and was impaled on a pitchfork; a man had a hand drawn into a threshing machine; a man fell from the shafts of his van and the wheels passed over him and he died 'within the hour'; a blacksmith was kicked in the face by a horse; and a child was burnt to death in a cottage.

Over the century the life-expectancy figure rose, and some improvement in general health began, thanks to medical care, the new Sanitary Authority, and to work performed by the Witheridge Union Society. However, it was not until the 1900s that local funds were raised to employ a village nurse.

COOMBE & THE CUTCLIFFE FAMILY

The Revd J.A.S. Castlehow identified Coombe in the Exeter Domesday of 1086 as follows:

The Bishop of Coutances has a manor called Coma, which Brongar held on the day on which King Edward was alive and dead and it rendered geld for one virgate. This can be ploughed with one plough. And Drogo holds this of the Bishop. On it he has one plough and he has there one serf and 10 head of cattle and 8 swine and 30 sheep and 2 acres of coppice and 3 acres of meadow and it is worth yearly 5 shillings and when the Bishop received it, it was worth 3 shillings.

Also, the Revd Castlehow noted William Mouncil at 'Comb Mouncell' in 1243, William de Monteaux at 'Combe Monteaux' in 1276, the le Marchant family there in 1302, 1303 and 1316; and a connection between the Martin/Marchant families and Combe Monceaux in 1326. There is a Deed of Release of 1367–78 from Richard de Brankescombe to Robert Cutteclyve of lands including 'Votheliswyke', identified as today's Buddleswick in the neighbouring parish of Thelbridge. In 1479 nearby lands were 'feoffed' by 'Richard Cutteclyf of Northcote, gent to Richard Cuttedlyff of Trentham in the County of Stafford, gent.' A deed of 'Feoffment to Uses', dated 24 February 1498 from 'Richard Cuttlyff the elder' to Richard Chichester, Thomas Cutclyff the elder and others, has the names of three attorneys on it, one of which is 'Thomas Cutclyff of Wutherygge'. This appears to be the earliest connection between the Cutcliffes and Witheridge.

By 1505 it seems the family were in possession of lands including Damage Barton and Morthoe, North Devon, where they remained until 1922.

Within these lands was property in the parishes of Witheridge and Thelbridge; these may have been theirs before their arrival at Damage.

In 1637 the Inquisition Post Mortem on Charles Cutcliffe included Coombe, described as '3 messuages, gardens, orchards, 60 acres of land, 10 of meadow, 60 of pasture, 4 of wood and 40 of down etc called Come Monceaux.' It also included the farms called Heiffers and Myncham Bradford – the latter may be today's Menchine.

The Cutcliffe possessions remained as one unit until 1745 when, under the will of Charles Cutcliffe, the main body of land was left to his eldest son Charles. However, the Witheridge and Thelbridge property, including Coombe, passed to his second surviving son John, rector of Ashreigney. The closer connection between the family and Witheridge may be said to have begun at this point, although it was not until the beginning of the nineteenth century that we can be sure of Cutcliffes living at Coombe. As to Thelbridge (or Delbridge as some old documents and maps call it) the Land Tax returns show no Cutcliffe ownership of Buddleswick in 1780 or afterwards. They do, however, show 'Mr Cutcliffe' as part owner of 'Chapmer' (today's Chapner). By 1797 Chapner had been sold to Jacob Cobley. The 1840 Tithe Apportionment for Thelbridge reveals there is no land in Cutcliffe ownership. Nor in 1840 is there confirmation of Menchine ownership.

The Revd John's son, Charles George, was born on 16 February 1754 and was baptised in Ashreigney. In 1785 this Charles George married a South Molton girl, Hannah Elworthy. There is a deed of marriage settlement dated 10 September 1785 by which Charles' father guarantees £500 and the farm 'Heiffers' to Hannah in the event of Charles' death. The Land Tax assessment for 1780 shows 'Heiffers' ('Heavers' in the document) as being then owned by the Revd John Cutcliffe and rated at £3.12s. per annum, whereas Coombe, also owned by the Revd John, was rated at £5.8s. (for comparison, Dart Raffe was also rated at £5.8s.).

Both sons of Charles and Hannah were baptised in South Molton – Charles John on 23 July 1786 and John Elworthy on 17 June 1789. With this generation we can place Cutcliffes at Coombe. Charles John married a Witheridge girl, Mary Besley, on 11 May 1811 in Witheridge, where their two sons were baptised (John Elworthy on 17 July 1816 and George on 17 May 1825). Their father was a Witheridge churchwarden from 1817 to 1830 and again in 1833. Coombe House is described as 'early-nineteenth century', so it may well have been built by Charles John about the time of his marriage in 1811. It was built on the site of an older farmhouse; in the 1970s an old bread oven was discovered, which may have been part of that older house.

In the Tithe Apportionment of 1840 Coombe is shown as belonging to Charles John Cutcliffe, and to

comprise 168 acres. Also recorded is Newhouse, of 275 acres (it then included what later became Broadridge) in the joint ownership of Charles John Cutcliffe and Francis William Cutcliffe. By the time of the 1841 census the family no longer lived at Coombe. In 1851 Charles John is recorded as being a land agent and surveyor, living in Back Lane, South Molton, as a widower with his daughter Mary Ann. Near him, in Broad Street, lived his brother John, surgeon, with his wife and two children.

Not until 1882 would there be Cutcliffes back at Coombe. In the intervening years the house was occupied either by a tenant or a bailiff. The following advertisement was published in Trewman's *Exeter Flying Post* on 29 May 1861:

To be let by tender for the term of 14 years from Lady Day 1862 determinable by either party at the end of the first 10 years on giving 12 months notice.

A desirable messuage and farm called Coombe and Cannington situate in Witheridge aforesaid and now in the several occupations of Messrs White and Mogford, consisting of a good dwelling house with convenient outbuildings, 4 labourers' cottages and gardens and about 169 acres of arable, meadow, orchard and pasture-land. The taker will have to discharge the Land Tax, Tithe Rent Charges, all other outgoings and to keep the premises in repair (except the walls and timber work of the roofs) on being found rough timber. The estate is desirably situated both for markets and manure. It adjoins good roads and is capable of much improvement. Mr Joseph Dinner, of Witheridge, will show the lands any Monday or Thursday, full particulars may be obtained of either J.E. Cutcliffe Esq., surgeon, Silverton, or Charles John Cutcliffe Esq. of South Molton.

The 1891 census for Witheridge shows George Cutcliffe and his wife Mary at Coombe with the younger members of the family – Grace (b.1860), Edith (b.1864), Gertrude (b.1865) and Montagu (b.1869). George had been actuary and secretary to the Clerical and Medical and General Assurance Company in London for 24 years. In June 1882 he retired and was presented with an engraved salver inscribed thus: 'In token of the affectionate regard and with the best wishes of the United Staff of the office.' In the centre of the salver is the Cutcliffe crest of three pruning knives. George spent his retirement at Coombe, and may have been responsible for the late-nineteenth century chimney pieces in the house, and for the very fine range of farm buildings behind the house.

George Cutcliffe took an active part in local affairs. He died after a long illness in 1900. His widow and two daughters continued to live at Coombe until Mary died in 1917. The estate was sold in 1919. Coombe was bought by Mr Counter, who two or three years later sold it to Mr William Cox.

The family did not lose touch with Witheridge,

Coombe House.

*Coombe in 1900.
Smith was a coachman
to George Cutcliffe.
He lived in a room
above the harness room,
which had a fire with
a tap for hot water for
shaving. He washed in
the horse trough.*

*The Cutcliffes in the
1930s. Michael
Cutcliffe is at the back,
with (left to right) his
brother Dick and his
parents Mr and Mrs
Ernest Cutcliffe.*

and in the 1930s Ernest Cutcliffe, son of George Cutcliffe's brother John, and his family paid visits, staying either in Cypress House, West Street, or with James and Ethel Woollacott at West Yeo. In 1940 Ernest bought Coombe and the family were back after a break of 21 years. Ernest's son Michael and his wife Sue and their daughters lived there for a number of years before the property was finally sold in the early 1980s.

The connection of the Cutcliffes with Witheridge goes back certainly to 1497, and with Coombe to 1637.

George Cutcliffe at Coombe, 1882–1900

On 17 November 1900 the *South Molton Gazette* announced the death of 'Mr George Cutcliffe, JP of Coombe House, Witheridge after a long illness.' The report continued:

Mr Cutcliffe for many years occupied the important position of actuary to the Clerical Medical and General Assurance Company... On retiring about 20 years ago he settled at Witheridge, devoting himself to the duties and recreation of a rural landowner. His kindness and geniality made him universally popular among all classes. The Lord Lieutenant placed him on the roll of County Magistrates, and he was returned as representative of the District on the County Council.

On 22 December 1900 the paper reported that the executors of the late Mr George Cutcliffe, were two of his sons, 'Mr George Cutcliffe of Cheapside, Solicitor, and Mr John Cutcliffe of the Stock Exchange.' Other reports in the *South Molton Gazette* give some indication of Mr George Cutliffe's life in Witheridge, following his retirement to Coombe in June 1882.

He was clearly not a man to waste time, for only two months after his retirement he decided to put an end to the vagaries of Witheridge's church clock, which had been an annoyance for years, and offered to provide a 'new clock with modern appliances' to the value of £200. The offer was accepted and the order was placed with Messrs Ellis, Depree and Tucker of Exeter. It included 'the newest improvements' and would strike on one of the large bells 'so that it will be heard for a long distance.'

On 26 December 1882 it was noted that 'the new turret clock' had been 'opened'. It was first set going on Wednesday afternoon a few minutes before four o'clock. The clock first chimed and then struck the hour. The vicar, the Revd J.P. Benson, told the crowd that they were deeply indebted to Mr Cutcliffe for his magnificent gift to his native parish. They should all rejoice that he had come back to reside with them after an absence of some years. He wished Mr Cutcliffe a long life. Mr Cutcliffe thanked the vicar for his kind words and said he 'felt great pleasure in

presenting the clock to the parish, which he believed was one of the best that skill could produce.' The report said that the clock had two dials of 6ft 4in. diameter, fixed to the eastern and southern sides of the tower. The western and northern sides of the tower were not visible to the people in the village.

Mr Cutcliffe's duties as a magistrate sometimes made the news. In August 1885 he was on the bench in South Molton when a local man was charged with assault and threats of bodily harm. He and his fellow magistrate dismissed the charge of assault but bound the man over for six months for the threats.

At some point Mr Cutcliffe must have purchased a marquee, for when the Alswear Wesleyan Chapel was opened in 1887 he lent it to them for the occasion. This is likely to be the marquee that did much service for Witheridge Flower Show in later years.

In the spring of 1887 he took the chair at a meeting to discuss how to celebrate Queen Victoria's golden jubilee. His suggestion that a dinner be provided for the men and a tea for the women and children was not accepted. It was decided that there should be a free tea for all, but that the tea for the men should include meat. There was to be a special church service, sports in the afternoon, and a concert in the evening. Among the ladies on the committee was a Miss Cutcliffe. Subscriptions of £5 each had already been received from Mr G. Cutcliffe, the Earl of Portsmouth (local landowner) and Dr Llewellyn, the Witheridge doctor. A total of £45 was raised, and on the last Tuesday in June:

... the celebration passed off most successfully. There was a church service in the morning, ending with the National Anthem and the Hallelujah Chorus. Just before 2p.m. 200 children marched to a field lent by Mr Partridge, where sports and amusements were provided. At 3p.m. the children had tea in the large marquee, and sports for the adults began. At half past four the adults commenced to take their places at the tables where they found a plentiful supply of boiled and roast beef, cake etc, awaiting them. Altogether about 400 adults took tea. Dancing to music supplied by a string band brought a pleasant day to a close.

In October 1888 it was reported that 'Mr Cutcliffe, JP of Coombe House, Witheridge' was a candidate for the local seat on the County Council. He was duly elected and served for one term of office.

On 12 October 1889 the *Gazette* devoted two full broadsheet columns to a report on the 'Wedding of Miss Edith Cutcliffe and Mr Richard Davey at Witheridge.' The road leading up from Coombe and the streets of Witheridge were 'profusely decorated with floral arches and festoons and a large number of flags and banners floated in the breeze'. The children of both schools were entertained to a 'sumptuous tea in the National Schoolroom, followed by dancing for all until 11 o'clock.' The same evening all the estate workers 'numbering over 60', were entertained to supper at the Angel Hotel. During the day the Witheridge Brass Band 'paraded the streets in their new uniforms, discoursing appropriate music.' They also paid a visit to Coombe House.

On Wednesday the presents of the bride and groom were on exhibition at Coombe House and the adult population of Witheridge were invited to see them. On entering the drawing room where the presents were laid out, each individual was requested to partake of the bridecake, and after having completed the inspection of the presents, all were directed to the barn where a substantial tea had been laid out.

The reporter's verdict on the occasion was that 'altogether the wedding is considered to be the finest celebrated in Witheridge within memory.'

At Christmas 1889 'Mr G. Cutcliffe and the Misses Cutcliffe' gave the church Sunday school their annual treat and Christmas tree. There was tea and presents and 'the remainder of a very enjoyable evening was filled up with seasonable amusements.' Each child got a present from Mr Cutcliffe: the juniors 6d. and the seniors 1s.

In December 1893 it was announced that Mr Montagu Cutcliffe (son of George) had been appointed medical officer of the North Tawton district of the Okehampton Union, after a spell as assistant surgeon at the Devon and Exeter Hospital. In the previous year the *Gazette* had noted that 'G. Cutcliffe Esq. had been made Vice Chairman of the South Molton Board of Guardians.'

In March 1894 Mr Cutcliffe at the South Molton Petty Sessions seconded a motion by Lord Ebrington drawing attention to 'the urgent necessity of another constable being stationed at Witheridge, that parish having been undermanned for several months.'

This is the last mention of George Cutcliffe in the *Gazette* until his death in 1900, when his obituary referred to 'his long illness'.

The Cutcliffe involvement with Witheridge was continued by his widow, Mary, and by two of his daughters. January 1903 saw Mrs Cutcliffe's representatives in action over recompense for stone taken from Coombe Quarry.

November 1904 brought a report that £57.16s.6d. had been collected towards the 100 guineas needed to provide heating apparatus for Witheridge church. One of the collectors was 'Miss Cutcliffe' who handed in £20.10s. Next year Miss Cutcliffe joined the vicar's family in providing the annual parochial tea, for which 173 people paid for admission. This was followed by an 'exceptionally good entertainment'.

In late 1908 Miss Gertrude Cutcliffe organised a class that met every Friday at Coombe House, working for the Toy Fair at Plaistow, London. After a month's work they sent up '30 very prettily dressed dolls and 30 Santa Claus stockings.' Several members

of the class sent financial contributions. The class planned to work during lent for the YMCA. In 1911 Miss Cutcliffe became a member of the committee set up to raise money towards the appointment of a district nurse. (Note: only rarely did the *Gazette* specify to which Miss Cutcliffe it was referring.) The class mentioned above continued to work, and in 1912 there was a report that the Misses Cutcliffe had organised an annual outing to Teignmouth for class members.

In 1913 the Annual Witheridge Ploughing Match was held at Cobley Farm 'kindly lent by Mrs Cutcliffe of Coombe House'. In 1914 the family allowed 450 yards of stone to be taken from Coombe Quarry to build the new Drayford Bridge. In 1916 the *Gazette* announced that Miss Gertrude Cutcliffe was canvassing the village for the names of ladies willing to help (although the nature of the help was not described).

August 1916 saw 25 wounded soldiers from Knightshayes Hospital, Tiverton, brought by 'motor car and motor cycle' and entertained at Coombe House by Mrs and the Misses Cutcliffe. Tea was served on the lawn. A Mr Charles Pickard had paraded the village with his accordion and had collected £2.3s.9d., which was spent on 'smokes' for the visitors and for the other soldiers at the hospital.

The *Gazette* did not report the death of Mrs Cutcliffe in 1917, nor the sale in 1919.

ARTICLES TAKEN FROM THE SOUTH MOLTON & TIVERTON GAZETTES

3 January 1865
On Thursday next a prize ringing match and grand doings amongst the residents of this neighbourhood will take place as announced in our advertising columns. After the match a dinner will be given at the Angel Inn, where the prizes will be distributed to the successful competitors.

17 January 1865 and 16 May 1865
Lengthy County Court reports of the case of Frost v Selley (damage to flock by a diseased sheep).

24 January 1865
The Princess of Witheridge & Caraboo.
Some of our readers may have read in The Times *a fortnight since the following passage: 'Death of the 'Princess Caraboo''. Such of our readers as are interested in the history of impostors will remember that many years since a person who styled herself the 'Princess Caraboo' created a sensation in the literary and fashionable circles of Bath and other places, which lasted until it was discovered that the whole affair was a romance, cleverly sustained and acted out by a young and prepossessing girl. On being deposed from the honours that had been accorded to her, the 'Princess' accepted the situation, retired into comparatively*

humble life, and married. There was a kind of grim humour in the occupation which she subsequently followed – that of an importer of leeches; but she conducted her operations with much judgement and ability, and carried on her trade with credit to herself and satisfaction to her customers. The quondam 'Princess' died recently at Bristol, leaving a daughter who, like her mother, is said to be of considerable personal attractions.

It will be interesting to the public of this neighbourhood to learn that this strange, indeed extraordinary woman is a native of this town, the daughter of a shoemaker named Wilcox, and the sister of a man whose remarkable eccentricities are within the recollection of many of the inhabitants of Witheridge, and who was very generally known here and elsewhere in Devon as 'Old Harry'. Some years ago the 'Princess' left Witheridge to enter service at Bristol, and shortly after her advent at Bristol the Western Times reported that she was found wandering the streets there in oriental costume. She appeared to speak English with considerable difficulty and could scarcely make herself understood; she represented herself as an Eastern Princess come to England in search of a lost relative. She was of a dark complexion, and so well did she impersonate the character she had assumed that her story received universal belief, and upon the strength thereof she was admitted to the best society in Bristol and Bath. The secret was at last betrayed by a female friend of whom she had made a confidant. Upon being taxed with the importune, the princess confessed the whole truth, asserting that she had no intention of carrying the hoax so far, but that once begun she was afraid to retrace her steps.

18 September 1866
The Ploughing Match is fixed for the 20th of October. Sir Stafford Northcote MP is expected to preside.

18 December 1866
A mechanics institute and reading room has recently been opened in this town. The Vicar (Revd J.P. Benson) offered the use of the National Schoolroom, and kindly consented to be the president. He opened the meeting with appropriate remarks, when Mr Veysey, of Bideford, gave a lecture to the satisfaction of a respectable and attentive audience. It is hoped that the secretary and committee will meet with generous support so as to enable them to carry on the cause to a successful issue.

27 February 1872
Think of the Poor.
On Monday a good substantial tea was provided for about one hundred and fifty of the poor by Host Mead, Commercial Hotel. The Ploughing Match Committee supplied the requisite funds, and the whole affair was in every respect a success.

12 December 1887
Witheridge Races.
These races which came off on Thursday attained as high

a degree of success as could reasonably be expected, considering the lateness of the season and the consequent uncertainty of the weather. As the latter turned out favourable, however, the course was in very good condition for racing, and the attendance was fairly large.

Darkness setting in at an early hour in the evening prevented the hurdles, Galloway and consolation races announced on the posters from being run. The Witheridge Brass Band was present, and rendered in their usual efficient style a good selection of popular music. Refreshments were supplied by Mr Jas Baker, of the Angel Hotel, at which place the winners were awarded prizes later on in the evening.

3 March 1888
Funeral of Dr Llewellyn.
On Friday morning the inhabitants of Witheridge were deeply grieved to hear of the death of one of the kindest-hearted gentlemen, Dr Llewellyn. He had spent the previous evening with Mr Hill Partridge. About three in the morning the latter was called up to go to the doctor, who said he knew his attack was serious and at once made preparations by writing a few important directions, and shortly afterwards passed away. Thus Witheridge loses one of the most benevolent gentlemen in the county. He was a splendid angler and an ardent general sportsman. He was admired by all with whom he came in contact. His age was only a little over 60... Many reasons have been assigned for the late doctor's popularity, but one is obvious, that is his kindness to the poor. In all weathers and at all times he was at their call, and this when he often knew that this poverty would prove an impediment to the smallest payment.

2 March 1889
Witheridge Music Society.
The local celebrity which the Society has attained on account of the popularity and general excellence of its performance was the means of drawing a large concourse of people to the National Schoolroom on Friday evening last week to witness the closing entertainment of the season. The platform, which had been prettily decorated by Miss French and Mrs Llewellyn, presented a very gay appearance. Dr Haydon occupied the chair. The programme had been carefully arranged by the Committee – Messrs Cornish, Mansfield and Pullen – with a view to gratifying the varied tastes of a mixed audience, and the hearty and enthusiastic reception which greeted its several items testified to the fact that the object had been attained. Parts one and two of the programme were each opened by the Witheridge Subscription brass band, who acquitted themselves capitally, thereby reflecting great credit upon their efficient and painstaking leader, Mr S. Hill. Mr G. Selley presided at the pianoforte as accompanist. The part singing bore ample evidence of the care that had bestowed upon its preparation, the expression, precision and spirit which characterised it calling forth most flattering remarks. The ladies solos, which were mainly of

a sentimental character, were sung with considerable taste and feeling and evoked spontaneous applause. There was a good sprinkling of character and humorous songs, etc., into which local and topical 'hits' were freely introduced, to the great amusement of the audience.

11 May 1889

Mr Cheriton's Otter Hounds met at New Bridge on Saturday... Just after nine o'clock the huntsman, Mr Budget, started the pack up stream as far as the junction, but without success. The hounds were then turned downstream, just below the starting point, under Little Newhouses. They struck the trail of an otter and everyone was eagerly expecting a find in Drayford weirpool, but they were disappointed. As the pack passed the weir to a pool some distance below, where the trail was lost, the huntsman called back, and retried many a likely place, but without success, although no doubt the otter was hiding in some secret spot close by. The pack once more took downstream but without finding an otter. Many complimentary remarks were passed at Witheridge on the healthy state of the pack.

7 December 1889

Progress.

Witheridge, like many other small centres, was at one time very dull during the long winter evenings. The streets were unlit, and there was nothing from without to induce either young or old to leave their firesides. A gradual change has been making itself felt these last two winters. Thirteen street lamps have been erected and kept lit. The Musical Society, which started just two years ago, has attained celebrity on account of the excellence of the concerts given by it. For some time past the Society, now numbering over 30, have been busily practising, and are announced to come before the public again very shortly. There are no less than three dancing classes held periodically for the amusement of those

whose tastes lie in that direction; while the science and practice of ringing is monopolising the spare time and attention of another section of the young men of the parish. Last, but not least, there is the Subscription Brass Band.

24 May 1890

A rick belonging to a farmer here looked as though it was infested with rats. Holes were numerous in the thatch, and it appeared to be a regular rats nest. The farmer thought he would put an end to their work of destruction and had the rick removed to the barn. Then he found it was not rats but mice that were working such havoc with the corn, and he and his helpers and dogs killed over 1,000 of the little creatures.

27 February 1892

The Weather.

On Friday the snow fell very heavily during the whole of the day with a strong northeast wind, causing very large drifts in the road, so that vehicular travelling was stopped. The mail cart was able to come yesterday, but unable to go out again in the evening. The rural postmen were unable to go on their rounds. The carriers from Exeter took their vans laden with goods as far as possible, and left them at a farm near the road, and then took home their horses. It is to be hoped that men will soon be put on so as to clear the roads, that traffic may resume its usual course. The thunder on Saturday morning seems to have cleared the atmosphere and we are glad to see the sun making its appearance again, although a little more snow has fallen. I hope that frost and snow will soon bid us adieu for this season.

2 December 1893

Dairy Company.

With a view of establishing a butter factory in Witheridge on the same principles as that successfully

This is our earliest photograph, taken before 1886. The thatched houses on the far side were burned down in February 1886. They were occupied by Mr J. Churchill (saddler), Mr J. Dinner (wheelwright), Mr W. Way (carpenter) and Mr H. Trawin (wool merchant).

carried out by the Culm Valley Dairy Company at Hemyock, it is proposed to form a Witheridge and District Dairy Company Limited, with a capital of £1,000, in shares of £5 each. The directors and hon. secretary, all practical men, will give their services for the first year without remuneration and judging by the promises of support already received, there is every reason to hope that the Company will be successful.

27 January 1894

Proposed Butter Factory.

The Committee have accepted Mr Robert Lee's tender for the erection of the Butter Factory in Fore Street. Mr T.S. Mitchell is the architect and Mr Stenner of Tiverton will supply and fit up all necessary machinery. This will be on the ground floor. Above this will be a large room over fifty feet long which will be, it is stated, available for public meetings. If that is the case it will be a valuable acquisition to the town. Work will commence at once and it is to be completed by the second week in April.

11 August 1894

A large excursion party of over 120 visited Teignmouth on Wednesday in connection with our Young Peoples Guild. The outing was thoroughly enjoyed by all. Horses were kindly lent by Mr Maunder, Mr James Partridge and Mr J. Lake to convey the young folks to Crediton. They returned by the 6 o'clock train.

5 November 1894

Technical Instruction.

The first of a series of lectures on horticulture was given by Mr John Haynes of Barnstaple, in the National Schoolroom on Monday, when a good number of people were present to improve their knowledge on the above subject... Practical hints on budding, grafting, pruning and fruit-growing generally.

17 November 1894

Floods at Witheridge.

After the heavy rains of Sunday and Monday the streams rose rapidly and overflowed the adjoining land. At mid-day the Little Dart had become a swollen torrent quite 50 yards wide and was flowing quite over the bridge. The valley at the bottom of Commercial Mead was soon full of water and the cottages in Pullens Row were flooded. In Tonkins Cottage there were several feet of water, which kept pouring from front to back in a perfect torrent. During Tuesday night a terrific gale was blowing, which died away before morning, and a heavy rain set in which continued all day and threatened another flood. The mail cart from Morchard Bishop did not reach until 1.30p.m. on Monday. It is many years since such floods visited Witheridge.

27 April 1895

A preliminary meeting in connection with the proposed Witheridge Light Railway was held at the Angel Hotel on Thursday after the fair, and was well attended.

Mr T.L. Lee of Crediton presided and the subject was introduced by Mr W. Hannaford, auctioneer, who invited Mr R.B. Mildon of Ash Thomas, the originator of the scheme to give the company an account of it. This he did at some length, remarking that he was aware that in years gone by similar schemes had been proposed for the district, but with the aid of the Government measure now before Parliament there should be no serious obstacle in the way of the present project.

3 August 1895

Revd J.P. Benson's rent audit was held at the Angel Hotel. Present were the Revd Benson, and Messrs Wreford, Vickery, Blackmore, Lee Maunder, Lewing, Matthews, Besley, etc. Mr Wreford in proposing the health of Mr Benson hinted that no land bill could benefit a set of tenants where such mutual understanding and kindly feeling existed as between them and their landlord. In response to the toast most heartily drunk, Mr Benson said it was his pleasure at all times to make his tenants comfortable and whenever he had any spare cash necessary repairs should be attended to. He also hoped the parishioners would assist him in church and school expenses.

2 November 1895

Reading Room.

A general meeting was held at the Reading Room on Saturday last when about 20 members were present, Mr J.W. Partridge, hon. sec. occupied the chair. The Chairman said Mr Thomas had made a complaint respecting the unnecessary noise that had been made in the room for the past few weeks. One of the committee said it was no doubt owing to the young men stamping to the tunes played on the piano, and visitors would be asked to be less boisterous in future. It was proposed that matting be put down to overcome the difficulty but it was thought that funds were not adequate to cope with the extra expense, consequently the motion was overthrown.

30 January 1897

The Witheridge Railway Scheme.

In attendance was Mr Pain, the Civil Engineer who supervised the construction of the Culm Valley Railway. The meeting was informed that they must set aside altogether the idea of coquetting between two schemes and of playing off the South Western Railway against the Great Western, otherwise between the two stools they might come to the ground and have no railway at all. A narrow gauge was the only possibility, two and a half feet or three feet, and must come into Tiverton town to get Tiverton support.

13 March 1897

The hopes and anticipations of many have been realised at last. The steamroller visited in the early part of the week and made a stay of several days. Not only has the main thoroughfare received attention, but the other streets have been rolled, so that the roads are now in a better condition than they have been for years. The hope is that the steamroller will become more general in the near future, as many believe this method of road making is the most economical in the long run.

25 December 1897
An extension was granted until 3 o'clock to Sidney Cox, landlord of the Angel Hotel, on 31st December for a dinner and ball held by the local Sick and Burial Society.

12 February 1898
Influenza – and in many cases it has developed into other diseases – is still holding its sway here. Many are even now just recovering from a very serious illness.

Rooks are doing a lot of damage to turnips in this area rendering them liable to rot if we experience much hard frost – a preventive of this evil would be a boon to farmers.

25 June 1898
A lawn tennis club has been formed here and the opening matches will take place in a few days.

6 August 1898
Great inconvenience is being experienced just now through the great scarcity of water in this town, a fact which is made more apparent by the waterworks being as yet incomplete. Hopes are entertained that this state of things will not last much longer or the outlook will be serious.

19 August 1899
Vehicles without lights.
At the South Molton County Petty Sessions several from Witheridge were summoned for driving at night without lights as required by the new county byelaws. As these were the first offences under the new regulations the Bench let the defendants off on payment of costs.

Left: *The Vicarage, c.1900.*

Founded in June 1898, the tennis club played on three courts on rented ground behind the manse. Players identified include Annie Trawin, Connie Selley, Phyllis Andrews, Vera Selley, Wilfred Comins, Kitty Way.

Chapter 4

PEACE & WAR

THE BRITISH SCHOOL 1896–1921

William Charles Carter began his duties as head-master on 4 September 1896, enrolling his own three children on the same day. He at once drew up a new timetable and syllabus and aroused hitherto unheard-of enthusiasm in the managers, for the school instantly became the best staffed it had ever been. Mrs Carter, as an assistant teacher, took charge of the infants and Standards One and Two, helped by her daughter Fanny and Helena Holcombe as monitors. Mr Carter had a trainee teacher, Miss E.G. Trawin, to help him with Standards Three to Six. He was an efficient, determined and dedicated teacher, with few other interests outside the school. He was not even very interested in the change brought by the 1902 Education Act. On the other hand the school numbers rose from 80 in 1896 to over 100 in 1909, and he dealt smoothly with the move to the new building in 1898.

Being the only Chapel school in the immediate area it attracted pupils from a far wider catchment than the National (Church) School, drawing from Poughill, Nomansland, Cruwys Morchard, Puddington, East Worlington, Rose Ash and Meshaw. All of these, except Nomansland, had only Church schools of their own. Considerable distances had to be covered by pupils to attend the British School, for it was not until 1906 that the County Council began to provide school transport, which at the start consisted only of a single horse-drawn van from the Creacombe and Rose Ash direction. This van was shared by both schools and at one time managers insisted that the van discharge its passengers half a mile from the schools, so that the children should arrive almost as wet as the others.

Although rivalry existed between the schools there was little acrimony. In Mr Carter's first 18 years, his school lost eight pupils to the National School and gained 15 from it. On rare occasions a pupil would 'vote with his feet'. In October 1904 an 11-year-old lad named William took himself off to the other school. He had been at the British School since the tender age of two and a half and must have fancied a change. There is no reference to his parents' wishes in the log-book.

Both schools increased their numbers in the early 1900s, although there was some decline in rural

A postman in the early 1900s.

Witheridge church in 1931.
Oil-lamps were still in use at this time.

populations. There were three reasons for this. Firstly the four private or 'Dame' schools in Witheridge went out of business. Secondly, the 1902 Act brought improved attendance, including a number of children who had not previously attended school. Two of these aged 13 and 14 came to the British School and had to start with the infants. Thirdly, the introduction of the school van helped some of those in remote areas.

The most important event in the life of the British School was drily recorded by Mr Carter on 6 July 1898: 'Closed School today in the old schoolroom, reopen on Monday in the new one.' On 9 July he continued: 'The scholars were arranged in their fresh

Left: *The Methodist Chapel. In 1855 a cob-and-thatch barn (on the site where the chapel stands in 2003) was bought for £30 and converted into a 'neat little sanctuary' with pulpit and pews. It soon became clear that more space was needed as numbers steadily increased. Two cottages close by were purchased and the present building was erected at a cost of £220. It was opened on 23 June 1859. Leading lights at the time were Mrs Clapp, who lived at Belmont, and Mr and Mrs Gill of Foxdon. Difficult times followed and by 1881 £50 was still owing. This was cleared in 1886. A stalwart of that age was Mr James Greenslade, who was the superintendent of the Sunday school for over 50 years. In 1903, the schoolroom was built at a cost of over £300. By the 1920s the large choir was in demand for concerts in the area. Electric lights were installed in 1931 and in 1935 electric heaters replaced the stove.*

Left: *The Square in the 1890s. The children are from the British School, which had no playground.*

Below: *The British School in 1910, as it was when Sarah Trawin taught there. The headmaster was William Charles Carter.*

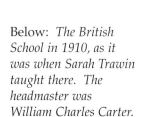

Above: *The British School c.1890. Second from the right, back row is William Partridge. Sarah Trawin is on the right in a white blouse and dark skirt. She was assistant to Mr Carter. She left for Canada in 1911 where her brother Frank had been farming for five years. Her sister Annie and 15-year-old brother Arthur (fifth from left, back row) went with her. The school made her a number of gifts including an album with a list of subscribers and photographs to remind her of Witheridge. The album is still with the family in Canada.*

The British School in 1898. It later became the primary school, and in 2003 is the village GP surgery.

The British School in 1917.

classes on Monday morning in the new schoolroom.' The new building had two snug and relatively well-lit rooms. There were toilets (known as 'offices'), playgrounds for boys, girls and infants, and a bell on the roof. At times there were over 100 children being taught there. Perhaps proximity helped to keep them warm for in the log-book for 6 February 1899, he noted 'that the temperature stood at 48 degrees in the school this afternoon.'

Mr Carter introduced monthly exams for each standard and regularly taught the school new songs. He brought in magic lantern shows, taught pupils how to write letters, and began military drill for the boys. However, it was with his introduction of nature study rambles, that sparks of enthusiasm appear in the log-book: wild flowers were 'found and identified' and spiders, frogs and grasshoppers all got a mention. In 1907 he began a 'School Calendar of Nature Observations', and in 1913 gardening classes started, after inspection of the 'garden plots and fruit plot' by HMI. One year Mr Carter recorded 117 pounds of fruit from a single apple tree. Seeds such as cucumber were planted in pots on the window-sills.

At times the wider world affected the school. In 1905 the High Commissioner for Emigration to Canada sent to each school a wall map of the country with glowing reports of the opportunities there. Sarah Trawin had entered the school in 1892 at the age of seven and became a monitor at 15. She worked a few years as a pupil-teacher and became an uncertified teacher at the school. In 1911 she resigned to go to Canada to join her brother who had already emigrated. On her last day she was presented with a number of gifts, including an album of views of Witheridge, which her descendants still treasure.

We can gain an idea of Mr Carter's teaching abilities from HMI's reports, which had to be recorded in the log-book. Early on HMI noted that the children of the lower standards were reading and writing indifferently, and appeared listless. More than once he noted that 'instruction in the lower part of the school is unintelligent and should improve in method and Reading should be more systematically

taught.' By 1905 there was some improvement, but it was not maintained. In 1912 HMI put his finger on one particular fault. He said 'The methods of teaching have been in some respects misapplied. The children should be encouraged to overcome difficulties for themselves.' A punishment book was started in 1911, but only 18 entries were made in the space of a decade (although this only covered use of the cane). Pupils of the time remembered being punched in the back and on the side of the head; a favourite trick of Mr Carter's was to come up behind a pupil and box his ears. When children complained to their parents, they usually sided with the head, but the village doctor made frequent protests at the blows received by the children. One lad, who was big for his age, returned to the school after he had officially left in order to gain revenge. He set about Mr Carter, knocked him down, smashed his glasses and trampled on him, shouting 'you done it to me, now I'll do it to you.' Mrs Carter was well aware of her husband's temper, and as soon as she heard him shouting she would hurry in from the infants' room and try to calm him down.

The log-book shows rare recognition of events outside the school. In May 1900 the managers ordered a half holiday to celebrate the capture of Pretoria in the Boer War. At the coronation of King George V, the lord of the manor presented each child with a medal and some sweets. The outbreak of war in 1914 passed without comment in the log-book, but in January 1915 the children had a half holiday to see a contingent of the Devonshire Regiment, with band, march by on a recruiting drive. In 1916 a collection was made for prisoners of war in Germany. There is no log-book reference to the Armistice on 11 November 1918.

Few visitors, other than those in an official capacity, came to the school during Mr Carter's headship. Parents, if the log-book is to be believed, were rarely seen. Pupil numbers rose under Mr Carter, several pupils got county scholarships, and his pupil-teachers seem to have received much consideration. His authoritarian methods and choleric nature told against him, and yet on nature rambles and in the school garden he was a different man.

THE NATIONAL SCHOOL 1894–1930

Augustus Andrews began by commenting on the looseness of the discipline and the low state of the stock, and added cheerfully, 'these little defects can be easily remedied', and he was as good as his word. Books and materials flowed in and the managers supported him by authorising the partitioning of the room, and provision of a gallery for the infants. These benefits were merited for he was a certificated teacher, his wife was a provisionally certificated mistress, and with them was Eva Tucker, a candidate on probation. HMI was full of praise but urged that a boys' urinal be provided (it is unclear what had they been using all this time). In his first year attendance averaged over 70; the Diocesan report classed the school as excellent, and HMI recommended the high grant figure of 20s.6d. per head. Local subscriptions amounted to nearly £27 out of a total income of £154, allowing up to £10 a year for books, materials and apparatus. Mr Andrews was brisk and businesslike and by 1896 the roll had risen to 109, with an average attendance of 90. Some of these extra pupils may have come from the two or three private or 'Dame' schools that closed about this time.

In May 1897 an average attendance of 97 was recorded, and the head suggested that more space could be found by using the master's house and garden, and housing the master elsewhere. The managers acted with speed; a house was rented for the master and his previous house was converted to classrooms. In addition, new cloakrooms and lavatory basins were installed and a new well was sunk and a force pump installed. The 'force' for the next 40 years would be provided by the caretaker.

Unlike his predecessors Mr Andrews recorded the syllabus for each standard for the coming year. Standards Four to Seven were taught such topics in medieval history as: Thomas à Becket, the Third Crusade, the Magna Carta, the foundation of the House of Commons, the Black Prince, Wat Tyler's Rebellion, social conditions. Current history was studied too, for in 1900 the school had a special holiday 'to commemorate Lord Roberts' success in the Transvaal', and in 1902 the end of the Boer War was celebrated with a half holiday on 2 June.

In 1901 Mr Andrews introduced a long-lasting and popular innovation, namely walks and visits to local places such as Yeo Woods, Bradford Pond, the sewage works, New Bridge, and Coombe Quarry. In 1902 the average attendance topped 100 for the first time, and the school was praised by HMI. The roll reached an all-time high of 129 in 1909. To cope with these numbers, the staff was increased to five, and the following year the school van ran for the first time. Special lessons noted in the log-book included 'Rain', 'The Post Office', 'The Empire', 'The Danger of Lamps', and in November 1902 a Mr Gunn gave an entertainment on the gramophone. At this time labour certificates to leave school early were granted

The National School, 1887. Henry P. Cornish was the sole teacher and head, 1886–93.
Annie Nott is second from left, back row.

The National School in 1918.

to children between 12 and 13 who had reached the Standard, whereas children to be employed in agriculture could leave at those ages without reaching any standard at all.

The outside world pressed more and more on the school, with visits from inspectors, managers, attendance officers, the photographer, the dentist, the medical inspector, the sanitary inspector. The children were regularly weighed and measured. County Council circulars flowed in. On one visit HMI inspected a site for a school garden and on 31 March 1913 Mr Andrews used capital letters to celebrate: 'RECEIVED GARDEN TOOLS AND COMMENCED GARDENING'. The same year he was recognised as a 'Teacher of Gardening', and in the autumn the County Council supplied the 'Approved Garden Syllabus'. The year 1902 had seen the establishment of Local Education Authorities on a county basis. This led to a nominee being added from the County and Parish Councils onto the original governing body. In spite of this Witheridge did not become a 'County School' but remained a 'Voluntary School', although it came under the County Education Authority with regard to administration, standards and finance. The managers were quite ready to strike out on their own on occasion, for at their first meeting they 'disapproved of the idea of starting a conveyance to bring in children living at a distance.' This, however, was a battle that they could not win. Although they turned down flat the County Council's suggestion that they give lectures to mothers and provide swimming-baths, they did agree to put the playground in order. On being told that toilets needed to be flushed more frequently, the managers replied that once a day was enough and greater frequency would increase the caretaker's salary.

To their credit the managers became involved in fund-raising for the school and in 1908 thanked the vicar's wife, Mrs Benson, for organising a dance in aid of the funds. In the same year they awarded all teachers a bonus of £2, due to excellent reports. The following year they displayed leniency in not discharging the school cleaner (referred to as 'Gooding') when he admitted 'smashing the Flushing

Apparatus'. When the County Council offered the sum of £5 towards the cost of a piano, the managers bought a harmonium instead for exactly £5, and so contributed nothing. They were ready to defy 'Exeter' if necessary, so when a circular arrived demanding a sub-committee of ladies to be set up to visit all mothers and lecture them on the importance of proper clothing, food and sleep for their children and the advantages of fresh air and cleanliness, they (perhaps foreseeing the reception they might get) rejected the idea outright, saying that no one would serve on such a committee.

The managers' defiance of Exeter took another turn in 1913, when they were contacted about school dinners. Their reply shows that 65 pupils had dinner in their own homes, 30 took their food into nearby cottages, and 25 ate their own food in school. The managers refused outright to provide dinners, but as a concession offered boiling water for the cocoa of those who ate in school. It was a further 33 years before school dinners were made available.

Ex-pupils had lively memories of pre-1914 days. Mrs Emily Williams recalled the horse-drawn van that brought them from Creacombe and Bradford, and the large buns baked by Churchills and Whitfields, known as 'three ha'penny busters'. There was great rivalry between the schools and battles took place, with Trafalgar Square serving as a kind of frontier between the sides. Gladys Ford (later Bristow) started school at the age of three and her brother Fred started aged two and a half. She had memories of the tortoise stove that did little to heat the building, but did help to dry out clothes. On dark days oil-lamps were lit morning and afternoon. Each child had his or her place, and was unlucky if he or she had to sit next to someone who had fleas or head-lice, or who didn't wash (although there were regular health inspections). At break time there were separate areas for boys, girls and infants. The surface of the play area was rough and injuries were common.

Mr Andrews kept a cane in the cupboard, but seldom used it. In fact the punishment book has no record of caning from 1905 to 1931. Old pupils recalled that 'if he looked at you, that was enough'. Mrs Bristow had memories of his keenness for rambles, particularly those to Bradford Pond and Drayford, followed by essays about the places they had visited and what they had seen. Each of the 12- and 13-year-olds had their own strip of garden, and prizes were given for the best. Gladys Ford used to say that she had enjoyed her time at his school and that he was much liked.

Evelyn Robins did not start school until the age of five, as her parents had decided that the two-mile walk from Lower Adworthy was too far for someone under five, and if the Adworthy Brook was flooded, then the long way round over Drayford Bridge added another mile. She liked and respected Mr Andrews. She recalls, 'he wasn't soft but he kept good discipline without bringing the cane out of the cupboard.' Amy Alford took the same view, but had amusing memories of the political rivalry between the schools at election time, with the National School and pupils decked out in blue, and the British School in Liberal yellow.

The log-book entry for 4 September 1914 brings a note of war, 'took the upper children to The Square to see the recruits start for Kitchener's army'. In November a Belgian refugee child was admitted (no details were given). Mr Andrews lectured on 'The Navy' and 'The Red Cross Movement'. Life continued much the same – ice delayed Mr Davey's van, the garden continued to be planted, measles and diphtheria occurred. The school held a Red Cross sale in 1916, and in the same year '12 children joined the cheesemaking classes'. In May 1917 the upper Standards were taken 'to see the Steam Plough at work'. Mr Andrews got his call-up papers in June 1918, but in July he was told he was not needed. School numbers gradually fell throughout the war, primarily due to the shortage of labour that forced farmers to keep boys of 12 in full-time work.

Mr Andrews had to leave the house he was renting, and the managers obtained a grant from the National Society to help them buy Orford House in The Square for £300, for which they charged Mr Andrews £21 a year rent. The end of the war brought physical

exercises, insurance for the 'van children' and 'useful training in independent study for the older children.' In 1923 a government decision was taken to cut teachers' salaries by five per cent. The teachers refused to accept this and the managers were forced to sack them. Despite this, they strongly backed them and allowed Mr Andrews to stay rent free in Orford House until the dispute was settled.

Between the early 1920s and 1933 the log-book notes are quite brief. Attendance fell to around 70, HMI's reports were a touch more critical and there was a sense of an era coming to an end. There was a novelty on 9 January 1930 when 'The Airship R100 passed over Witheridge at 9.45.' The two schools shared the new motor transport that replaced the old horse-drawn van. The managers continued to fight the County Council when they could. For example, when the Council insisted that school coal came from Lapford rather than Tiverton, they thought this pointless and said so.

On 13 October 1930, Mr Andrews resigned as head after 37 years. He had introduced ideas of his own and easily coped with the pressures, changes and demands of the authorities. His enthusiasm for teaching is clear in the log-book, and his managers' appreciation is apparent in their minutes. Those of his pupils who shared their memories of the school spoke highly of him. He was a good teacher and a good headmaster.

The National School, 1927. Left to right, back row: *Bob Southcott, Tom Bucknell, Reg Drew, Archie Nott, Gilbert Pincombe, Sid Gibbs, Archie Beer, Charlie Gard;* middle row: *? Moyse, ?, ?, Ruth Southcott, Kitty Morrish, Millie Beer, Doris Ford, Stella Baker, Vernon Reed;* front: *Fred Ashelford, Wilf Down, Reg Cole, ?, Wilf ?, Muriel Prentice, Emma Westcott, Chick Voysey, Lionel Gunn, ? Pyne.*

The National School, 1929. Left to right, back row: *Phyllis Hill, Betty Nott, Kathleen Lamprey, Rita Selley, Marjorie Ayre, Loveday Stoneman, Nora Holmes, Betty Manley, ?;* fourth row: *Arthur Ayre, Sylvia Leach, Evelyn Criddle, Doreen Tanner, Vera Manley, Hazel Fewings, Jose Baker, Rosalind Hartnell, Dora Bourne, Arthur Stenner;* third row: *Cecil Reed, Ben Rowcliffe, Bill Woollacott, Cyril Windsor, Eric Selley, Reginald Bucknell, Herbert Bucknell, Stafford Hartnell;* second row: *Percy Middleton, ? Kingdom, Cedric Chapple, Kenneth Criddle, Alan Vernon, Geoffrey Hill;* front row: *Reginald Windsor, Stanley Selley, ? Holmes, Henry Beer, Philip Dunn, Bill Blackford.*

Kelly's Directory 1902

Witheridge is a parish and village on the road from South Molton to Tiverton, 7 miles north-east from Lapford Station on the North Devon branch of the London and South Western Railway, and about 8 south east from Bishopsnympton station on the Barnstaple section of the Great Western Railway, and about 10½ south-east from South Molton and 10½ west by north from Tiverton, in the Northern division of the county, Witheridge hundred, South Molton petty sessional division, union and county court district, and in the rural deanery of South Molton, archdeaconry of Barnstaple and diocese of Exeter. The church of St John the Baptist is an edifice of stone in the Early Perpendicular style, consisting of chancel, nave of four bays, aisles, south porch and an embattled western tower with pinnacle.

Private Residents

Adams, William, The Square
Benson, (Miss) E T, The Lawn
Charlton, Thomas William,
  Colleton Hall, Hill Town
Cutcliffe, (Mrs), Coombe House
Fernie, (Miss), The Square
Holt, Geo. Frederick, Lawn Cottage
Partridge, (Mrs) Ellen, South Street
Shelley, Percy Wilfred Graham MRCS Eng.
  LRCP Lond., Cypress House.

Bennett, Thomas, North Street
Benson, Revd John Peter MA (vicar and rural dean), Vicarage
Cheney, Revd Henry (Congregational), The Manse
Cock, George, Commercial Cottage
Elworthy, (Mrs), Lashbrook
Folland, Frank, Burn House
Partridge, (Mrs) Elizabeth, Fern Cottage
Pullen, Geo. Henry, sen. Rosemont Vil
Tucker, Mrs, Fore Street

Commercial

Adams, Richard, Dairyman, The Lawn
Addicott, Fanny (Mrs), Nurse
Ayre, George Thomas, Farmer, Lower Queendart
Ayre, Thomas, Farmer, Witheridge Moor
Baker, William, Blacksmith
Bennett, James, Shoe Maker, Fore Street
Blackford, Henry, Miller (water), Bradford Mill
Bodley, Thos, Carpenter, Pullen's Row
Bowden, Robt, Jobbing, Gardener, Gunn Hole
Bradford, Wm, Chimney swpr, Penford
Bulled, Edmund, Wheelwright, The Square
Burnett, Ann (Miss), Dressmaker, West Street
Churchill, Herbert, Baker, West Street
Clark, Ephraim, Black Dog, PH
Conner, Wm, Tailor and Draper, South Street
Cruwys, George, Farmer, W. Piliven
Dart, William, Farm Bailiff to
  Mrs Cutcliffe, Cannington and Coombe House
Dummett, Thomas, Angel PH
Eastmond, Edmund, Farmer, Muxeries
Fox, Fowler and Co, Bankers (branch)
  (Herbert John Mansfield, Manager),
  Wed and Fri 11 to 2; draw on
  Barclay & Co Ltd EC
Greenslade, Wm, Shoemaker, Bow Court
Gunn, Charles, Wheelwright
Harris, John, Farmer, Foxdon
Hodge, Hy, Mason and Shopkeeper, North Street
Holcombe, William, Tailor, Fore Street
Hooper, Robert, Piano Tuner, Fore Street
Huxtable, James, Farm bailiff to
  Mrs Cutcliffe, New House
Maire, Amos, Miller (water) and Shopkeeper
Munley, Wm, Butcher, Gunn Hole
Matthews, Harold, Farmer North Coombe
Maunder, Lloyd, Farmer, East Essebere
Partridge, Charles, Farmer, Lakelands
Phillips, Ann (Mrs), Nurse, The Square
Pullen, George Henry, junr, Draper & Grocer,
  Post Office
Rowcliffe, Issac, Farmer, Penford

Adams, Richard, Farmer, Hole
Alford, William, Blacksmith, West Street
Ayre, Michael, Farmer, Downe
Baker, Charles, Dairyman, Litterbarn
Bennett, Harriet (Miss), Shopkeeper, Fore Street
Besley, Henry, Farmer, East Piliven
Board, Thos, Farmer, Higher Adworthy
Boundy, Frederick, Farmer, Horestone
Bowden, Robt, jun. Mason, Gunn Hole
Bucknell, Robert, Farmer, Westeria House
Bulled, John, Dog Trainer
Chapple, Sarah Jane (Mrs), Farmer, Bythen
Churchill, Joseph, Saddler
Clotworthy, John, Builder, Fore Street
Cox, Henry, Farmer, Heiffers
Cutcliffe (Mrs), Farmer and Landowner, Coombe and New House
Davey, John and William, Farmers, Malson and Wilson
Dinner, William, Blacksmith, Fore Street
Eastman, James, Police Constable
Fewings, Edmund, Farmer, Wheadon
Gill, Hedley Thorne, Assistant Overseer & Clerk to Parish
  Council, Lakelands
Greenslade, James, Shopkeeper, Fore Street
Greenslade, Susan (Mrs), Newsagent, Rose Cottage
Gunn, Charles, Hare and Hounds, PH
Gunn, Ellen (Mrs), Nurse, South Street
Hill, John, Farmer, South Grendon
Holcombe, Claude and Mary (Misses), Dressmakers
Holt, George Frederick MRCS Eng., LRCP Lond., Physician
  and Surgeon Lawn Cottage
Lee, Robert, Builder, Ebrington's Row
Lee, William, Farmer, South Coombe
Maire, Harriet (Mrs), Dairy, Mitre House
Mansfield, Herbert junr, Grocer and Draper
Maunder, Frank, Butcher, Fore Street
Norrish, Geo, Gardener to Mrs Cutcliffe
Partridge, William, Shoemaker, Rosemont
Pickard, Ann (Mrs), Tailoress, West Street
Roberts, Thomas, Farmer, Newland
Robins, George, Farmer, Adworthy
Selley, George, Butcher, South Street

Selley, John, Farmer, Hill Town
Stone, Sidney John, Resident Sergeant, Police Station
Stoneman, Richard, Miller (water), Drayford Mill
Thomas, Richard, Farmer, Leat
Tolley, Wm, Insurance Agent, Rosemont
Trawin, Henry Tapp, Wool Stapler and Drug Stores
Tucker, George (Mrs), Farmer, Wilson
Tucker, Wm Henry, Shoemaker, West Street
Venner, Thomas, Thatcher, Godswell
Volunteer Battalion (4th) Devonshire Regiment
  (L Co. Capt. Percy W. G. Shelley,
  Wm. C. Carter, Drill Instructor)
  White, Frank, Farmer, Fore Down
Wreford, William, Farmer, Bradford.

Shelley, Percy Wilfred Graham, MRCS, LRCP, Physician and
  Surgeon,
Medical Officer and Public Vaccinator, No 6 district, South Molton
  Union and Cruwys Morchard district, Tiverton Union,
  Cypress House
Tolley, John, Farmer, Hellinghayes
Tucker, William Henry, Farmer, Higher Queendart
Venner, Robert, Thatcher, Drayford
Vicary, Charles, Farmer, Dart Raffe
Way, James, Carpenter
Way, Mary (Mrs), Dressmaker
Whitfield, Selina (Mrs), Baker
Witheridge District, (The) Dairy Co. Ltd (William Greenslade, sec.),
  Dairymen.

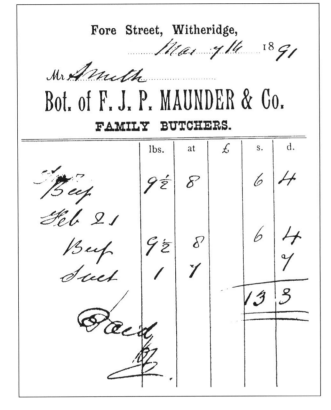

Above: *Cows passing the Mitre.*

*Mr and Mrs Woolway and
their daughter Sarah outside
Peartree Cottage, later known
as Mitre Cottage.*

EXTRACT FROM THE SOUTH MOLTON GAZETTE

21 August 1897

Breeze at Witheridge Flower Show.
George Henry Selley, of Witheridge, was summoned by Frederick Phipps, for wilfully damaging a 'striking' machine, his property, on 12th August at Witheridge Flower Show.

Mr W.B. Seldon, Barnstaple, appeared for the complainant, and Mr R.S. Crosse for the defendant. Complainant said he was a licensed Hawker and travelled with a toy stall and striking machine. He arrived at Witheridge and paid 2s.6d. for a stall. Shortly afterwards a second half crown was demanded, which he refused to pay. Defendant then said he would knock the thing down; he cut the rope and struck the machine with a mallet, damaging it to such an extent that he had not been able to use it since... The second half crown was subsequently paid... The machine cost him £5.10s., this was exclusive of the plume of feathers and the bell. William and Louisa Hurford corroborated as to seeing the defendant commit and damage. Evidence was given on behalf of the defendant as to the usual charge for stalls, etc., by Robert Way and Herbert Mansfield. The latter heard Mr Selley tell the complainant to shift the machine or he would do it for him. Selley struck the machine, and made a crack large enough to admit a penknife. Witness considered that 3d. to 6d. would meet the damages... The bench fined the defendant 2s.6d. and expenses and allowed the complainant £1 for the damage done. The amount of £2.13s.6d. was paid.

EXTRACTS FROM THE TIVERTON & SOUTH MOLTON GAZETTE

24 May 1902

Rifle Range for Witheridge.
The Volunteer Movement in Witheridge has made rapid strides since a section was formed in March 1900... The Company now numbers about 110 men under Captain Shelley and Lieutenants Cruwys and Gurney. The Vicar readily assented to a range on his property at Bradford in the tenancy of Mr Wreford, who also gave his consent. It was decided to make Saturday week the opening day. The weather was very rough, the honour of firing the first shot was accorded to Mrs Shelley, and when the signal was given for a bull there was a hearty cheer. The Vicar also proved himself a steady shot. All present then had a few shots each at 200 and 500 yards, and returned to the village to partake of a luncheon provided at the Angel Hotel by Host Fradd. The afternoon was spent in the Drill Hall, where there was some very good Morris Tube shooting.

16 August 1902

Coronation.
The festivities were initiated by the Parish Council, who appointed a committee for June 26th and reappointed it for Saturday [the coronation date had to be postponed due to the illness of King Edward VII]. Among those who worked the hardest to bring the proceedings to a successful issue were Mrs Clatworthy, Miss Meadows, Mesdames Selley, G. Selley and Cheney, the Misses Pullen and Hayter, Mr and Mrs Tolley, Mr and Mrs Andrews, Mr and Mrs Carter and Mr and Mrs Benson. The village was gay with flags and bunting. The Volunteers paraded the town in the morning and attended divine service in the Parish Church at 11.30, where the Vicar gave a brief address. The school children were given a tea, and a programme of sports was done through.

29 August 1903

Motor Cars for Rural Districts.
At their recent meeting the Tiverton and District Agricultural Association passed a resolution calling on the Great Western Railway Company to bring about at the earliest possible moment a motorcar service between Tiverton and Witheridge.

3 October 1903

Crops.
Wheat not average, barley ditto; oats average crop; swedes not average, many turned to finger and toe; turnip, failure; potatoes above average; mangold very good; apples quite a failure; grass very plentiful; hay ditto; straw not up to average.

6 August 1904

Motor Car Traffic.
The Chairman of South Molton RDC brought up the report of the Committee with respect to the regulation of motorcar traffic in the district. After consideration of what would best tend to public safety the Committee said they could not recommend such traffic on district roads. They suggested with regard to main roads that the speed permitted should not exceed 12 miles an hour.

4 November 1905

A correspondent writes 'If the Great Western Railway Company fight shy of [a] starting motor car from Tiverton to Witheridge, why does not the South Western Railway run one between Lapford and Witheridge? The distance is only 8 miles and the road is level for a great part of the way'.

1 February 1908

A lantern Lecture was given in the British Schoolroom on Thursday, entitled 'Peary's Dash for the North Pole'. There was a large and appreciative gathering. Mr Cole of Newhouse came with his lantern and the pictures were very clearly shown.

2 May 1908

Witheridge as a Health Resort.
Witheridge being 10 miles away from a station does not get so many visitors as it deserves. However, this Easter a medical man in flourishing practice in Monmouth

sought change of air and rest at Witheridge, and found both much to his satisfaction. He tells us that although he had been round the world, taking 6 years in the process, he was never in Devon before save for one day in Ilfracombe.

Of the beautiful scenery around Witheridge our medical friend spoke with warm appreciation. He was specially struck with the beauties of Bradford Pond, a fine stretch of water three quarters of a mile in length, embowered among trees and teeming with fish – an ideal spot for a picnic in fine weather. There are swans and heron in the vicinity. It forms part of the estate of the Vicar, the Revd J.P. Benson.

From a doctor's point of view the chief drawback of Witheridge, apart from its isolation, seems to be extreme healthiness. Nobody ever seems to be ill there. There is however plenty of sport.

29 October 1910
Theft from Witheridge Church.
At the Devon assizes, before Mr Justice Bankes, a labourer was indicted for breaking and entering a church and stealing a penny, the money of the Vicar of the parish, at Witheridge between 15th and 18th June... he denied the charge, marks on the offertory box corresponded with a knife and a pair of scissors found on the accused... and his boots fitted imprints discovered near the church, he was found guilty and sentenced to penal servitude to three years – previously he had served two periods of five years penal servitude.

11 March 1911
A meeting has been held in the National School for the purpose of hearing a report as to the canvass for the appointment of a District Nurse... notice has been received of 80 subscribers. The cost was estimated at about £60, of which £40 had already been promised. A committee was formed for the purpose of making all inquiries concerning the matter. A vote of thanks was accorded the members of the Parish Council for the trouble they had taken.

24 June 1911
Coronation Rejoicings.
Church and Chapel services... sports... 200 children have tea in the marquee, meat tea for 400 adults, dancing and games 'until the time arrived for the large bonfire to be lit, when there was a general move to Providence, where a huge bonfire, the wood for which had been given by the farmers, had been erected in a field belonging to Mr Tucker. Before setting the fire alight, Mr Churchill gave a good display of fireworks, and then amidst many cheers and much excitement the pile was set ablaze, which signalled for miles around that Witheridge and Thelbridge were ending the day's rejoicing in the generally approved fashion.

21 February 1914
Disturbing Salmon.
Five Witheridge young men were summoned with disturbing salmon in certain waters called the Queen Dart at Witheridge, contrary to section 16 of the Salmon Fishery Act 1861, the defence was that the defendants while searching for cattle, disturbed a rabbit and they crossed the stream in pursuit of it, they admitted ignorance of what a spawning bed was. They were each fined a shilling and costs.

11 April 1914
At a meeting of the Bowling Club in the National School, the Vicar presided. The Hon. Sec. Mr G.H. Pullen, made a statement of the formation of the Club, and read letters from well-wishers, among whom were Mr Cutcliffe (Dawlish), Messrs Amory, Cottrell (Hon. Sec. Tiverton Bowls Club) and W. Howe (South Molton Bowls Club). It was decided that bona fide working men of the parish should be allowed use of the green during the evenings on payment of two pence.

28 April 1917
South Molton RDC.
Mr Trawin said, 'I should like to ask who would be answerable if an accident occurred through the condition of our roads. Take the Witheridge roads. If you fell out of a trap and pitched in one of the ruts, people would pass and never see you (laughter). The state of the roads wants looking into'.

19 May 1917
The first motor plough seen in Witheridge arrived a few days ago and proceeded to Newhouse for Mr E.J. Cole.

23 June 1917
Witheridge Auction.
The largest entry of stock ever recorded for a June market, nearly 1,000 sheep and 150 bullocks, besides pigs and horses.

26 January 1918
There are nearly 100 members in the local war Savings Association, and 72 certificates have been purchased during the present week.

Sayings from *Witheridge Memories*

'I don't care what the law is, I produce it and if I'm eating cream I'm not eating anything else.'

'I maybe cabbage-looking but I'm not green.'

'Smoke a pipe to get the fleas out the cat's ear.'

'And George Mayne's jacket went down into the thresher and the thresher went 'woomf', and Hughie said 'was you wearing it, George?''

'Dick Middleton was a rabbit trapper; when he was in the Army his wife addressed a letter to him: Dick Middleton, Rabbit Catcher, Somewhere in France.'

18 October 1918
Mr G.H. Pullen, Chairman of the Parish Council, presided at a meeting in the National School on Saturday October 18th, called to make final arrangements respecting the War Memorial. There was only a fair attendance, and the report showed that the response to the appeal made for funds had fallen far short of what was anticipated, the amount reached being some little over £80. As there seemed a bar to fixing the wayside cross in The Square, it was decided to place the memorial just inside the churchyard rails.

29 May 1920
Men engaged in the building trades at Witheridge are asking for an increase in wages of two pence an hour – mechanics from 1s.5d. to 2s.3d. an hour, and labourers from 1s. to 1s.2d. per hour. Mr W.H. Hobbs, District Organiser of the Workers Union, on Saturday had an interview with Messrs Way Bros, the principal firm in the locality concerned, who however it is understood, refused to accede to the request. It is probable that the matter will be referred to the Ministry of Labour to decide, so that a strike may be avoided.

30 October 1920
South Molton RDC.
It was reported that the Postmaster General's representative would meet parish representatives and 'explain the position'. 'We don't want the position explained', said a member, 'we want the telephone'. Mr Trawin hoped they would not have the state of affairs that existed in housing, for if so they would not have the telephone until some of them were in their graves.

18 December 1920
The attempt to inaugurate a Football Club for Witheridge has proved successful. A meeting was held in the Church Rooms when it was decided to enrol members and elect officers. The Revd M.W. Melrose was elected President, and a number of Vice Presidents were nominated. Mr Stanley Leach was appointed Secretary, and Mr Gunn Treasurer, Mr Gilbert Maunder was elected temporary Captain, and Messrs F. Leach, S. Selley, W. Baker, Edworthy and J. Churchill were chosen to constitute the Committee.

5 April 1924
A Witheridge Nonagenarian.
A South Wales journal contains an interesting sketch of Mr Henry Ford, a native of Witheridge, who has just celebrated his 95th birthday. Born at Witheridge in 1829, Mr Ford comes of proud old Devon stock, the family being known throughout that county for their skill as coopers, a craft that they have been engaged in for over 300 years. In the year 1850 Mr Ford, who had completed his training to follow the family craft, left Witheridge and made his way to Bristol, where in due course he took to the sea and signed on as a ship's cooper in one of Bristol's old sailing vessels, his first voyage was to the West Coast of Africa,

a voyage that occupied 17 months overall. He continued in active work until the age of 79 years. Mrs Ford is now 88, and there are 6 children and 25 grandchildren.

21 February 1925
Recently a wireless concert took place in the British School in aid of the Congregational Church. The programme was received clearly and of ample volume, arrangements being carried out by Mr W.J. Cole, wireless dealer of South Molton. There was a crowded attendance.

16 October 1928
Eight Houses for Witheridge.
Five tenders have been received for the erection of eight houses at Witheridge. The lowest tender has been accepted, that of Messrs J. Morrish and Sons, at £3,123, conditional on their giving an undertaking to erect the houses by 15th March next.

29 June 1929
Thursday will be a day long remembered by the inhabitants of Witheridge who gathered in full force for the opening of a recreation ground of about an acre at Providence. The arrangements were made by the local Playing Fields Association. The programme opened with a procession through the village, organised by Miss Margaret Mansfield, of children in fancy costumes. After the ceremony the children attending the local undenominational school gave a folk dancing display, which was followed by sports and sideshows. Refreshments were dispensed by a Ladies Committee under Mrs Lewis and Mrs Silliphant [sic]. The Vicar, Revd J.A.S. Castlehow presided. He was supported by the Earl of Devon, Sir Ian Amory Bt MFH, and others, thanks were expressed to Miss Mansfield for so generously buying the ground in memory of her father, who had been a great sportsman.

21 February 1931
Inquiry at Witheridge on New Sewerage Scheme.
At present 90% of houses have WCs, the Council will bear the cost of connecting them. The Inspector said it was impossible to connect the Vicarage as it was at a lower level that other houses nearby, the annual loan charges would be £169.15s.3d.

23 June 1932
A Friend to Witheridge. Passing of Miss Mansfield.
A large congregation attended the Parish Church... To pay their last respects to Miss Harriett Comins Mansfield, who passed away last Thursday after a brief illness. Miss Mansfield was a nurse by profession; she served with distinction during the war when she was 'mentioned in dispatches'. A few years ago she fulfilled one of her heart's desires by providing Witheridge children with a playing field. This is situated on a pleasant eminence just outside the village on the Tiverton road, and is equipped with a sandpit, swings and seesaws, which seem thoroughly to be appreciated. Her passing at the age of 48 is deeply deplored.

A hoist for batteries at the Exe Valley Electricity Co. The building lies behind Cypress House.

15 April 1931
Lighting.

The Parish Clerk read a letter from the Exe Valley Electricity Company re the proposed electric lighting of Witheridge. The Company were prepared to make a reduction, provided the street lights were switched off at 11pm instead of midnight. The following reduction was suggested; 20 watt standards, 2s.6d., 60 watt 3s.11d., 100 watt 6s.2d. There were 16 lights in the town, which have hitherto been extinguished at 10pm. Mr Churchill considered the Company's scheme too expensive and thought that in five years' time they would probably have a Government supply which would be cheaper.

Water.
Worms and snails were said to be still present in the water.

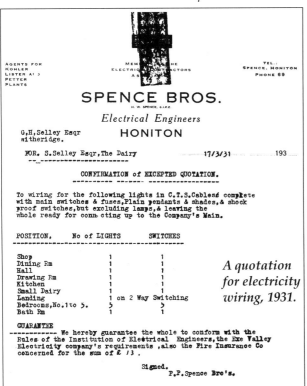

A quotation for electricity wiring, 1931.

28 September 1933
Witheridge Young Farmers Club.

Witheridge is to be congratulated upon the membership of its YFC. Their keenness is unrivalled, as was shown on Saturday when they met at West Yeo Farm kindly placed at their disposal by Mr and Mrs Woollacott, the ages range from 10 to 21, the club is the largest in Devon.

7 December 1933
Foolish Cyclist.

A local man was fined 5 shillings for riding a bicycle while under the influence of drink. His defence was that his bicycle seat caught in his trousers and threw him off, and he staggered about due to anger.

2 August 1934
Witheridge Scouts in Latvia.

Two Witheridge Rover Scouts and the District Scoutmaster formed part of the British Group of 35 in the Latvian National Camp near Riga, the capital.

4 April 1935

Application was received for the alteration of the name 'Cannington Villas', as at present applied to the Witheridge council houses. It was agreed they be renamed 'Merryside Villas'.

15 April 1937
Witheridge Housing Inquiry.

Clearance Order affecting Anstey's Court – 22 buildings including outhouses and woodsheds. One of the owners, Mr Palfreyman, said there was little wrong with the cottages and he had had no complaints, Dr Mortimer said they were all unfit for human habitation.

THE RAILWAY

A public meeting for Witheridge and surrounding parishes was held on Monday 8 February 1897, in the National Schoolroom, at 7p.m., for the purpose of considering a light railway scheme from Tiverton to Witheridge. The Revd J.P. Benson presided. Mr F.J.P. Maunder moved that a railway communication would be beneficial to Witheridge and the district; this was seconded by Mr Jas Brawn and carried unanimously. Mr Jas Partridge proposed that Witheridge should accept the help that Tiverton had offered, as it would be the cheapest option. Mr G.H. Pullen senr seconded this proposal, saying that the line would be the most direct. This was also carried without opposition. The chairman said the next question was what would Witheridge do towards helping to pay for the preliminary survey. He wanted to report to the public meeting to be held at Tiverton on Tuesday next that he had collected £20 from a public meeting at Witheridge, where volunteers had entered their names on a list for the above survey, which had thus far raised the sum of £10.

CORONATION OF GEORGE V, 22 JUNE 1911

Children of Witheridge and part of Thelbridge had tea with a meat sandwich, cutrounds and cream, bread and butter and cake. Adults had meat and beer or tea. In the evening a large bonfire was lit in a field of Chapner, the 12 loads of wood being given by

Revd J.P. Benson JP, and the farmers around. No expenses were incurred for the bonfire.

Receipts:

Mr Wreford's book	£4.4s.6d.
Mr Maire's book	£3.19s.6d.
Books of Messrs F. Selley, E. Hutchings,	
A Vicary	£14.3s.9d.
Luxmoore (lord of the manor)	£2.2s.
F. Tucker's book	£5.17s.6d.
Book for Aunt Sully	2s.
Total	£31.7s.1d.

Expenditure amounted to £25.19s. The balance of £5.8s.1d. was given to the Nursing Fund.

PARISH COUNCIL, FEBRUARY 1910

It was unanimously agreed to accept the tender of Mr Tucker at £8.15s. for street lighting. Considering a recent fire that had taken place in the village, it was thought desirable that the exact position of the several water hydrants should be known. On the proposition of Mr Gunn, seconded by Mr Churchill, it was resolved that Mr Gardner, surveyor, be asked to point this out, with a view to having marks placed on the nearest building as to their position.

It was thought advisable by some of the members present that some steps should be taken to procure a fire engine for this locality, and after a long discussion Mr Carter proposed and Mr Rogers seconded that the several insurance companies interested in this neighbourhood should be approached with a view to their granting a sum of money towards the expense. This was unanimously agreed.

PARISH COUNCIL, SEPTEMBER 1907

The report of the committee respecting the cleansing of the streets after market days was considered. A discussion took place regarding how the cost of this would be met, and whether a charge for cattle driven through the town should be made. This, it was thought, would be detrimental to the market, and the cost of collecting waste would leave very little for other expenses. Mr Trawin proposed that tenders be invited for cleansing and disinfecting the streets after the markets in April, June, September and November.

PARISH COUNCIL, DECEMBER 1907

Applications for allotment yardage were received from Messrs Holcombe, Dinner, Cheney, Crook, Bennett, Greenslade, Gard, Tolley, Bulled, Carter and Leach. On the proposition of Mr Gunn, seconded by Mr Huxtable, it was unanimously decided that Lime Close should be rented for the purpose of allotments. (Lime Close is now the Parish Hall field).

FIRES

The combination of close-packed houses and highly inflammable material such as thatch and wood made village fires an almost inevitable nightmare. Witheridge was no exception. Water was always in short supply. Some properties had their own wells, while others relied on the small reservoir in the corner of the sports field, fed by springs in the nearby Lakelands field (now houses). In the twentieth century this was supplemented by a pumped supply in the field beyond Merryside. Even so, there were times when demand was heavy and there was nothing left in the pipes and taps for those at the bottom of the village. Witheridge was, however, lucky in having The Square, which acted as a fire-break, when for example in the 1880s the Bell Inn and houses along the north side of The Square caught fire and burnt out. The fire brigade at Tiverton had been telegraphed and came galloping, but the fire had too strong a hold and as there was little water anyway, all the brigade could do was go home again.

In the 1830s the Old Parsonage farmhouse went up in flames; 50 years later it was replaced by the present Hope House (then the Vicarage). In the 1930s the farmhouse at Dart Raffe was destroyed by fire. In 1947 Tracy Green cottages burnt, and the wind blew sparks from the burning thatch over to the thatched Venbridge cottages beside the Drayford road; they went up as well. Very soon afterwards the village got not only its own fire brigade but a mains water-supply as well – at last!

This excerpt from the *Tiverton Gazette* shows the story of what happened in 1909:

Tuesday 29 June 1909
Fire at Witheridge, four houses burnt.
A disastrous fire destroyed four houses in Fore Street, Witheridge, early on Saturday morning. Just before six o'clock smoke was observed coming from the house of Mr Rogers, builder, undertaker, etc. – one of a row of eight. Mr James Greenslade, who lives near, assisted in conveying Mr Rogers' children to a place of safety, while Mr W.C. Carter informed P.S. Luxton. That officer was soon on the spot, together with Mr Rogers' workmen and many others. It was impossible to prevent the fire spreading to the shop adjacent, occupied by the Misses Holcombe, dressmakers, and the dwellings of Mrs Tucker and Mrs Hooper. The Misses Holcombe lost a sewing machine, and Mrs Tucker some furniture, but a good deal was conveyed to other houses.

Considerable anxiety was felt respecting the house occupied by Mr W. Dinner, who is dangerously ill, as is also Mrs Dinner. However, Messrs C. Maire, H. Gunn, W. Drew, J. Mogford, J. Crook and several others stationed themselves upon the roof and threw buckets of water upon the thatch. In this way the fire was kept from spreading in a westerly direction. Messrs A.

Vicary, F. Leach, J. Phillips, E. Gunn and others in a similar manner prevented the fire from travelling towards Mr Rogers' workshops, engine shed, and timber yard at the rear.

Perhaps the hardest fight with flames was that which resulted in saving Mr James Bennett's house. The wind was blowing up the street in the direction of that house, and already the houses between Mr Rogers' and Mr Bennett's were hopelessly involved. A large party commenced to strip the thatch off an empty cottage which separated Mr Bennett's from Mrs Hooper's. Numbers of willing hands conveyed the thatch further up the street, where it would be altogether clear of the flames. Others mounted ladders and threw water which was handed up in buckets. It seemed very doubtful which would win, and many looked anxiously up the Tiverton road and hoped the Tiverton Fire Brigade would soon arrive. Mr W. Greenslade of the Witheridge Dairy Co. had cycled to Tiverton immediately upon seeing the flames; and about eight o'clock he brought back the welcome news that he had met the Brigade at the bottom of Long Drag, they having received a telegram previously. Not long after the Brigade arrived, and all anxiety with regard to the further spreading of the conflagration was at an end. The promptitude with which they had acted upon receiving the message was much admired. They quickly poured a heavy stream of water upon the flames and then proceeded to pull down dangerous beams and walls, their operations being watched by an interested crowd of people.

It would be impossible to enumerate all the helpers. Mr J. Way, builder, rendered valuable help by fixing a standpipe in the water main and also by the loan of ladders, etc. Messrs E. Hutchings, R. and F. Bowden, J. and P. Gard, J. Davey, J. Burnett, J. Southwood worked hard at saving the buildings; and men and women alike copied the example set by the Vicar and his wife, and carried hundreds of buckets of water from the pumps to the ladders.

Nearly all the property in Fore Street is thatched and the danger at one time was very great. Fortunately the water-supply held out well. The heavy rains of the past week rendered the thatch less liable to be set on fire by sparks. The street is narrow, and this makes it more surprising that the property on the other side of the street did not take flame.

The fire is said to have originated in a defective flue. The damage is estimated at over £1,000. The owners and occupiers were insured. As the Tiverton firemen left on Saturday evening they were heartily cheered.

Captain Mercer's Narrative

Interviewed by a *Tiverton Gazette* reporter, Mr Mercer, captain of the fire brigade, said:

We received a telegram from the police at Witheridge stating that there was a large fire in the village, and asking us to bring out the engine. I rang up the firemen and fired off the maroon; and in a short time we started with the engine and eight men. We reached Witheridge just after eight and found that four houses were well alight, the roofs having fallen in. The villagers were hard at work preventing the fire from spreading. They were drawing their water from a hydrant connected with a reservoir just outside the village. They were doing very good work. In one place they had cut the thatch in two to prevent the fire spreading in that direction. At another place they had got on top of a house throwing water on the thatch. At this place the fire was burning furiously, and was getting very dangerous, as there was a long row of thatched cottages very near. We found some difficulty in getting the engine to work owing to the standpipe of the hydrant not having the same coupling as ours, theirs being a screw and ours instantaneous. Another difficulty was that the stand-pipe was low on the ground, and so we could not get anything to catch the water. A number of men, however, set to work with picks and spades and sank a pit underneath, into which we put a tin bath, the water from the hydrant being thus able to flow into it. After this we soon got to work with one jet, there not being sufficient water to keep two jets going. We played on the flames first at one end and then at the other. We kept the hose going until between five and six in the evening, when all danger of the fire spreading was at an end. There were one or two exciting incidents. Soon after we got there I was on top of one of the houses when the roof gave way. I spread out my arms to save myself and fell into the room below, carrying the ceiling with me. I was partially buried, but escaped with a few scratches and a damaged uniform.

At one time the risk to surrounding property was very grave, the burning buildings being surrounded with thatched buildings, while at the back of Mr Rogers' buildings was a long row of cottages. We concentrated our attention first of all to the old place next to Mr Dinner's house. The roof had fallen in, the woodwork underneath had become ignited and was blazing furiously. At one time the firemen were driven back in consequence of the intense heat and the smoke. They stuck manfully to their work, however, and prevented the fire spreading to Mr Dinner's house, which was only separated from the burning buildings by a narrow cartway. At the rear of Mr Rogers' house were a lot of outbuildings: had these become involved a big range of buildings would have been swept down.

JUDY ROAKE

Judy Roake has written the following:

My grandmother Ellen Edith (Nellie) Gard was the third daughter and seventh child of Philip and Mary Lee Gard (née Woolway). She was born at Yeo Cottage in the village of Witheridge on 8th May 1886, and went to school at the National School until she was 12 years

Watercolour of The Square, c.1910.

Judy Roake with her husband Peter and their son Jarrett.

old. After that, she went into service, both in London and up near John o'Groats in Scotland. I think she was in Scotland for two years. On December 20th 1903, she was in London to witness her sister Alice marry Albert Green at Holy Trinity Church, Wimbledon. The other witness was John Gard, who I think was their brother, also named Charles John Gard. (There was a lot of repetitious naming with the children of the Gard brothers which is a bit confusing at times).

On 14th January 1911 Ellen, her sister Alice and her brother-in-law Bert Green, set sail on the Wilcannia for Australia. I also have a photo of this ship. According to Grandma she didn't enjoy the trip at all, and I have since thought that if the Titanic had sailed a year earlier, Grandma would never have left England. I got the impression she had suffered a broken romance before coming out here. After meeting her cousins, Lydia and Percy, when they docked at Melbourne, another romance blossomed and she married Percy at the Parsonage in the suburb of Richmond, Melbourne, on 26th February 1912. At the time of the marriage Percy was a carpenter but on 9th April of the same year he commenced employment with the Victorian Railways. This occupation was the cause of the family living quite a nomadic life for a number of years, as he moved to different areas in South Gippsland. My mother Violet Ena was born on 18th November 1912 at North Melbourne, and was followed by her brother, Leslie Percival on 13th July 1914 at Korumburra.

My grandmother and I were very close and I can remember her telling me stories of her life in England – how I wish I could remember all the details now!

Although she couldn't play a musical instrument, she liked music, was a good knitter – which she passed on to both her daughter and granddaughter – and enjoyed herself. She also liked to dress well and was interested in the supernatural and royalty. I remember her telling me that she used to walk around the fence of Buckingham Palace on her days off. She would read anything she could about the royal family. She also used to attend the Christian Science Church at times. In her later years she developed... Alzheimer's Disease and eventually went to live in a retirement home. Except for a few lucid moments,

most often she didn't recognise any of her family. She died of heart failure on 6th November 1967.

As well as the Gard family. I have other family interests in Witheridge too. Grandma's grandmother, Mary Gard, was born in Witheridge in 1797, although she was baptised in Thelbridge. Her parents were Richard Brewer and Ann (née Veysey), and her siblings were Ambrouss 1778–97, William (b.1781), Emlin (b.1785) and Richard (b.1789). So far I have traced this family back to the baptism of Ambrose Brewer in Rose Ash in 1639 and he and his wife Joan appear to have settled in Witheridge by 1681. His third son, Richard, was baptised there on 22nd May 1681. Other names associated with the Brewers are Trix, Bowden, Melhuish and Zeldon.

WITHERIDGE & LLOYD MAUNDER

In the year 2000 Lloyd Maunder employed over 900 people at the Tiverton Junction business. The company had its origins in Witheridge and the material that follows gives an outline of the part played by Witheridge in the early years of their success.

The father of the founder of the company was born in Witheridge in 1838 and was christened Frederick James Partridge Maunder. After being educated at boarding school at Ashburton, he inherited much of his father's estate on his death in 1856, including Middlewick Barton, Thelbridge. In 1864 he married Elizabeth Elworthy in South Molton. Whilst they were on honeymoon Middlewick Barton burnt down; it was in due course replaced with something a little more grand. There were close ties between Thelbridge and Witheridge, particularly between those families who were both Liberal and Nonconformist, such as the Lakes and the Maunders. The Maunders had nine children, of whom Lloyd was the seventh. Along with his siblings he attended the British (Chapel) School in Witheridge, and in 1888 he passed HMI's examination successfully in Standard Seven. By this time Frederick was using Lapford Station to send sheep carcasses to London and wool to merchants; he also built up a local dairy-fed pork business, as well as a market for his 'Red Ruby' Devon cattle.

Dorrie and Winston Maunder, with Keeper, in 1911.

In 1890 Lloyd left school to learn more of the butcher's trade in London. Two years later he and his brother Hugh, in partnership with their father, opened a shop in Twickenham. Back in Devon Frederick never slaughtered cattle himself; they were slaughtered at an abattoir in Witheridge, and the meat was sold in local butchers' shops, including the one belonging to the family. Hugh and Lloyd came back to Devon in 1893. Lloyd married Beatrice Goatly and by 1898 was farming East Essebeare, bought for him by his father. In 1900 he moved to The Lawn in

Outside the butcher's shop in Fore Street, between 1914 and 1918. Left to right: ?, Tom Nott, E. Hill, L. Thomas, Frank Maunder, ?.

Witheridge and in 1903 he moved a few yards up Fore Street to Mill Park, a house almost opposite the family's shop.

In the meantime Frederick had taken a leading part in setting up the Witheridge and District Dairy Company in 1893. He and his sons plus some of the wives bought shares in this limited-liability company, itself something of a rarity in the rural world at that time. Early success did not last, and in 1901 the company went into voluntary liquidation. Frederick had the money to purchase the assets and the company passed into Maunder hands. Lloyd took over the business, and at once expanded into sending fresh eggs, butter, poultry and rabbits to London by train, collected locally by pony and trap.

One day in 1898 Lloyd was down at Witheridge Mill when the miller, Amos Maire, showed him a letter from London asking for regular supplies of poultry. Amos could not supply the quantities required, but it was a breakthrough for Lloyd, for the author of the letter was John James Sainsbury. This was to prove to be the start of a business relationship between the two firms that endured for 100 years.

When Lloyd moved into Mill Park he converted the barn; the ground floor was for slaughtering pigs, which were then hoisted by winch to the first floor for storage and despatch. Local men Bert Westcott, Charlie Bowden and Ernie Hill worked there. The butter factory was run by William ('Billy Butterdabs') Greenslade. All goods destined for Sainsbury's were taken to Lapford Station by Fred Leach and his horse and trap, loaded onto trains for Exeter St David's, and there transferred to London trains for Blackfriars. Sainsbury's duly collected the meat and took it to a depot. This arrangement was unusual for the times because it bypassed Smithfield market and consequently caused a certain amount of friction.

By 1910 it was clear that the Witheridge site could not meet the demands made by Sainsbury's and others, so Tiverton Junction was chosen for the availability of industrial land and its proximity to the railway. In 1914 new premises were built and the Witheridge slaughterhouse was closed down. The butter factory continued until 1933 when William Greenslade retired and the factory closed. Nearby the Witheridge butcher's shop continued with Lloyd acquiring control in 1929. The butter factory became a mill and feedstore.

CLOCKS

In the book *Clocks and Clockmakers of Tiverton* there is a photograph of a 30-hour brass-dialled clock of the 1760–70 period. It has the maker's signature 'Wm Bradford of Drayford'. The centre of the dial features a well-engraved shipping scene, possibly of Plymouth Sound, with ships, buildings and fortifications. William and his wife Elinor had a son William baptised in Witheridge church in 1776. William senr was mentioned in the will of James Bradford of Stockleigh English, dated 4 June 1779.

Father and son were clockmakers and clock repairers. In 1789 William senr was paid 14s. for repairing the church clock at Cheriton Fitzpaine, and in 1838 William junr did two years' work on the same clock for £4.18s. In 1801 and 1802 a William Bradford was paid for repairing the clock at Rewe.

By 1808 the younger William had moved to Tiverton, where he was listed as a watch- and clock-maker in the *Directories* for 1822–23 and 1830. Some time later he moved his business to Mary Arches Street, Exeter. The Vestry minutes of Exeter St Thomas for 2 May 1846 noted an agreement with him to repair, improve and maintain the church clock there. He died in 1849.

William senr lived in a cottage halfway between the bottom of Have's Hill and Drayford Bridge. A photo shows the board on the wall which featured Roman numerals and the words 'Wm Bradford, Clockmaker' on it. Both board and cottage were demolished in the 1960s.

In the *Devon Directory* for 1878 a Witheridge clock- and watchmaker is listed called Robert Edward Downing, about whom nothing is known.

The Church Clock

The only reference to Witheridge's early clock occurred in this rather dry report in the *Tiverton Gazette* on 15 August 1882:

> *Possibly nothing except the weather was ever more abused than our church clock. Sometimes it has been too slow, and sometimes, but rarely, too fast, and some-times, like grandfather's, it has stopped short for a week or two and then off again.*

As described in Chapter Three, George Cutcliffe donated the funds for a new turret clock. The clock had to be wound manually each week, which involved a long and steep climb and descent, but this poorly paid task was faithfully carried out for many years. The clock suffered the occasional misfortune. Indeed, one evening it came under fire. A few locals had been out hunting rabbits for the day. They had had a good day and celebrated with plenty of cider on their return. It seems, however, that on being chucked out at closing time, they blamed the clock and on reaching The Square attempted to shoot the hands off it. Their aim was surprisingly good – the clock face still shows shot marks – but the hands remained in place.

On another occasion the clock was ridiculed. It had been stopped for some time and the explanation given was that in certain weather conditions the tower leaned, causing the mechanism to stop. This reached the ears of the local press, whose photogra-pher's sense of humour got the better of him; in taking the photo he leant his camera so far sideways that when the picture was printed the tower appeared to lean at an angle of 45 degrees!

By the end of the year 2000 the winding mechanism had come to the end of its useful life. Repairs would have cost approximately £2,500, so it was decided to replace it with an electric automatic system, which required the raising of some £5,000. An appeal was launched and the response was generous. Among the donors were the Viscount Amory Trust, The Allchurches Trust, local businesses, private donations, local fund-raising, including a hymnathon, a coffee morning at The Firs, and sales of copies of a water-colour of The Square that had been in Australia for about 90 years. (see page 89). In 2003 the clock is once again in full working order.

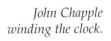

John Chapple winding the clock.

Tower and scaffolding in the 1980s.

THE TRAWIN FAMILY OF WITHERIDGE & SASKATCHEWAN

In the nineteenth century there were several branches of the Trawin (pronounced 'Troyne') family in South Molton. One of these in particular was deeply involved in the wool business. In 1861 Joshua Trawin (b.1785), a wool sorter, and his wife Mary (b.1790) were living in East Street, South Molton, with their son Samuel, a wool agent, and his wife Sarah (born Sarah Baston Tapp) and their three children, William, Sarah and Henry Tapp Trawin (b.1855). By 1891 Henry Tapp Trawin, a wool stapler, had a wife Sarah, and eight children. They had a wool business at Lashbrook House, North Street, Witheridge. Later they moved to No. 19 The Square.

Their second son, Frank, was trained as a tinsmith, but at the age of 28 he emigrated to Canada. In 1904 the Canadian High Commissioner for Immigration had sent posters and maps promoting the prospects of

Frank Trawin in the Canadian Army during the First World War.

Sarah Trawin.

life in Canada to all schools, and Witheridge was no exception. Frank may have seen these and they may have helped make up his mind. He sailed for Canada in 1905, and obtained entry for his homestead on 25 October of that year: it was near the Carrot River in Saskatchewan.

A homestead was 160 acres and cost $10. If after three years a house had been built, 40 acres of land had been cleared and cultivated, and the home-steader had lived there for six months in each year, then title to the property was his. In 1906 Frank built his 12ft by 12ft house for $100 and cleared land. In 1907 he sowed his first crops of oats and barley, and built a 16ft by 30ft stable and a granary, dug a well and put up 1½ miles of wire fencing. He spent the long cold winter months in the Carrot River lumber camps to supplement his income. In 1908 Frank's elder brother Harry came out and joined him in time for harvest. Later Harry took up a homestead of his own, but things did not work out, and he abandoned it for work on farms and in lumber camps. He enlisted when war broke out in 1914 and was killed by gas in France.

In December 1909 Frank's farm was inspected, and in January 1910 a patent was issued granting him title to the land. After harvest the same year he returned to Witheridge and spent the winter there. His account of life in Canada must have enthused two of his sisters, Annie and Sarah, and his youngest brother Arthur, who was 15, for in March 1911 all four set off for Canada from Avonmouth on the *Royal George* steamship.

Frank's first-class ticket had cost him £100, but the other three travelled third class at £25 each. During the voyage the emigrants were all examined by the ship's surgeon to see that they met the health regulations of the Canadian Immigration Act. The examination was to see that they were 'believed not to be insane, epileptic or consumptive or idiotic, feeble-minded or afflicted with a contagious infec-tion or loathsome disease', and to see if they were 'deaf, dumb or blind or otherwise physically or mentally defective.' The ship docked at Halifax on 28 March. From there they went by train to Melfort in Saskatchewan, where they loaded their belong-ings onto a wagon for the 15-mile journey to Frank's homestead.

Sarah, or Sally as the family knew her, had been a pupil-teacher at the British (Chapel) School in Witheridge, which she and her brothers and sisters had attended as pupils. She had passed her Standard 8 by the age of 15. There was no money for her to continue her education, so to become a teacher (her ambition) she became a pupil-teacher at the British School and taught Standards One, Two and Three. The schoolroom was open and the headmaster, who taught the remaining Standards, was able to keep his eye on her and supervise when neces-sary. When her youngest brother, Arthur, came to the school, he tended to play his sister up. She mentioned this to her father, who punished Arthur so severely that she never reported him again. She taught there for 11 years until she left for Canada in March 1911. She was popular, for when she left she received a presentation of a dressing case, handbag and an album of Witheridge that contained photographs and the signa-tures of all the contributors. This is still in the family's possession. Soon after she arrived in Saskatchewan a teacher vacancy occurred locally and Sally was taken on; she taught there until her marriage to Bert Whittome in 1912. The couple had three children and lived in the Naisbury district until 1940, when they retired to Melfort, north of Regina.

When Annie (known as Nancy) arrived at Frank's homestead she took over as housekeeper for her bachelor brothers and her sister Sally. When the brothers enlisted in the First World War, she engaged a farmhand to do the work under the supervision of her brother-in-law Bert Whittome. After Arthur married in 1921 Nancy worked in various homes, and looked after the Whittome farm when Bert and Sally and their young son Steve went to England in the winter of 1922–23 to visit their families.

Arthur was 15 when he arrived in Canada, and initially he worked on Frank's farm. When his broth-ers enlisted and his sister Sally married Bert Whittome, Arthur farmed the land at Belgrave and Annie kept house for him. In 1919 he enlisted and was drafted overseas, being stationed at Ripon in Yorkshire. After his discharge from the Army he came back to Belgrave and purchased a homestead of his own. It had a 16ft by 20ft frame house with a lean-to kitchen, a 24ft by 26ft frame barn, and three granaries. Boarding with the Trawins at the time was Jessie Robertson, who was a teacher at Belgrave School. Arthur and Jessie were married in 1921. Their children were Bill, Ellen Margaret, John and Jean.

Ellen Thorne Trawin ('Nellie') was born in 1878 and, like her brothers and sisters attended Witheridge British School. On finishing her time as a pupil there she was made a monitor and in 1893 she became pupil-teacher. She held this post for five years; at the same time she was studying for her teaching qualifications and passing exams. On one occasion her father, Henry Tapp Trawin, persuaded the head to allow her two days off for extra private study. She took music lessons and became quite an accomplished pianist. The Trawins all loved music and spent hours singing while one of the girls played the organ or the piano. Nellie taught piano and played at many Christmas concerts, socials and weddings throughout her life.

In 1898 she left Witheridge and taught in London and Edinburgh. In 1912 she booked on the *Titanic* to cross the Atlantic, but fortunately for her an earlier passage became available and she took it. She arrived in Halifax in April and joined her siblings on Frank's homestead. She was quickly taken on as a teacher at Belgrave School. In 1915 she married Newman Holmes. They had two sons, Edward Trawin and Arthur Newman. Nellie taught at local schools and died in 1955.

Back in Witheridge the old couple, Henry and Sarah, moved their business across The Square to Leigh House, where there was still room for them to milk their cows round the back. This was in 1923. In 1924 Henry Tapp Trawin died, and Frank returned to Witheridge to take over the family business. He died in 1936. Nancy (Annie) also came back to live with her mother, her two brothers and her sister Ella. Her mother died in 1957, and Nancy in 1962.

In 1939 Arthur purchased Frank's land, which he had been renting for some years. Arthur had been the secretary-treasurer of Belgrave School in 1917 at the age of 21, and played an active part in the community. In 1944 he and Jessie sold their land and moved to Naisbury, where they farmed and established a pedigree seeds firm. At the time of writing, Trawins

Seeds Ltd is run by their sons Bill and John, and John's sons Ross and Brent. Jessie died in 1957, and Arthur in 1976.

ANSTEY'S COURT
The Ministry of Health Inspector's Inquiry, 1937.

Mr Palfreman owned three cottages and outbuildings. His solicitor said they were very nice and pleasantly situated cottages, although the Sanitary Inspector disagreed. The solicitor said that Mr Palfreman had never received any complaints from his tenants, and that he himself would suffer considerable loss and hardship if such an unreasonable clearance order was made. In his view the cottages were in a more than average state of repair for that type of property (cob and thatch construction). The tenants had made no complaints and had in one instance expressed considerable appreciation of the property. His client would be unable to bear the losses brought by clearance.

Anstey's Court.

Mr Dallyn owned three cottages and outbuildings. He had never had any complaints. It was not half as bad as had been stated. Dr W.G. Mortimer said the whole property was unfit for human habitation. Mr Dallyn said the cottages were not badly out of order; they had cost him a lot of money and he felt it was hard on a man of his age to have his cottages taken away. He had had them for 12 years and during that time he had spent £50 or £60 on repairs. The inspector asked for details of this work, but Mr Dallyn could not provide any.

The inspector then dealt with a fowl house and a wash-house owned by Mr F.R. Maunder, who was represented by his brother, Mr L. Maunder.

Mr Palfreman's solicitor pointed out that there was no evidence of alternative accommodation, to which the inspector replied that rehousing was outside the terms of reference of the inquiry. He would inspect the property.

The Trawins outside their home, Leigh House, The Square, 1925. Left to right: *Harry, Annie, Ella, Sarah (Henry Tapp Trawin's widow), Frank. The car is Frank Trawin's Bullnose Morris Tourer.*

Anstey's Court, c.1914. Jack Rice (owner of the grocers shop) and his daughter Eliza.

There is no press report of his findings, but local memory is of dwellings in very poor repair, of inadequate sanitation and water-supply, and of pest infestation. The inspector made up his mind, and on the front page of the *Gazette* for 24 June appeared the clearance order, with vacation to be completed within ten months.

It is interesting to note that the local Witheridge doctor, Dr Ernest A. Price, owned one of the cottages, with its woodshed and water-closet. Any opinions he had on the matter did not appear in the press.

On 17 June of the same year under the headline 'Witheridge Housing Site' the *Gazette* reported the Rural District Council's Finance Committee had been informed that the District Valuer had approved of the new Witheridge housing site being purchased at a cost of £200. This was, and is, a little further up and on the other side of the road from Anstey's Court. So the plea for alternative accommodation was in fact answered.

South Molton Rural (Witheridge) Housing Confirmation Order.
Taken from the *South Molton Gazette* 24 June 1937.

Clearance of the following properties at Anstey's Court:

Property	Owner	Occupier
Cottage	*Robert Lee Palfreman*	*Charles Leach*
Cottage	*Robert Lee Palfreman*	*D.E. Tucker*
Cottage	*Robert Lee Palfreman*	*J. Dart*
Water Closet	*Robert Lee Palfreman*	*J. Dart*
Woodshed	*Robert Lee Palfreman*	*J. Dart*
Water Closet	*Robert Lee Palfreman*	*Charles Leach*
Woodshed	*Robert Lee Palfreman*	*Charles Leach*
Water Closet	*Robert Lee Palfreman*	*D.E. Tucker*
Woodshed	*Robert Lee Palfreman*	*D.E. Tucker*
Water Closet	*Dr Ernest A. Price*	*W. Brent*
Woodshed	*Dr Ernest A. Price*	*W. Brent*
Cottage	*Dr Ernest A. Price*	*W. Brent*
Cottage	*W. Dallyn*	*W. Gibbs*
Woodshed	*W. Dallyn*	*W. Gibbs*
Woodshed	*W. Dallyn*	*A. Adams*
Water Closet	*J. Norrish*	*S.A. Sowden*
Cottage	*J. Norrish*	*S.A. Sowden*
Woodshed	*J. Norrish*	*S.A. Sowden*
Water Closet	*W. Dallyn*	*W. Gibbs*
Cottage	*W. Dallyn*	*E.M. Perkins*
Cottage	*W. Dallyn*	*A. Adams*

Chairmen of Witheridge Parish Council

1894–97	Revd P.M. Benson	1958–63	S. Stoneman
1897–99	Dr E.S. Pollock	1963–66	J.M. Adams
1899–1913	J. Clotworthy	1966–70	A.J. Knight
1913–19	W. Carter	1970–71	S. Stoneman
1919–26	G.H. Pullen	1971–72	Revd A. Jones
1926–34	G.H. Selley	1972–82	W. Stoddard
1934–46	E. Hutchings	1982–87	F. Venner
1946–48	B. Cox	1987–93	P. Miles
1948–52	J. Woollacott	1993–2000	R. Alleyne
1952–55	W.S. Selley	2000–02	F.J. Woollacott
1955–58	Revd J.A.S. Castlehow	2002–present	E. Martin

WAR, 1914 – 1918

Excerpts from the *South Molton Gazette.*

31 October 1914

A meeting to arrange for the reception of a Belgian family in Witheridge was held in the National Schoolroom on Monday evening. Mr G.H. Pullen offered a cottage, rent and rates free and many offers of furniture to furnish a home were made, also promises of money and food per week for the refugees' support.

12 September 1914

The Square in the centre of the old market town of Witheridge was the scene of a remarkable demonstration on Thursday evening. Drawn together by the announcement of a meeting on the subject of 'The War and our Country's Call' about 300 people assembled, chiefly men. Among those standing in The Square around a wagonette, which served as a platform for the speakers, were Sir Ian Heathcoat Amory, Mr W.C.L. Unwin, JP, Mr W. Lake, Mr Carter, etc. The Vicar, the Revd J.P. Benson presided, and in introducing the speakers referred to the crisis as the most serious which the nation had ever been called upon to pass through. Mr L. Mackenzie JP, CC, spoke next, pointing out that the war was brought about by the overweening ambition of Germany, and that it would have been impossible for Great Britain to have held aloof and allowed Belgium and France to be wiped out. The Mayor followed with an appeal to employers of labour, woman, men fit for service to respond to the call of duty. A resolution pledging the meeting to promote recruiting was carried with acclamation, and after the National Anthem had been sung, and cheers given for King, Army and Navy, a number of young men came forward and joined Kitchener's Army. Next day Sergeant Beer, the recruiting officer, took away from Witheridge about 20 likely recruits, who were hospitably entertained at Tiverton in the afternoon, and left for the Higher Barracks, Exeter, on Saturday morning.

5 December 1914

It is with deep regret that the inhabitants have heard that Private Cecil Facey of the 2nd Battalion Coldstream Guards has been killed in Belgium. His brother, of the 1st Battalion, is home at present, having been wounded in the shoulder at the battle of the Aisne. Much sympathy is felt for the family in their bereavement. The father is Sergeant in the Devon Constabulary and stationed here.

15 May 1915

Much sympathy is felt in Witheridge with Sergeant and Mrs Facey, who have lost their eldest son, Private William Facey, 1st Coldstream, on the battlefield in Flanders. He returned to the front a short time ago after recovering from injuries in the shoulder. He was found dead between the trenches having received the full effect of shrapnel fire. His younger brother Cecil lost his life in the autumn by shellfire.

January 1915

Soldiers Route Marches Local Recruiting.
The journey on from West Worlington was the most difficult part of the day's march. A short distance out of Worlington a half-built bridge had to be negotiated, and a little further on, a stream, several inches in depth, flowed across the road necessitating walking in single file over a footbridge. The hills too were long and steep and winding. However, 'all's well that ends well' and the company looked none the worse for their 12 mile tramp when they arrived at Witheridge at 12.40, 40 minutes behind scheduled time. Witheridge has been aptly described as '10 miles from anywhere', but the news of the coming of the soldiers had penetrated even to these remote regions. As soon as the first strains of the band were heard, the school children, who had been given a half day holiday in honour of the event, rushed forth to greet the arrivals, and their parents followed more sedately but no less eagerly. After forming up in The Square, the band played selections and the men dispersed to their billets. They had plenty of eligible material to work on in Witheridge and did not fail to make the most of their opportunity. In the evening an enjoyable smoking concert was held in the Angel Assembly Rooms.

Sergeant Samuel James Way, Devon Yeomanry,
First World War.

Corporal Bill Gold.

Percival Blackford, Gloucestershire
Regiment, 1914–18. He was the
father of Olive and Vera,
of Malson Farm.

Those killed during the First World War 1914–18

A. Bodley	F.A. Kingdom
H. Boundy	C. Matthews
E.F. Burridge	S.W.P. Partridge
F.C. Crook	H. Phillips
C.H. Facey	A. Roberts
W.R.E. Facey	J. Rowcliffe
W.H. Ford	S.R. Selley
P. Gard	J. Tarr
A.H. Hill	

The two families of George Henry Selley, 1914.
Left to right, back row: Fred, Stanley, Bert
and Francis; middle: Stephen, Emily and George
(parents), Sidney; front row: Constance and Vera.
All six boys served in the First World War.

Outside the bomb factory in Gallipoli.

*Ammunition stores on the beach at Anzac Cove,
on the island of Lemnos.*

Camel ambulance.

21 August 1915

The number of eggs sent from Witheridge in July for the National Egg Collection for Wounded Soldiers and Sailors is 1,017. Up to the end of July 1,791 eggs have been sent from the village.

19 February 1916

Mrs Benson took the chair at a meeting organised by the Agricultural Committee to consider the question of employing female labour on farms. Mrs C. Vicars Boyle explained the details of the scheme and said that in the near future the young men on the farms would be called up for service, and women must be ready to do their bit. A motion was carried without a dissentient vote. Five members were elected to the canvassing committee.

25 March 1916

Private Frank Kingdom 6th Devons, has been seriously wounded in Mesopotamia. The many friends of Mr Charles Gunn will be pleased to hear that his youngest son, Corporal Hugh Gunn, of the Royal Engineers, has been mentioned in dispatches for conspicuous bravery in France.

28 April 1917

Private F. Pincombe, of the Worcestershire Regiment, who was injured in the left leg by shrapnel many months ago so that an amputation below the knee was necessary, has arrived home at Queen Dart Farm. He gets along very well by the aid of crutches. He will proceed to Roehampton later to be fitted with an artificial limb.

In the First World War Francis Selley served in the 1st Devon Yeomanry. In 1915 the regiment was at Gallipoli, and Francis brought home many photographs of the campaign there (*see page 97*). By 1915 there was a stalemate on the Western Front, and Churchill's plan to attack Germany through her ally, Turkey, was adopted. The spot chosen for the assault was Gallipoli, a 60-mile-long peninsula sticking out into the Aegean Sea, bounded on the south by the channel known as the Dardenelles. The base chosen was Mudros Bay on the island of Lemnos, 40 miles away.

In April the British and French landed. In addition, the Australian and New Zealand Army Corps (ANZAC) landed at what became known as Anzac Cove. More troops were soon needed, and transatlantic liners were hired to take them out. The *Olympic* arrived at Mudros in early autumn with 6,000 men, including the 1st Devon Yeomanry. The campaign was a disaster and by the end of December all troops had been evacuated.

The Devons found themselves in Alexandria, where Francis distinguished himself, as the *Gazette* shows: 'Corporal Francis Selley, who has been in the Dardenelles, won first prize in a donkey race at Alexandria, there were 44 starters.' In 1924 the

Gazette reported: 'Mr Francis Selley (Essebeare) has been one of the four chosen to represent the 1st Devon Yeomanry at the unveiling of the cavalry memorial at Hyde Park on May 1st.'

Percy Whitfield

Late of 2548 South Broadway, Denver 80210 Colorado, USA.
(Thanks to Mrs Dorothy Lee Cann for notes of a visit she paid to Percy in Denver, 1980.)

Percy Whitfield was born in 1900 in No. 18 West Street. His grandmother was 'Granny' Whitfield, who lived where Reed's bakery is now located. At the age of ten Percy used to stand on a chair to help mix the dough. He joined the Army in 1917, but was wounded; he used his Army gratuity to start a new life. He, Charlie Brent, Arthur Churchill and Leslie Baker tossed a coin – heads for the USA, tails for Australia. It came down heads, so they went to America in December 1919.

Percy found work in the Cadillac Car Company, and then moved to Colorado where he married an English girl. They moved east where he had a number of jobs – he worked in car factories, for Hotpoint, drove a yellow cab and dispatched newspapers. In 1947 he started a financial advisory business, calling it Whitfields Tax Services, in Denver, Colorado, which he was still running at the age of 80. He kept his Witheridge school photographs on the mantelpiece, and had youthful memories of the village. He died in 1982, leaving six children, 20 grandchildren and nine great-grandchildren.

WITHERIDGE & TRANSPORT

The earliest form of transport here, as elsewhere in North Devon, was the packhorse, with a pannier on either side of the animal. With these, limestone could be brought from Watchet, corn and hay (among other things) could be carried and dung could be dropped on fields by means of panniers with removable bottoms. As roads and lanes were improved, carts became more common, and from these it was only a short step to the horse and cart. Better roads were brought about by the Turnpike Acts in the mid-eighteenth century. Carriers came into business, and a new wave of Turnpike Acts in the 1830s and 1840s encouraged the establishment of regular services. By 1878 the Witheridge carrier John Tidball had the following weekly timetable:

Tuesday: to and from Tiverton for the market.
Thursday: to Exeter, staying overnight at the Crown and Sceptre by the Iron Bridge.
Friday: return to Witheridge via Kennerleigh and Black Dog.
Saturday: to South Molton, delivering parcels from Exeter along the way, and picking up goods and passengers at Meshaw or Alswear en route.

No. 1 Ebrington Row. Mrs Jack Rice and John Bryant.

By 1900 John had retired and his son Thomas had taken over the service. Thomas Tidball had an assistant. Arthur Bryant was born in Witheridge in 1903, and at the age of 13 started work. When Thomas drove to Exeter, Arthur would go with him in charge of a pony and trap. This was used to deliver eggs, butter and other produce from the Witheridge area to customers in Exeter, and to collect orders from town traders for Witheridge shops, farms, blacksmiths, etc. On the return journey on Friday the steep hills up through Sandford and Tridley Foot might prove too much for the laden cart. In such a case the trap horse would be unhitched to help, or extra horses (known as tracers) would be used. In icy conditions frost nails were put into the horses' shoes, but there were times when snowdrifts were insurmountable.

Behind High Cross, the Tidballs' house in North Street, the family stabled eight or nine horses. Arthur Bryant recalled cutting chaff here at 10.30p.m. after a long day on the road, and all for 3s. a week.

In addition to their van and trap, the Tidballs had a landau, a smart conveyance which they hired out, with Arthur driving. He would also drive Revd Benson's cart, and a four-wheeled carriage. Witheridge people enjoyed their annual outings, which often involved Arthur driving the party to Lapford Station to catch the Exeter train for Exmouth or Teignmouth.

Next door to the Tidballs were the Thomases in Trafalgar House. Mark Thomas is listed as a local carrier in the 1870s. His service stayed the same until the outbreak of war in 1914. He did the return journey to Tiverton three times a week. On Thursdays he drove to Exeter via Black Dog, Morchard Bishop and Crediton. Mark put up at the Elephant in North Street, Exeter, and in Tiverton his terminus was the Prince Regent at Lowman Green. Mark Thomas died young in 1902; the *Tiverton Gazette* paid him this tribute:

Death of a Witheridge Carrier.
A familiar figure on the road, in person of Mr Mark Thomas, of Witheridge, passed away on Wednesday morning last. For the last 25 years Mr Thomas has been engaged in conveying persons to and from Tiverton in his covered van. Of a bright and cheerful disposition, the deceased had won many friends in the township of Witheridge as well as at Tiverton, where he was well known. Mr Thomas started the business of carrier in a small way, and as the number of passengers to and from Witheridge increased he was obliged to provide a larger conveyance, a pair of horses attached to a roomy four-wheeled van being substituted for a horse and trap. Prior to his death the deceased had three carrier vans plying between Witheridge and Tiverton, which he visited three times a week. He also worked with the London and South Western Railway, taking passengers from Witheridge to Lapford Station every Friday. Some time ago Mr Thomas underwent an operation for cancer in the head, and great benefit appeared to result. The relief afforded however did not last long, but despite this Mr Thomas did not give up his duties and continued to be about up to Tuesday May 27th [when] he drove his van to Tiverton. On the following Saturday he was taken ill while engaged in work on his farm. He expired three days later. For a number of years the deceased took a prominent part in the musical portion of the Witheridge Bible Christian Chapel, and was for some time Superintendent of the Sunday school there, in which work he took a keen interest. Nothing appeared too much trouble to him if he could perform a kind act, and on many occasions he has driven preachers and laymen to and from their appointments. The deceased, who was about 50 years of age, leaves a widow and eight children, with whom much sympathy is felt.

Mark's eldest son, Bill, was barely in his teens when he had to take over the business. A new contract was to take the laundry from Coombe House and the Vicarages at Witheridge and Cruwys Morchard to Tiverton. The business grew, and soon Bill had two traps, a Brougham and a Victoria, and a two-horse brake used for outings. For the Brougham and the Victoria the drivers wore bowler hats, and for weddings grey horses were expected and provided. The horses were stabled in West Street, although the carriage yard was beside the Tidballs in North Street. Winter weather was a challenge, and for snow soft soap was applied to the horses' hooves. Now and

The horses belonging to Thomases the carriers, August 1914.

The wedding day of Mr and Mrs Bill Thomas, 1920s.

This bus is the Scout, bought by Bill Thomas in the summer of 1914.

Right: *Witheridge Transport Co. Arthur Thomas, Walter Tidball, Lamberet Thomas and Fred Tidball at Woolacombe Sands in June 1921.*

Below: *Witheridge Transport Co. buses in the early 1920s. The drivers were either Thomases or Tidballs.*

Above and left: *Witheridge Transport Co., 1920s. This charabanc was built by the Tiverton Motor Co. on a former War Department Dennis chassis. Too much overhang at the back led to it being banned because it was deemed too dangerous. The problem was solved by cutting off the back row of seats.*

again there would be complaints about the slowness of the journey. The response from the driver would be to suggest the passenger got out and walked, to which came the reply 'I would if I was in a hurry'.

In 1914 the advantages of the new motor transport struck both families. Tidballs got in first in July with a 30hp Overland, registration T 4442. The Thomases were close behind, for in September they took delivery of their 52.6hp Scout Motor Service Bus, which took over the routes to Tiverton and Exeter. The new motorbuses could be hired for outings, and offered both speed and comfort (padded benches instead of wooden forms). The horsemen of the two families taught themselves to drive the new vehicles and gained their mechanical knowledge as they went along. By 1919 the war and a railway strike had made motor transport a key feature for the future. In August 1918 Tidballs bought a 1915 Willys Overland (T 6396) and replaced it the next spring with a big 36/40hp Leyland (T 6746). In May 1919 Thomases acquired T 6872, a 38hp Dennis capable of carrying 25 passengers plus luggage and parcels.

The two families decided that there was likely to be strength in union and jointly formed in 1920 the Witheridge Transport Company. This was a limited liability company with an authorised capital of £8,000, of which £4,630 was issued. The directors were Arthur and Lambert Thomas, Walter and Fred Tidball, and Charlie and Bill Maire. The Maires were millers and shopkeepers in Witheridge; they contributed capital and their Foden Steam Wagon. This capital helped the new firm to buy a new Dennis charabanc (T 9795), a Ford 14-seater bus and a Bedford bus (T 9795). The charabanc had an open body, with a canvas hood which could be pulled forward in bad weather, stretched on wooden hoops. In 2002 these wooden hoops hang on the wall in the old Tidball premises. These vehicles proved popular, even though Chapel beliefs prevented their use on Sundays.

In the 1920s there were regular return runs to Tiverton, South Molton, Barnstaple and Exeter. Special excursions were made to fairs, carnivals and shows and as early as 1921 there was a special trip to the Bath and West Show at Bristol. At that time the drivers, Arthur, Bill, Lambert, Walter and Fred not only drove but at the end of each day cleared out and washed the buses. In the early 1920s cans of petrol were used to top up the tanks, but soon a hand-operated pump and tank were installed. The pump is still evident in 2003.

Some of the early vehicles were versatile in the sense that they could have their seats removed and be used as lorries or vans. Every opportunity was taken to cram in goods, and a ladder fixed to the back allowed goods, including timber, to be carried on the roof, covered with a tarpaulin. In 1926 a Witheridge Transport Co. bus took the place of the horse-drawn van used to bring in schoolchildren

Bill Thomas and an early taxi.

from the Creacombe area. By the end of the 1920s the fleet had been increased by another Dennis, and several small buses. The adverts for these ran: '32, 20, 18, seater Pneumatic-tyred Motor Coaches for hire, also 18 seater De Luxe Coach for long journeys.'

With the 1930s came disagreement within the company about the future. Fred Tidball was keen to expand, but Lambert Thomas preferred to keep the level of operation as it had been. The result was that in 1932 control of Witheridge Transport passed to Greenslade Brothers of Exeter, which the following year became Greenslades Tours Ltd. Fred Tidball managed the Witheridge branch of the firm, which was still referred to as Witheridge Transport. Under Fred the coach-hire business expanded and the transport of livestock began. Greenslades had not bought the North Street premises, so it acquired a field in Fore Street opposite The Firs and built a new garage there. This was closed and knocked down in 2000; houses have since been built on the site.

There was a considerable business in parcels. Arthur Buckingham remembered parking his bus in The Square in South Molton with the door open. When he came back, parcels would have been left with the money – 3d. or 6d. – on top. Nothing ever went missing. Newspapers were also delivered, and a skilled driver could throw a newspaper out of his window onto a doorstep without stopping or even slowing down. In 1936 daily return buses ran for pupils attending schools in Tiverton. In 1934 the older boys from Cruwys Morchard School were brought to Witheridge. In 1937 senior pupils from Meshaw were similarly transported. In 1935 Greenslades lent their big garage for the celebrations on the occasion of King George V's silver jubilee; here the children had their tea and received jubilee cups and saucers.

In May 1939 a special bus service took a Witheridge platoon of 20 Territorials to South Molton for regular training. In 1939–40 Canadian troops were ferried about and in 1940, when invasion was feared, drivers slept by their buses in case they were needed in an emergency. Evacuees doubled the populations of the two Witheridge schools and extra buses became necessary. In 1942–43 Fred Tidball and his wife suffered tragedy, when their twin sons, Len and Roy, were killed in separate incidents while serving with the RAF Volunteer Reserve with Bomber Command. They were in their early twenties.

With peace in 1945 the bus business boomed. Tiverton, Witheridge and South Molton were linked four times a day. Greenslade's coach hire and touring business expanded, but before long local services became less attractive to the firm. In 1947 Devon General bought the Witheridge services, but Greenslades retained the garage and the private-hire business.

In 1949 the Witheridge–Chulmleigh School run began and Greenslades sold its business to Douglas Venner, a thatcher from Drayford. Venners continued the Witheridge business and in 1966 bought Scarlet Coaches of Minehead. The business was sold in 1973 to Powells of Lapford. In the early 1950s Devon General had introduced double-decker buses to the Witheridge–Tiverton and Witheridge–Exeter routes, but car ownership increased and the bus office in The Square closed in 1955. During the 1970s services were drastically reduced and in November 1980 buses ceased to be parked in The Square. The era of Witheridge Transport Co. had come to an end.

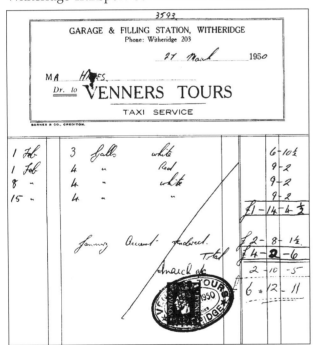

REVD J.A.S CASTLEHOW

On 24 January 1925 the *South Molton Gazette* reported the arrival of the new vicar of Witheridge, the Revd J.A.S. Castlehow. 'Jas' as he soon became known to the village, had been ordained in 1913 and had previously served as curate in Exeter, Plymouth and Northam. He was a very keen scoutmaster and former scouts have happy memories of, among other things, scout camps at Mamhead and elsewhere. Sport was a great interest of his, and he enjoyed

Stone-crushing plant at Coombe Quarry.

Road repairs on Newbridge Hill in the 1920s. Left to right: Fred Leach, Fred Bryant, Wally Manley, Fred Ward, Sid Leach. Farmer Jones is with the cart and Farmer Tucker is on the horse.

Left to right: *Gilbert Maunder, John Gibson, Christine Gibson (née Maunder), Toz Gibson (with school cap), Bill Buchanan, Miss Sloman and Mr Roberts in the 1920s. They are pictured with the Vauxhall 14–40 that belonged to the Gibsons and was known in the area for 40 years.*

many a day watching the Somerset team play cricket at Taunton. An enthusiastic tennis player, he relied on cunning rather than power. Some remember, on a

Fred Gibbs on pillion of a Royal Enfield motorbike in the 1940s.

Grass tennis court. The house, now South Park, was the chapel manse. The ground is now part of Appletree Close.

The Gard family. Left to right, back row: Josie, Albert, Ross, Roy, Eric, Faye; front row: Char, Stella, Greta, Joseph, Mary, George, Molly, Bob. During the Second World War George was in the Eighth Army and was taken prisoner by the Germans in 1942. After being held captive in both Italy and Germany, where he worked in mines, he was released by the Russians before making his own way back to American lines. Many of the other siblings saw action in the war: Albert served in the Middle East, Greece and North Africa as a member of the Tank Corps; Roy served in Iraq in 1942 and returned home in 1946; Eric served in the RAF in the Middle East between 1945–48; Ross was also in the RAF (1948–50); Char was wounded during the invasion of France and airlifted home; Bob joined up in November 1939 with the Queens Royal Regiment in France, before returning to England to guard against invasion and then serving as a gunner on a merchant ship all over the world; Stella served the ack-ack as a rangefinder in Yorkshire in 1942–45, although she was wounded by shrapnel in her hand.

summer evening when it was almost impossible to see across the net, his urgent cries of 'don't waste the light'. He provided the pony boots for the pony that pulled the roller over the three courts at the back of the manse; he probably provided the roller as well.

He was always to the fore in battling for the interests of his parish. He never owned or drove a car, but put his faith in his trusty bicycle, until his increasing weight proved too much for it. In later years the rambling Vicarage was beyond his needs, and he settled happily in the Well House in The Square. He took a great and scholarly interest in the history of Witheridge, and he left us 70 foolscap pages to prove it. Some of his work is included in this book.

WITHERIDGE BOWLING CLUB, 1925

The AGM was held in the Church Hall on 19 February 1925. Mr H. Maunder presided. Also present were: Messrs Pullen, Andrews, Ford, Gunn, Heal, Hutchings, Kingdom, C. Leach, F.G. and W.S. Selley, H. Way and H. Whitfield. The minutes being signed, the balance sheet was presented showing a debit balance of £1.6s.5d. This was promptly subscribed by members, so the season opened with the club being debt free.

The back of the Commercial Inn. Left to right: Mr and Mrs Herbert Partridge, Mr W. Partridge, Moira Partridge.

In his report, the secretary referred to the abnormally wet weather of 1924, which completely upset all the club's arrangements. Letters were read from supporters showing unabated interest in the club and an increase in the amount of subscriptions. A vote of thanks to all kind helpers was carried unanimously.

Annie Gard (1873–1950) was the
eldest daughter of Philip and
Mary Gard, and cousin to Joseph.
In 1901 she was housemaid to a
General Whisk in London.
Later she was head cook to a
General Buller, also in London.

Mr and Mrs George Pullen at Rosemont.

Charles Gunn (b.1 October 1846)
married Mary Ann Churchill
(b.7 November 1852) at
Witheridge church on
19 March 1873.

Above right: The Gunn family
at May Cottage, West Street
(cottage now demolished), c.1908.
Left to right, back row: Jeanette
(Nett), Ern, Walter (Joe), Hugh,
Francis (Frank), Reg; middle
row: Doll, Marge, Eleanor (wife
of Frank); front row: Charles and
Mary Ann Gunn (née Churchill).
Marge and Doll were the
daughters of Frank and Eleanor.

The bowling club: Frank and Charlie Leach, Frank Maunder,
Ernest Hutchings, George Selley.

The following elections were then made: secretary-treasurer Mr Pullen, president and vice-presidents, Captain Mr F.G. Gunn, Vice Captain Mr H. Maunder. The resignations from the committee of Messrs Andrews and Mansfield were received with much regret. Messrs W.J. Kingdom and F.P. Selley were unanimously elected to the vacancies. The new committee was as follows: S. Heal, E. Hutchings, C. Leach, Fred Leach, W.J. Kingdom, F.K. Maunder, F.G. Selley, H. Way and H. Whitfield. Mr Frank Leach was unanimously appointed groundsman. His keenness and enthusiasm were suitably acknowledged.

FARMING IN THE 1930S & '40S

Notes made by Mr and Mrs R. Woollacott, West Yeo, Witheridge, now of Appletree Close, on 14 May 1999.

James Woollacott with his wife and three sons, Bob, John and Bill, came in over Exmoor from Kipscombe to West Yeo in 1929. The move took three days. The first day saw the horses and carts reach Kinsford Water, from where the ponies were ridden back to Kipscombe for the night. At the end of the second day they reached Ash Mill, and the ponies were ridden to West Yeo for the night. On the third day they arrived at West Yeo with their belongings. The sheep and cattle came by lorry – the pigs had been killed and salted before the move. James Woollacott came on his BSA belt-driven motorbike, with Bob on the pillion, but coming up Rockford Hill near Brendon the bike failed and Bob came off. The bike surged forward and climbed the hill to James' surprise, as he had not noticed Bob's fall. At West Yeo the bike was kept in the cider house; James never owned a car.

Harvesting.

Another 'Vigilo' wedding rhyme.

The groom came in a motor
The bride in travelling dress
Went down the church as Miss Edith
And came back as Mrs Bur-gess.
When returning from the altar,
We freely scattered the rice
Said Mrs Smith to Walter,
Caw! don't her look awfully nice?
The Vicar made a pretty speech
In accents sweet and mild,
For you see, he used to teach
Miss Edith when a child.
May Heaven their footsteps bless,
May flowers bestrew their path!
May Mr and Mrs Burgess
Make their home an Eden at Bath.

Wedding of Miss Mansfield and Mr Burgess, celebrated in verse by 'Vigilo'.

Marion Rice in the 1920s in the pram made by her father, Jack Rice, who was carpenter, wheelwright, postman and lamp-lighter.

Mrs Benson and Mr Rogers, ('Vigilo') at the opening of Bradford Bridge in 1927.

Plaque recording the opening of Bradford Bridge.

*Ralph Tarr on his Fordson tractor, TA 395,
in the 1960s.*

Left to right: *James, John and Robert Woollacott, 1940s.*

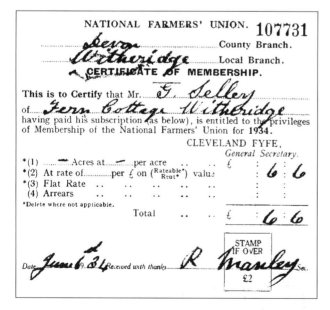

Winter

Once a week chaff was cut for the horses in the chaff-house. An engine powered the belt-driven barn

machinery, which drove not only the chaff-cutter, but also the winnower, the thresher and the grinding stones. Mending bags for corn was a winter task. Wheat was in 2¼cwt bags, and barley 2cwt bags; a man was expected to be able to carry one of these under each arm.

Spar gads for thatching, usually of withy or hazel, were cut in the kitchen. When finished the floor was swept and the sweepings used for the fire. The spar gads were for thatching farm ricks, and for sale to Venners, the local thatchers.

Hedging was done in winter. Hedge material, especially whitehorn and beech, had to be steeped towards the sun, otherwise new growth could pull them up. Steepers were held in place by crooks, cut from hedge stuff and driven into the bank. It was best to steep beech at the end of the winter, because of the rising of the sap. No saws were used, but the cuts were made with hooks (billhooks) after the grass had been cut with a paring hook. Before the hedge could be made, however, the bank had to be cast up with clats (turf) taken from the hedge trough. In North Devon this was done with the long-handled Devon shovel, but the Woollacotts preferred to use a stone fork, as was the practice the other side of Exmoor. Where banks ended at gateways, or where they were weak, stonewalling was used. For this it was essential for the bottom layer of stones to be three quarters under the ground for stability. The angle of the stonewalling had to be right – too flat and the sheep would get up it, too steep and frost could get in and bring it down. Several long stones would be driven into the bank for extra firmness. Banks suffered damage by rabbits, and with the help of ferrets these would be netted, 40 rabbits a day being the target.

Winter was the time for making gates, and the Woollacotts made their own from oak. The cross-pieces were known as shuttles, and at the ends were the hanging post and the hapsing post. It was said that if a gate was well hung it should be possible to open it, place a full glass of water on the top shuttle, let it go, and see it close so softly that not a drop was spilt. Gateposts were also made of oak; the bark had to be removed or water would get in, and the cuts of the bark had to be made with upward strokes, again to avoid the entry of water.

Sometimes corn ricks had to be made away from the farm buildings. For these Nott's steam threshing tackle would be booked, and enough coal ordered. Two men came with the tackle and stayed overnight, ready for an early start to get steam up in the engine before breakfast. A dozen men would sit on forms at the kitchen table, and they included Perce Woodman, Ned Partridge, Webber from Adworthy, and Charlie Middleton. For spring threshing a reed comber was added. Beans were grown, cut with the horse binder and threshed, but the threshing drum sometimes threw them back at the man feeding.

Reed combing at Leat Farm in the 1950s. George (left) *and Henry Blackford.*

Mole catching was another winter job. No traps were used at West Yeo, but a watch was kept for moles 'heaving', and then 'down with your heel'. Dry weather drove the moles down and wet weather brought them up. Bob's best was 37 in one day. The skins were dried and sent to Grantham; they fetched 4d. each.

Between 60 and 70 Devon cows were kept in the 1930s. It was just about possible to milk eight cows an hour. At that time about 500 sheep were kept. At the start they were Exmoor horns, but later Devon closewools were favoured. There were three

cart-horses and two ponies, one butt cart and one cart. The acreage included West Yeo Moor and amounted to 356.

Spring

One of the first signs of spring was the purchase of 25 or 30 chicks from Venners. As soon as the weather and the ground were right ploughing began. An acre a day was the target for horse ploughing. Implements also used were scuffles, heavy and light drags, flat stone rollers and Cambridge ring rollers. Grass fields were stone-rolled, and grass seeds were chain-harrowed. As soon as the bracken began to grow on the moor, the set of heavy drags would be turned upside down and dragged over the young shoots to check them. Between 30 and 40 acres of corn were tilled. The first tractor, a Fordson, was bought in 1940.

Lambing was planned for April; corners of fields were wired off and the ewes driven into them at the end of the day, so that it would be easy to find and inspect them at night. The meadow, or 'mead', was kept for the ewes and lambs.

Basic slag was applied in spring. A lorry would bring a ton or ton and a half and tip it out loose. It was then shovelled into a butt; one man led the horse

Bert, Christine, Fred and George Blackford with Winston Chapple in the 1930s.

and the other spread the slag off the back with a saucer. Oats were followed by barley, roots (with sheep folded on them) and wheat. Dung was taken out in the butt and put in heaps (two heaps per load) and then spread manually with a dung fork. The Devon cattle might be turned out in mid-April, but the sheep always had priority on early grass.

Summer

Bob remembers hay being once made in May, but June was the usual hay month. Grass for hay was never cut when damp. After being tedded, hay was brought in with a double horse sweep to an engine-powered elevator for rick-making. In damp weather the hay 'yetted a bit' (heated) and smaller ricks were made. A long iron bar used to be inserted

Bert and Christine Blackford and their children Henry, Fred, George and Cyril. Also pictured are two evacuees with their parents. Leat Farm, 1941.

into the rick to test for overheating. There were other hazards; on one occasion hay was being gathered in Lower Park when a whirlwind caught it and left it strewn along the main road. Ricks were thatched as soon as possible with wheat reed or rushes.

Roots were horse-hoed, then singled by hand-hoe. In steep fields the soil accumulated at the bottom and from time to time had to be drawn back up.

At times pigeons were such a plague on the swede greens that it was possible to shoot three with one shot; they were sent to Nott's, the poultry packers in Nomansland. During the Second World War the government provided ammunition for pigeon shooting and neighbours worked together. Also during the war West Yeo was made a depot for government machinery.

Usual clothes for farm work in the 1930s were breeches, leggings, hob-nailed boots and a waistcoat. A sack round the shoulders and another round the waist kept out the rain. However, the shearers wore white trousers and jackets, which had to be clean every morning. When hands were washed during shearing a bucket of water with ferns in it was used instead of soap, another idea from 'out over' (Exmoor). Several from there came to help with the shearing; they either rode over or came by taxi. A retired Witheridge butcher, Reg Rodd, tied the wool. Charlie Middleton always helped, and at the end of the day, after food and beer, the kitchen table would be pushed to the side. Charlie would put two crossed brooms in the middle of the floor and do his 'broom dance' to music played by James Woollacott on his accordion.

Among the wives who came to help on those occasions were Mrs Rodd and Mrs Webber. Beer was brewed in three grades at West Yeo; the best for parson and doctor, the next for farmers, and the last for everyone else. Bill Woollacott started keeping bees in the 1930s. When he went into the Army Bob took over the 14 hives. Orders for honey came from

places such as Exmouth, Teignmouth and Minehead, and deliveries became family outings paid for by the money received.

Autumn

Paring hooks were used to clear the edges of the cornfields, then scythes cut room for the horse and binder. As the area of uncut corn became less many rabbits bolted and were killed.

There were a couple of two-acre orchards, mainly of cider apples, but there was a Russet tree in the garden, and a tree of 'Listener', a yellow apple shaped like a quince and the size of a breakfast cup. Maunds were used to carry in the apples. There was a two-screw cider-press in the cider house; all cider was consumed on the farm. Mangolds were gathered in by butt and stored in 'caves', long heaps against a wall or bank, covered with rushes, bracken or browse against the frost. Late summer was 'maggot time'; a dead rabbit was hung on a bough near where sheep gathered, with a bath filled with a Jeyes Fluid mix underneath. The flies left the sheep and laid their eggs on the dead rabbit. When the eggs hatched the maggots fell into the bath of disinfectant and died.

The only vet in the area was Matthews of Rackenford. If he was needed someone had to ride over to fetch him. West Yeo had no telephone until the Ministry of Agriculture put one in during the war. Stanley Andrews of Romansleigh travelled for an animal medicine firm and visited from time to time. Cattle would be 'drenched' by having medicine poured down their throats by means of a cow's horn with a hole drilled in the bottom.

In the Second World War John served in the Life Guards and Bill in the Marines. In 1940 the Woollacotts were allocated six evacuee boys aged from three to ten. Queenie Long had been a land girl at Newhouse, but had left. She was asked to come to West Yeo to help look after the evacuees and give a hand at harvest time. In autumn 1940 Bob and Queenie were married.

One autumn a couple of years later John Woollacott was on leave and went rabbiting on North Hill with Bob. Queenie remembers pushing the pram carrying young Robin and Fred all the way out to meet them with a hot drink and some food, and returning with rabbits hanging from the pram handle.

WITHERIDGE CARNIVAL 1930–53

On 27 September 1930, at a meeting in the Church Rooms, the decision was taken to arrange a carnival in Witheridge. Officers were appointed (Mr A. Chamberlain as president, Revd J.A.S. Castlehow as chairman, Messrs L.C. Thomas and C. Thorne as secretaries, Mr W. Thomas as treasurer) and a committee plus several subcommittees were set up to cover the procession, sideshows, dance, auction, confetti and mascots, collection boxes, torches and judges. Little time was wasted, for they met again on 8 October to decide to allocate £5 for prizes, to assemble the procession 'at 6.45p.m. at Nothernhay Bank' (North Street) and to note that the superintendent of police had granted a permit for street collections (no person under 16 to collect). They met again briefly on 10 November to change the assembly point to The Square, and the carnival took place on 20 November. It was a success; when the accounts were presented on 6 December it was reported that total receipts were £201.10s.6d., that total expenses were £25.15s.9d., and that there was a profit of £175.14s.9d. This was a big sum: to put it in context, in 1930 £170 would buy a new Morris Cowley saloon car, £140 would buy a fully equipped Austin Seven saloon, and for £16 you could get a good three-piece suite. A donation of £60 was given to Tiverton Hospital, £30 to South Molton Cottage Hospital, £25 to the Devon and Exeter Hospital, £15 to the West of England Eye Infirmary and £30 to the Witheridge Nursing Association.

The *Crediton Chronicle* of 22 November gave a short report of the occasion under the headline 'Witheridge Beats the Weather – Fine Carnival Effort'. It went on to say:

Witheridge rose superior to the handicap of bad weather... soaking rain fell before the procession, and continued intermittently during the evening, saturating tableaux and fancy dress, onlookers and masqueraders alike, damping everything but high spirits.

The prize winners were:

Best tableau: first, 'Gipsy's Warning' (Mrs Lee, Misses Mitchell, D. Turl, L. Baker, E. Trawin); second, 'Dresden China Shepherd and Shepherdess' (Misses J. Townsend and J. Seal); third, 'Guardian Angel' (Mrs Payne, Miss Fulford, and Joyce Litton).

Humorous tableau: first, 'Windwhistle Villas' (Mr and Mrs Jones, Renee Jones, Gwennie Sculpar); second, 'Every Copper Helps' (Messrs Bert Ostler, Percy Johnson, Alf Tidball); third, 'Everyone Works but Father' (Mrs Gunn, Mrs Maire, Misses R. Reed, P. Lamprey, Messrs E. Tucker and J. Gunn).

Tableau (under 16): first, 'Wedding Group' (Messrs B. and J. Nott, J. Windsor, W. Blackford, Masters A., G., K. and S. Nott); second, 'Fairy Dyes' (Marjorie Southcott, Phyllis Chapple, Sylvia Leach, Dora Bourne and Sylvia Bolland).

Decorated motorcars: first, 'Silver Paper' (Mr Ollerenshaw); second, 'Powder Puffs' (Messrs Bragg, Fewings and Coles).

Pedestrians: first, Mr Gunn, 'When Mother was 21' (Mrs Palfreyman); third, 'Eastern Lady' (Miss V. Scantlebury).

Decorated bicycles: first, Pearl Smith; second, George Knight.

Mounted riders: first, 'Jockey' (J. Keenor); second, 'Mounted Guard' (H. Boundy); third, 'Carnival Star' (Mr L. Carter).

Pedestrians (children): first, Bernard Whittock as 'Wee Willie Winkie'.

The following years the organisation committee meetings were held in September. There was a committee for the procession and for the dance, as well as an organiser for: refreshments, dance refreshments, lighting, stalls and sideshows, a jazz band, whist drive, clay-pigeon shoot, football match, skittles, auction. Nearly 50 names appear in the minutes of the meeting of people involved in the organisation. The profits continued to be allocated on a percentage basis to local hospitals and nursing associations. A balance of about £15 was kept in hand. In 1931 the prize money was increased to £12.0s.6d., and 'the Witheridge Comedy Band's offer of their services free for the Dance in the Angel Assembly Room' was accepted. The carnival included the following classes:

Class 1   Mounted horseman.
Class 2   Best tableau: steam wagon/motor lorry.
Class 3   Best comic tableau: steam wagon/motor lorry.
Class 4   Best tableau: horse wagon.
Class 5   Best comic tableau: horse wagon.
Class 6   Decorated motor car.
Class 7   Decorated tradesman's vehicle.
Class 8   Novelty entry.
Class 9   Decorated cycle or motor cycle.
Class 10   Pedestrian: schoolchildren.
Class 11   Pedestrian: single entry.
Class 12   Pedestrians: Best pair.
Class 13   Best decorated horse drawing a vehicle.

Final arrangements were made on 13 November, just six days before the carnival itself. Mr Maire was asked 'to roll more level the places where new drains have been laid'. Mrs Palfreyman reported a profit on the whist drive of around £4 and it was agreed that:

Free Refreshment Tickets should be given to the members of the three bands playing at the carnival and to the judges, and that Free Dance Tickets should be given to members of the Carnival Jazz Band.

Mr Moore of South Molton was invited to give a firework display, but was not to be allowed to sell fireworks to the public. Following the 1931 carnival, £110.6s.0d. was donated to the hospitals and nursing associations.

In contrast to the short report that the *Crediton Chronicle* gave the event in 1930, the 1931 carnival got the full treatment: nearly three full-length columns (not tabloid) containing about 3,500 words. The reporter set the scene like this:

Unless they are careful the promoters of Witheridge carnival will achieve the double-barrelled reputation of providing one of the best and most consistent carnivals in the district and, at the same time, some of the worst weather. Last year the procession was held in a downpour of rain and wind of gale force, on November 19th things were somewhat better, for a watery moon made valiant efforts to smile on the moving panorama of tableaux, but as soon as the procession was over the rain set in by the proverbial bucketful. Nothing daunted, the carnival went on, and proved if anything to be an improvement on the previous effort. Many factors combined to make the show better. The installation of electric lights in the village enabled a scheme of coloured lamps to be used in the centre of the town, a welcome innovation which did much to counterbalance the recent labours of sappers and miners who apparently had had most of the streets up. Without adequate illumination it would have been an unpleasant adventure to cross the roads. The allocation of special rooms for Judges, Officers and the Press was a thoughtful innovation on the part of those responsible for the arrangements. Whatever the weather or the exigencies of the national call for economy, Witheridge takes its pleasures cheerfully; on Thursday the village was en fête, and attracted many visitors.

There followed a list of committee members and judges, and details of the other activities such as the dance at the Angel, skittles, whist drive and auction. Next came the list of prizewinners:

Comic Tableau: first, 'Witheridge Past and Present' (Mrs Selley); second, 'Washing Day' (Mrs W. Venner); third, 'Cruwys Morchard 1961' (Mrs Greenslade).

Decorated lorries: first, 'Christmas Carol' (Mrs Greenslade); second, 'Convalescent Home' (Witheridge District Nursing Association); third, 'Japanese Lady' (South Molton Hospital Committee).

Decorated horses and wagon: first, 'Pageant of Empire' (Black Dog Nursing Association); second, 'Witheridge Beach Girls' (Mrs C. Maire); third, 'Christmas Eve' (Miss Ayre).

Comic lorries: first, 'Honeyman' (Yvonne Redwood and Roy Gunn); second, 'Before and After Treatment' (F. and M. Blackford); third, 'Witheridge Talkies' (Miss Southcott).

Novelty tableau: first, 'To Market in 1891' (Mrs A. Mills and Master E. Winner); second, 'Returning from School in Winter' (Ayre and Blackford).

Decorated motor cars: first, 'Powder Puff' (South Molton Cottage Hospital Committee); second, 'Silver Wings' (Mrs R. Selley).

Trade tableaux: first, 'Dog Biscuits' (Southcott); second, Gunn; third, Frisby.

Decorated motorcycles and bicycles: first, 'Tiny Fairy' (Mr L. Crispin); second, 'Chinese Lantern' (A. Leat); third, 'Buy British' (Dorothy Webber); fourth, 'Sitting on a Rainbow' (Marjorie Southcott).

Decorated horses: first, Phillips; second, Woodman; third, W. Earl; fourth, J. Beer.

Mounted: first, 'Jockey' (W. Pincombe); second, 'Soldier' (H. Boundy); third, K. Webber.

Pedestrians, Pair: first, 'Gipsies' (Henry Davey and Gwen Hooper); second, 'Hiking' (Gordon and James Luxton).

Pedestrians, singles: first, Mrs Palfreyman; second, J. Trevelyan.

Pedestrians, schoolchildren: first, Marjorie Keith; second, Eric and Stanley Selley; third, Sylvia Leach; fourth, Bernard Whittock; fifth, Christine and Stella Selley.

The remaining two columns of print were taken up under the heading 'The Procession Described' and began thus:

Last year Witheridge gave evidence as to what it could provide in the way of a spectacular procession; on this occasion the lesson was rammed home. In every way the line of tableaux, decorated motors and cycles was an effective sight. The coloured lights festooned over the main streets enhanced the spectacular effect, giving a top light to the torches and brightly illuminated cars. As many people as ever appeared to have flocked into the village from the surrounding districts, including visitors from the Chulmleigh and Chawleigh districts, who were engaged in comparing the effort with their own recently held carnivals... Encouraging music was dispensed by the Tiverton Town Band (Bandmaster W. Loosemore) and Crediton Town Band (Bandmaster L. Bennellick). The moist conditions did not affect the quality of music provided. Decorated horses were again a feature of the carnival, an attraction other centres would do well to emulate. Decorated manes and tails and shining coats, covered with polished and glittering harnesses were a tribute to many hours of work on the part of the drivers.

The report then gave a detailed description of many of the entries, of which the following are some examples:

'Witheridge Talkies Just Arrived' was a skit on the long-established illusion that women are the loquacious sex. Mr Nott's lorry, in the charge of Mr W. Chapple, was transformed from its everyday appearance into a local parliament of ladies with a sprinkling of men, busy engaged in knitting, drinking tea, and the most engrossing task of all – discussing the affairs of their neighbours. Looking at the tableau one quickly received the impression that no-one's reputation was safe for very long. The acting of the various occupants was realistic, and gave the impression of a number of animated conversations going on at one and the same time, in which each person was talking whether or not anyone was listening. Action was liberally used, looks of surprise and condemnation, generally of the 'I thought so' and 'told you so' variety predominating. The characters in this hard working entry were taken by Mr and Mrs Bristow, the Misses L.B. and P. Chapple, Mr J. Holmes, Mr B.

Stenner, Miss D. Ford and Master Billie Southcott.

'Witheridge Past and Present' was novel in conception. The lorry was divided to represent the living rooms of a house. In one half a party of gentleman, got up regardless, with fierce moustaches, fat cigars and all the trimmings, were engaged in a game which looked suspiciously like ha'penny nap. The cards went round and festivities were merry and bright, in contrast to the other portion of the tableau, where an old couple were sitting in domestic felicity round the teapot. The occupants were Messrs W. Kingdom, B. Nott, W. Gold, F. Kingdom, and Mr and Mrs W.H. Selley.

Amusement and fears for the old shirt and collar were provided by a glance at 'Drayford Washing Day, 1931', where laundry was being subjected to processes more suitable to sheet steel than linen. Inventive genius had been devoted to the appliances used; the washerwomen in the persons of Mrs W. Venner, Mrs Sanders, Miss I. Venner, Miss A. Venner and Master F. Venner spared no effort in playing their parts. Mr S. Stoneman drove the wagon.

Fashion's trend can always be trusted to reflect itself in a carnival, especially when it leads to pretty effects. A few years ago Venice and other Continental resorts set the pace in up-to-date beach attire; in time the vogue spread to Britain, and Witheridge took the lesson to heart and blossomed out upon an astonished world with a beauty chorus who termed themselves 'Witheridge Beach Girls'. Beach pyjamas of smart cut and vivid hue, with rush sombreros and sandals, were well displayed against a wagon decorated to represent a seaside scene. The lighting was particularly good. Those taking part were Mrs C. Maire, Misses E. Mitchell, J. Gunn, E. Whittock and E. Gold. Mr A. Haydon at the horse had a perilous cargo in his wake.

'Silver Wings' was a novel and pretty innovation in decorated motor cars. A saloon car, driven by Mr W. Brent, was decorated with a silver motif, ribbons, flowers etc., creating the effect; in the centre of the car was placed a large bowl of goldfish, whose movements were caught and reflected by the light, forming a charming contrast to the general colour scheme. Three little girls (Barbara Pickard, Kathleen Lamprey and Rita Selley) seated within, dressed in fairy-like frocks, completed a pretty picture.

The Witheridge Nursing Association entered an appropriate wagon – 'Convalescent Home'. Mrs Gard, Mrs Davies, Mrs Whittock, Mrs Sillifant, Jose Baker, Bert Winter, Leslie Criddle, and Nora Holmes were the central figures. Divided wagons are popular this year; the entry followed the fancy; on one side was shown the inner workings of a medical institution, and on the other patients in degrees varying from the hopeless ill-health to robust and bouncing restoration. The medical department were engaged in preparing prescriptions, looking after the commissariat and generally giving the public a glimpse of what goes on behind the scenes. The patients were skilfully made up to represent their condition of health.

A comic entry, 'O la la Beauty Parlour', created mirth, Mr G. Woodman drove, Messrs S.W. and C. Thorne, W. Maunder and J. Adams were the specialists and unfortunate victims. The title of the exhibit explained itself, a beauty parlour of the Heath Robinson variety, made all the funnier by the antics of the performers.

Mrs A. Mills and Master E. Winser had a turnout, 'Going to Market in 1891'. The idea was not unique, but there is a certain sham in the old dog-cart and the homely country figures of a past generation, with their baskets of produce, rattling along with a cracking whip.

'Before and after Treatment' was another humorous exhibit. The self-explanatory parts were taken by Messrs F. and M. Blackford, M. and K. Reed, J. Churchill, F. Leach, Tanner, Tucker, and B. Blackford.

There was a good entry of decorated cycles, Master A. Leat (Washford) wheeled a machine cleverly contrived to represent a 'Chinese Lantern'. Paper lanterns swinging on the body of the machine added to the effect. Another brilliantly-lit entry was 'Sitting on a Rainbow' (Marjorie Southcott). A large rainbow of vivid colours surmounted the machine. Stanley Hunt, wearing a mask, entered a cycle trimmed with coloured paper, and Gordon Reed (Hare and Hounds Hotel) was dressed up as Father Christmas. A 'Buy British' cycle was in charge of Dorothy Webber.

The report ended with a paragraph headed 'The Foot Brigade':

There did not appear to be as many pedestrians in fancy dress as last year. The most conspicuous gang was the jazz band under the leadership of Mr C. Pickard. His accomplices were Douglas, Frank and Fred Kingdom, S. Hitchcock, J. Ford and Arthur Brent. In costume and noise the band was distinguished. Others in fancy dress included: Henry Davey and Gwen Hooper attired as Gypsies, Gordon and James Luxton, who were out 'Hiking', and in similar vein Stanley Beer and Henry Down ('On the Road'). 'The White-eyed Kaffir' concealed Mr J. Trevelyan, while F. Hill (Crediton) impersonated Charlie Chaplin. Willie Knight was a study in 'Black and White', Sylvia Leach was a charming Father Christmas. Jean Keith, with picture hat, copied Gainsborough's 'Duchess of Devonshire', and the Red Cross was represented by C. and E. Selley. Messrs P. Courtenay and F. Long made a pair with Hiking and Grannie. R. Mildon advertised the Lido.

So it went on – the preliminary meetings took place in mid-September, and a further meeting or meetings shortly before the carnival itself. It was always held on a Thursday (early-closing day), but the actual date was 3 November in 1932, and 20 October in 1938. There was always a long and impressive list of those involved, and changes were confined to such matters as giving each bandsman a shilling rather than a free refreshment ticket, voting not to include the Black Dog Nursing Association as a beneficiary, deciding to hire a 'skittling alley' from South Molton, and so on. Occasionally there was disagreement, usually over the allocation of the profits.

The local jazz band attended regularly and in 1933 a request was made to the Exe Valley Electric Light Company (in West Street) for its help with extra lighting. In 1933 Mr Tudball tried again to propose that 'a Quarter of the proceeds be given to start a hut fund' but he got no support. However, Mrs Ollerenshaw's proposal that £10 be kept 'in trust for the hut fund' was carried, and Mr Selley's amendment that 'the sum be altered from £10 to £5' was defeated by six votes. Mr Selley then tried again, proposing that if the £10 for the hut fund was not claimed in six months it should revert to the carnival fund. Chairman, Revd J.A.S. Castlehow, had had enough of this subject and got a proposal through that 'the question of handing the money over should be left in abeyance until this time next year.' Mr Castlehow resigned the next year but was back again in 1935, when it was minuted that 'Through the Jazz Band being unable through lack of instruments to tour the district, Mr Knight be asked to fulfil these engagements with his radiogram.' In 1936 the September meeting had to be adjourned 'owing to there being such a small company present', but ten days later there was a better turnout, and preparations went ahead. In the event £90 was distributed to the usual hospitals and nursing associations; in 1934 and 1935 it had been £100.

In 1937 some apparently regular features got a mention, such as 'that the Boy Scouts again be asked to carry torchlights around as last year', and that 'Mr Knight with his radio and Mr Pickard with his band be again asked to tour the district as in other years.' This time the question of having a carnival queen was first discussed and agreed to, with Mr Culhene as convener. The year 1937 enjoyed a particularly successful carnival, with a detailed report in the *Crediton Chronicle*, and £140 available for distribution. The *Chronicle* used the headlines, 'Witheridge Carnival Success' and 'Carnival Queen Contest – A Magnificent Response'. It went on to say:

... a prelude to the carnival was staged on Monday evening when the 'Queen', Miss Joan Nott, aged 12 was crowned. She is the daughter of Mr and Mrs A. Nott of Eastway. There were 15 candidates, and between them they raised the magnificent sum of £58 in pennies... For several nights prior to the carnival a band of willing helpers toured the district with Mr Knight's radiogram, and a substantial sum was raised in this manner.

Tableaux that got most favourable mentions included 'The Sculptor', 'Rocky Mountaineers', 'HMS Witheridge', 'Varmer You Naw – Ee Makes Varming Pay', 'A Romany Camp', 'Kirk's Wool Bar', 'Coronation Dancers', 'Interval in Business'. Among the children's entries there was special praise for 'Carol Singers' (Joan Ratcliffe, Bryan Hitchcock, Kathleen Pyne, Gordon Pyne, Ivor Bourne and Les Tucker), 'Babes in the Wood' (Ronald Ashelford and Valerie Leach) and Betty Way as a 'Mounted Red Indian'. The report ended by saying:

The village was tastefully illuminated with coloured lights provided by the Exe Valley Electricity Company Ltd. Messrs Lock's amusements and sideshows were in The Square and contributed to the carnival funds.

Carnival, 1938. Bill Cox is in the driving seat and beside him is Bill Gold. Fred Rippon and Ted King are behind. Mrs Ayre is in the wheelchair (right). *In the autumn of 1938 newspapers were full of the country's lack of readiness should war come.*

In 1938 £100 was available, after a good carnival, for distribution, and in addition Mr Knight's radiogram was purchased. When they met on 28 August 1939, the shadow of war hung over their meeting – the attendance was poor – but nevertheless they fixed 26 October as carnival day. When they met again, however, on 11 September the minutes record that:

... owing to the declaration of war it was decided not to hold a carnival this year, but it was unanimously agreed to that an effort be made to collect as much money as possible by sending out the collecting books etc. [The proceeds were to be distributed as usual].

This they continued to do until 1943, after which there is a gap in the minutes until 22 July 1946. At this meeting Mr W. Thomas retired as treasurer, having done the job since 1930; Mr D. Kingdom was appointed in his place. Mr E. Hutchings became president and the vicar continued as chairman. The decision was taken to restart the carnival, and as judges the Earl and Countess of Eldon (Rackenford Manor), Mr and Mrs Allanson Bailey (Bradford Tracy), Mr F. Verney and Mrs Cruwys were invited. The effect of the war was still being felt, as they had to apply to the Regional Petroleum Officer for a petrol allowance for any car drivers who volunteered to drive collecting

Carnival, 1947. Left to right: Sheila Andrews, Sylvia Boundy, Stella Bourne, Doreen Manley (carnival queen), Mrs Price, Mary Gibbs, Sheila Leach.

parties. They also had to 'apply to the Food Office for a permit for light refreshments', and the radiogram was to be repaired. The 'Footlight Follies Concert Party' was invited to give an entertainment. Mechanisation on farms was recognised by the inclusion of a class for 'Agriculture, Drawn by Tractor'. This first postwar carnival turned out to be successful, as it made a profit of £183.15s.7d., of which £160 was allotted to the usual hospitals and nursing associations.

The year 1948 saw Mr Allanson Bailey take over as chairman, a competition to find 'Miss Witheridge' was added, prize money for the classes was increased, and there was a draw for a bicycle, 'value £12.12s.0d.'. This latter idea fell foul of the law of lotteries and had to be abandoned. Tradesmen were asked to keep their shop lights on, and £5 was offered to the South Molton Band for their attendance, 'should their fee exceed that sum the Committee would be unable to entertain same.' The result was another success, with £180 to be distributed, but with a difference: £100 stayed within the parish (£75 to the top playing-field and £25 to the Mitre Committee – the forerunners of the Parish Hall Committee) and £80 went to the nursing and hospital services. This was the last occasion on which these services benefited from Witheridge carnival, perhaps as a result of the introduction of the National Health Service.

Further changes took place, as it was decided for the first time to hold the event on a Saturday 'in the hope of lorries, etc. being available earlier in the day for those bringing tableaux and giving more time for stripping down during the weekend.' In addition, 90 per cent of the profits stayed in the village; they were distributed to the Witheridge British Legion, the Church Tower Repair Fund, the playing-field and the football, tennis and bowling clubs. There were no horse-wagon classes, just 'Mounted Horseman' and 'Best Decorated Horse' classes. There were only three candidates for carnival queen: Miss Sylvia Sowden collected £84.3s.0d. and was queen for the

second year in succession. A profit of £222.12s.3d. was made and 'the newly formed Cricket Club' was added to the list of beneficiaries.

Increased interest in the possibility of a Parish Hall for Witheridge was reflected in the 1949 decision that the whole of that year's profits should go to the Parish Hall Fund, in view of the fact that the Mitre Club was unlikely to materialise. Two dances were held on carnival night: the B and M Band played in the Angel Room, and the Ambassadors in the Church School. Perhaps it was increasing car ownership that brought Police Sergeant Bond to a meeting to make special arrangements for parking. There was a record profit of £291.15s.1d., all of which went to the Parish Hall Fund.

In 1950 more meetings than usual were needed. Lord Eldon was appointed president and concern was expressed over the fact that there was only one candidate for queen. A 'Portable Wireless' was purchased as first prize for the draw, and 'a cylinder of Hydrogen for a Balloon Competition'. The Skylarks Dance Band was engaged, the collecting boxes were renovated, and the usual extension of street lighting to midnight was requested. The parking problem was solved by offers of space at Lakelands, the Mitre Field, the Market Field and land next to Mr Venner's garage for buses. The Women's Institute took charge of the refreshments. Further meetings were held in September and October, when they were glad to learn that five queen candidates had come forward, with Miss Marion Holt as the winner. After the carnival the sum of £118.7s.8d. went to the Parish Hall Fund, followed by a further £183.15s.0d. in 1951. The accounts for this year make special reference to the payment of a half-crown toll to the lord of the manor for use of The Square, although this was almost certainly a regular outlay.

In 1952 there is a gap in the minute book and no carnival took place. There was a public meeting on 3 July 1953 to consider whether 'to revive the carnival', and a further meeting on 10 July resolved to go

A carnival float, early 1950s. Left to right: Dorothy Davey, ?, Jean Manley, Thelma Cole, Fred Davey.

ahead. After some hesitation two queen candidates came forward, but the committee had difficulty in securing judges, and the WI could not provide a convener for refreshments, although individual members would help; the minutes record that Mrs Williams saved the day. Nothing, however, could save the 1953 carnival from the weather; the headlines in the *Tiverton Gazette* told the story, 'Carnival Carries On Despite Weather' and 'Thunderstorms Swamp Tableaux and Spectators at Witheridge.' The report went on:

Thunder and lighting and hours of pouring rain terrified horses, swamped the gay tableaux, drenched competitors and spectators alike and turned the streets into swirling streams, but the organisers of Witheridge carnival on Saturday decided to carry on. 'What else can we do?' they asked when nine tableaux beat the weather and began to turn up for the procession. Most of the tableaux – which came from as far as Tiverton and West Anstey were well on their way when the storm broke. It had passed its heights by the time they reached Witheridge, but the damage was already done. Tarpaulin sheets, carried for emergency were brought into use but provided little resistance against the heavy downpour.

The children's decorated cycles and prams and adult walkers found refuge in the Angel Room, where they were marshalled and judged. But outside it was a different story. Gamely competitors mounted their tableaux and rolled back protective coverings for the judging. They stayed in position for a short parade round the village, led by the Tiverton and Crediton Town Bands and two machines from Witheridge Fire Brigade and the NFS huddled in doorways, the few drenched spectators cheered encouragement but could see little of the finer points of the entries... 'She won't burn tonight', quipped a spectator as Miss P. Davis, wearing a plastic mackintosh, was lashed to the stake on Tiverton Walronds Social Club's 'The Last Hours of Joan of Arc'. The other characters also bowed to the weather and wore galoshes and raincoats over their costumes. The four local entries were more fortunate because in most cases they were able to keep their tableaux under cover until the worst of the storm had passed. But even then Witheridge Poachers turned out in an open-top coach and kept up a non-stop pantomime while the water grew deeper around them.

The queen, 20-year-old Miss Margaret Parker, of the Post Office, was to have driven in state through the village in an open landau drawn by a pair of horses lent by Mr C. Perkins of Sandford. The carriage and pair arrived in fine weather, but with the first alarming flash of lightning the horses panicked and had to be freed from their traces and let out into a nearby field. Not to be outdone the queen led the parade in a car, lent by Mr F. Venner. With the queen in the car was her attendant, 26-year-old Miss Marcella Andrews of Mill Park, Witheridge. Between them they collected £75 in twopenny votes – Miss Parker £52 and Miss Andrews £23. Miss Parker was crowned at a concert at the Angel on Thursday by Lady McNair, wife of the President. The competition was organised by Mrs I. Way.

This year, in the light of past difficulties, the carnival committee decided to have car parks at each end of the village. But the scheme had to be dropped because both parks became little more than quagmires. As it was, very few cars were to be seen. The carnival was the first in the village since 1951, and from their original meeting in July the committee had been working against time to make arrangements. Faced with total loss through the weather, they spared no efforts to achieve some measure of success and keep up the reputation they had tried so hard to revive... The day was brought to a close with two dances at the Angel Room and the Schoolroom. Refreshments at Messrs Venner's garage were served by Mrs E. Williams, Mrs Parkhouse and helpers. List of prize winners:

Decorated Tableaux: first, 'The Last Hours of Joan of Arc' (Tiverton Walronds); second, 'Bunch of Rosebuds' (J. Southcott, J. Buckingham, J. Summerwell, A. Manley, M. Priest, C. Joslin, N. Southcott, C. Southcott); third, 'Cinderella' (Tiverton); fourth, 'Homage to the Throne' (South Molton).

Comic: first, 'Zaturday Night at Jan's' (Mrs Culhene, Mrs E. Knight, Misses Cannon, Gloyn and Way, Messrs I. Nott, K. Nott, S. Nott, and J. Bryant); second, 'Witheridge Christmas Market 1903' (Messrs F. Venner, G. Bamson, D. Elston, P. Farmer, M. Gard, B. McDonald and J. Yendell); third, 'Anstey Model Laundry' (West Anstey).

Trade: 'Thatched Cottage' (Mr Rice, Broadclyst).

Decorated Prams and Cycles: first, 'HMS Roses' (Mr W. Rose, Tiverton); second, 'Harvest Home' (Mrs L. Price); third, 'Jack and the Beanstalk' (Mr Moore, Tiverton).

Mounted: first, 'Trooping the Colour' (Ralph Tatlock); second, 'What no petrol?' (Mrs Vodden); third, 'Red Indian' (Gillian Thorn).

Children's Class: first, 'Stork' (John Sowden, Bampton); second, Elizabethan Page' (Michael Channing); third, 'Patriotic Miss' (Jennifer Phillips); fourth, 'Jockey' (Martin Champion).

Walking Guys, Adults: first, 'Sporting Achievements' (Mrs K. Sowden, Bampton); second, 'Nell Gwynn' (Mrs P.N. Phillips).

In spite of so much misfortune a profit of £51.16s.9d. was made and put into the Parish Hall Fund, which then stood at £632.10s.5d. Sadly it was to be the last carnival for 24 years. The next record of a meeting is dated 21 June 1956, where it was decided, subject to Charity Commission approval, to hand over the Parish Hall Fund to the Parish Hall Committee, and to retain the balance of funds 'to be used to promote any venture that would benefit the Parish, providing the Trustees were satisfied that a properly convened committee had been formed.' The minutes of this meeting were signed by Mr A.J. Knight on 11 March 1958, the same date the public meeting was wound up. The remaining balances of £141.12s.11d. were dispersed – £99.3s.0d. to the youth club, and £42.9s.11d. to the football club.

Witheridge carnival was revived in the jubilee year of 1977 on the initiative of the Witheridge Fire Brigade.

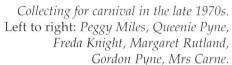

Collecting for carnival in the late 1970s. Left to right: Peggy Miles, Queenie Pyne, Freda Knight, Margaret Rutland, Gordon Pyne, Mrs Carne.

Carnival, 1981. Left to right: Ivan Leat, Mervyn Leach, Colin Leach, Den Cockram, Fred Leat, Cyril Leat.

Carnival, 1978.

'Rock Around the Clock', carnival, 1977. Left to right: Mark Woodall, Kath Reed (behind), David Bryant, Kim Payne, Toby Day, John Williams, Tony Short, David Ford, Graham Isaacs, Nicky Reed, Linda Bryant, Alison Reed.

The British School in 1928. Left to right, back row: *Mr Ollerenshaw (head), Tom Harris, Stanley Hayes, Henry Lynn, Reggie Ayre, Fred Tucker, Gilbert Bristow;* standing: *George Knight, Fred Ayre, Margaret Davies, Eileen Cox, Vera Lynn, Agnes Ayre, Orpah Mills, Gwen Maire, Nancy Knight, Phyllis Gard, Ida Brayley, Aubry Besley, Douglas Hayes;* sitting: *Edwin Tucker, Ian Ayre, Clarice Burridge, Beattie Chapple, Elsie Winter, Dorothy Winter, Bert Winter, Hilda Cox, Percy Holloway, Jack Beer;* kneeling: *Ida Beer, Evelyn Tucker, Gladys Cox, Molly Cockram, D. Leat, Ada Kingdom, Gladys Bristow, Phyllis Chapple.*

Below: *The British School, 1946.* Left to right, back row: *Bert Thomas, Ron Ashelford, Violet Thomas, Doris Dart, Margaret Grant, Derick Roberts, Tom Green;* middle row: *Ron Lewis, Jean Radford, Marianne Field, Eileen Bryant, Lucy Govier, Margaret Cole, Marion Nott, Doreen Arscott, Mr Ollerenshaw;* front: *Edna Radford, Evelyn Monteith, Mary Ash.*

Above: *The British School, 1936.* The picture includes: *Dorothy Davies, Irene Woodman, Gwen Drake, Freda Holloway, Pearl Cole, Doris Dart, George Parkhouse.*

Chapter 5

THE 1930S & '40S

THE BRITISH SCHOOL, 1921–46

In this school one long headship followed another. Mr Ollerenshaw served for 26 years – some of which were affected by talk of reorganisation and the problems of the war. An early success for Mr Ollerenshaw was to achieve an attendance of 90 per cent, whatever the weather, as these examples taken from his log-book show:

31 March 1922: *The Infants and Standard 1 have made a perfect attendance in spite of the wet weather.*
18 February 1924: *As the boys in the main room made 100 per cent attendance during last week, they have been allowed to play football for the last half hour this afternoon.*
19 February 1926: *It is rarely even on the stormiest morning that we find any absent on account of the weather.*
18 December 1930: *Evelyn Tucker has been presented with a pen and pencil on completing 6 years perfect attendance.*

Changing attitudes of parents, stricter enforcement, and school transport played a part in this improvement. The first school motorbus ran on 6 September 1926 on a route that took in the Venhays, Ashmoor, Creacombe, Bradford and Nomansland. During Mr Ollerenshaw's time school numbers varied. He inherited a roll of 52, which rose to 72 in 1925, 80 in 1927, 90 in 1932, and a peak of 107 in 1933. From then on the trend was downward, to 82 in 1936, 57 in 1940, followed by a big influx of evacuees in the early war years. In school history terms these were modern times, and yet the head must have been surprised in December 1935 to record:

... admitted two children aged 7 and 13 who declare that they have never been to school before. As neither can read or write I have been compelled to put them both in the infants class.

To help him Mr Ollerenshaw had Miss Mitchell, who taught the infants for 16 years and received many positive mentions from HMI. Mrs Ollerenshaw was a qualified teacher who helped out in emergencies and taught occasionally in her own right. The head had wide interests and his log-book entries include mentions of football and cricket equipment, health talks, domestic science classes, poultry keeping, the telephone, cookery, and royal weddings, as well as the day in 1928 when an aeroplane landed near the village, and the children were taken up to see it. In September 1931 'The Top Class visited the new Electric Power Plant at Cypress House' (Witheridge's first venture into electricity). There was co-operation with the National School, as in 1936, when a class from each school visited the Ambrosia milk factory at Lapford. Other joint ventures included visits to a dairy farm at Whipton, a poultry farm near Ottery St Mary, and Heathcoats factory in Tiverton.

In most years one or two pupils passed the scholarship exam, but parents were seldom able to accept this opportunity for their children. In 1934 the head noted that 'several children develop mentally after reaching the age-limit for scholarship and would benefit from a Secondary School education.' In his time the age range was 5 to 14, but in the 1930s there was already talk of separate senior schools for the older pupils.

Below are some excerpts from HMI reports in the 1920s and '30s.

12 July 1922: *... promising start... in the top grade the results in English, Arithmetic, Geography and drawing give evidence of sound teaching. The tone is excellent... the work is well planned to arouse the children's interest and cooperation... the teacher of the infants is earnest but inexperienced.*
27 May 1926: *... trying conditions, lighting and ventilation are poor, the Head has to treat Standards 4 to 7 as one class, changes must be made and better accommodation found for practical subjects.*
5 Jan 1933: *... poor lighting and ventilation, classes to be more quietly conducted, the Head's organisation is sensible and his syllabus detailed and carefully compiled but without distinctive features.* [For the infants] *the lessons in dramatisation have encouraged the children to speak freely and clearly.*
18 Nov 1937: [Praise was given throughout the school] *particularly standards 1 to 4 where the teaching marked by energy and intelligence.* [In general] *the teaching is successful in rousing the children's interest and many of them are obviously stimulated by it.*

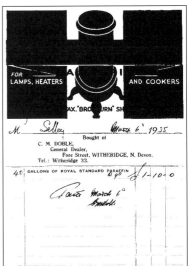

The British School, 1948. Left to right, back row: Joyce Radford, Vera Winter, ?, Sheila Andrews, Violet Dart, Edna Radford, Joan Brent; middle row: Roy Manley, Ivan Ashelford, Norman Lewis, Sheila Nott, Monica Maunder, ?, ?, Stanley Lewis; front row: Fred Leat, David Nott, Cyril Leat, Derrick Bryant, Rodney Grant.

Bill and Ruby Buchanan's wedding, 1934. Included in the picture are Annie and Les Baker, Stella Baker, Joe and Millie Churchill, William Baker.

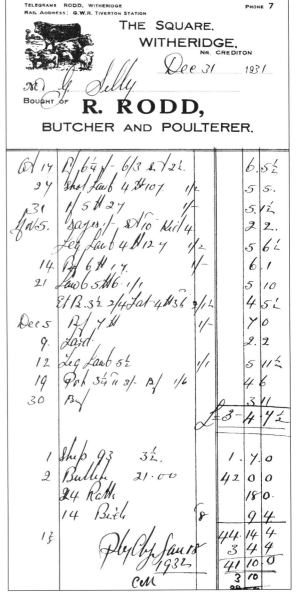

Contribution by 'Vigilo' (Mr W.H. Rogers)

In the *Western Times* on a Friday in the early 1930s.

To Mr Bourke whose electric work
Relieved the gloom of night.
He felt compassion in up-to-date fashion,
And said, 'Let there be light'.
At once it was so, and a mighty glow
Pervaded our streets so vitty
And strangers say as they pass our way
'Why this sure is a City'.

As remembered by Mr Leslie Knight, 1996.

The 'Electricity poem' by 'Vigilo'.

There are just 18 mentions of corporal punishment in 26 years; the most frequent offence was pupils throwing stones, usually at the 'School motor van', but sometimes at each other. The playground had always been too small and with 80–90 children out there falls were common, either in mud or on stones. Knees, arms and foreheads were often grazed or cut – so much so that one of Mr Ollerenshaw's first tasks was to provide a first-aid kit. Eventually the playground was tarred and such entries were much reduced.

Heat and light caused further problems. It was 25 years before a canteen was considered, but in 1923 a boiler was installed to heat food brought by the children. In 1926 water was laid on. By 1940 milk and hot water for cocoa were available, and talks had begun with the County Council about a canteen. They were still talking in 1946. There were no facilities for drying clothes: lack of ventilation kept the room fairly warm in winter but high-summer temperatures sometimes proved problematic. The main room, used for two widely differing age classes, was only divided by a curtain. Light too was a problem. In December 1934 'the lamps were lit until 10a.m.', but even then the light was not good. Work had to stop at 3p.m., as the children could not see. However, help was at hand and in September 1936 the head wrote, 'electric light installed'.

There was no land for gardening near the British School; instead a triangle of land was used at Chapner Cross. Here the boys (only the boys gardened) had their plots and grew flowers and vegetables from seeds supplied by Trumps or Toogoods. Income and expenditure accounts were kept, and the County Council provided tools, a wheelbarrow, a grant for a shed, and sent from time to time their 'Inspector of Gardening'. In 1926 the inspector was full of praise, but noted that the keeping of notebooks was inadequate. The County Council eventually bought the field (which has since become the sports field) and the garden moved to a

'30 square rod plot along the Manse boundary'.

In 1934 there was a change in the status of the school. Founded in 1845 on the principles of the Independent Chapel and confirmed in 1898, the school's Deed of Arrangement, dated 27 July 1934, was transferred to Devon County Council for a period of 999 years at a yearly rent of 1s.

War cast its shadow over the school: in February 1939 a site for an air-raid shelter was selected. School opened a week late in September 1939 'due to the declaration of war'. In October seven evacuees joined the school and gas masks were distributed. On 16 June 1940 the official evacuees arrived with their teacher, Mr Gates. At a stroke the roll rose from 57 to 125, which must have put a huge strain on staff and premises. The children arrived with their names and home addresses on labels that hung around their necks and were selected by those who had offered accommodation. Many were housed in the village but a substantial number were billeted on farms. Most came from the St Augustine Road School in Belvedere under the Erith Education Authority in Kent, but a few were from Willesden and Leytonstone in North London. A few drifted home but in early 1941 a further 29 arrived from Bristol and the roll showed the remarkable total of 133. At the peak there were between 75 and 80 evacuee pupils attending, but the drift home continued, leaving 53 evacuees in 1941–42. By summer 1942 there were 30, by summer 1945 only seven, and by autumn that year only one remained.

In July 1940 an air-raid disposal place was chosen in Dr Price's shrubbery next door and the school windows were covered in net to guard against splinters of glass. The two schools agreed to remain open for alternate weeks in the summer holidays although senior children were encouraged to work on farms. By 1942 all British School pupils had been supplied with the means to withstand air raids, namely earplugs, two buckets of sand, a stirrup pump and

Fancy-dress dance in the Angel Room, 1928. Included are: Mr and Mrs G.H. Selley, Mrs Leila Bryant, Mr W.S. Selley, Florrie Reed, Constance Selley, Aubrey Hosegood.

William Pyne up the greasy pole, 1936.

three sandbags 'filled ready for use'. It was fortunate that they were never needed. The log-book reveals little about the war, except that the main problem turned out not to be the Germans or Japanese but the difficulty in getting and keeping teachers. However, the school played its full part in the various 'Savings Weeks' and 'Drives for Victory', and the D-Day landings in June 1944 were celebrated with 'an extra Geography Lesson on Northern France'. In 1946 the roll was back to 67. The head's entry for 20 December that year was the last before he died. It seems clear that Mr Ollerenshaw was a good head and a good teacher, and this is born out by the recollections of former pupils.

Evelyn Tucker went to the British School in 1923 and remembered him as 'a wonderful master – if you did wrong he would punish you, but he was fair.' She recalled that the infants had their own room, but the main room was divided by a curtain and carpentry was taught in the cloakroom. The tree and high windows kept the school dark, but the fires and the tortoise stove kept it warm. The playground was rough, but the girls managed to play marbles, skipping and rounders. Cricket and football were played in the sports field; the girls were allowed to play cricket but not football. In Evelyn's time the infants used slates until they became juniors. The two schools joined together to send pupils to cookery classes in the Church Rooms; pupils had to bring their own ingredients but took home what they cooked. Evelyn had vivid memories of the visit to the electricity station, and of the time they were allowed up to Stretchdown to see their first aeroplane, and her excitement at seeing it 'run and take off'.

Greta Parkhouse attended the school in 1934, and she remembered the head for his firmness and fairness, and that his teaching method was to encourage them to learn, rather than to drum knowledge into them. She recalled his gramophone with which he taught country dancing in the playground; school teams had some success at this in competition. The school provided cups of hot cocoa at dinner time, and those who hadn't brought anything to eat would go to the butcher's shop opposite, 17 Fore Street, and collect the pasties they'd ordered on their way to school. Alternatively they would go across to Greenslade's shop for 3d. bags of broken biscuits. There was no school uniform; the children 'all wore what they had', and some lads were still wearing heavy nailed boots, while some of the girls had long button-up or lace-up boots.

THE NATIONAL SCHOOL, 1931–65

Mr Andrews left in 1932 and there were four more heads at the National School before the merger in 1965: Charles Luxton, Jack Dryer, Bernard Johnson and Frank Sellars. There were three main themes to this period, namely the war years, the introduction of the 11+, and the proposals for amalgamation of the two Witheridge schools.

Charles Luxton's headship of two years was marked by 67 uses of the cane, a stark contrast to the regime of his predecessor. The statistic must be balanced by the fact that there were 88 on the roll when he came, and 108 when he left. He was very keen on teaching materials as these examples taken from his log-book show: 'received first aid outfit', 'woodwork tools arrived', 'science apparatus arrived', '8 volumes of the Encyclopaedia were received from Mr John Benson', 'received sewing machine'.

Witheridge British School 1933. Left to right, back row: *Gladys Cox (teacher), Dick Roberts, Gordon Ayre, Bill Darch, John Rowcliffe, Gwen Nott, Phyllis Roberts, ? Braunton, Monica Rowcliffe, Olive Vicary, Claude Rolle, ?, Cyril Perkins, Harold Parkhouse, Eileen Williams (teacher);* middle row: *Percy Rolle, Aubrey Greenslade, ?, Grace Morgan, Barbara Pickard, Phyllis Rowcliffe, Nora Lang, Stella Selley, Florrie Sowden, Evelyn Dart, Clifford Bristow, Wallace Ayre, Bimbo Leach;* sitting: *Bernard Whittock, Percy Somerwill, Ron Vicary, Elsie Holloway, Vera Roberts, Joan Rowcliffe, ?, Doris Blackford, Arthur Hill, Aubrey Pike, Eddie Darch, Reg Nott.*

The wedding of Mr Andrews (head of the National School) and Miss Netty Gunn (teacher), 1930s. Eric and Stanley Selley, Cissie Bourne, Gladys Bristow, Edna Gold and Kathy Reed are also pictured.

It is to Mr Luxton's credit that he favoured co-operation between the schools. For example, when Miss Alford, in charge of the infants, was absent her place was taken by Mrs Ollerenshaw, wife of the head of the British School. Modern subjects such as Land Utilisation Surveying and Rural Sciences made their appearance and annual visits to Paignton Zoo began. Diocesan Reports were good, and HMI praised the new subjects, but asked for 'more self-reliance and free discipline for the pupils'. 'However, Mr Luxton could not wait to get away.' A fellow teacher's view was 'we didn't like Charlie Luxton, nobody did, he used to terrify us.'

Jack Dryer began as head in January 1934, with three assistant teachers and a roll of 105 pupils, which rose to 110 in 1935, then dropped to 80 in 1939. He introduced some innovations, such as taking the seniors to the river for swimming instruction, visiting Mr Selley's dairy and the Ambrosia Milk Factory at Lapford. An Aylesbeare dairy farm and the egg-laying trials at Whipton were also on the list. The school poultry section was popular and in 1939 the school won the County Challenge Cup for laying hens. A new and larger school garden was bought. The school introduced an annual 'open session' for parents and friends. In 1938 officials inspected the Church Rooms with a view to their use as a school canteen, but no canteen appeared until 1947, 40 years after it had first been suggested.

Relations between the two schools had improved over the years until the Milk Board Scheme for supplying milk to schools began in 1934. The Authority appointed Mr C. Maire (a manager of the British School) to supply milk to both schools. The National School preferred to get their milk from Mr Selley, one of their own managers. This row rumbled on for some time.

Diocesan Reports were so invariably good that they raised a flicker of doubt. Whether a 'quiet School' at assembly really showed the 'deeply reverential attitude' so often mentioned, or merely indicated that the children were quiet because they knew they would be in trouble if they weren't, is a moot point. In fact Mr Dryer's punishment book showed 136 canings between 1934 and 1939, for offences ranging from 'spitting at a man on the road' to 'cheeking the bus driver'.

In September 1938 the children were shown how to put on their gas masks, but not shown how to use them, as Mr Dryer thought they should have been. The school rented half an acre of land down Newbridge Hill from Mr Selley so that it could grow more food for victory. Probably the biggest event in the life of the school took place on 17 June 1940, when 107 evacuee children and two teachers arrived from Erith, a town five miles east of Greenwich. Many of them were billeted outside the village, and an extra school van was needed to carry a total of 90 children twice daily. In July they practised evacuating the

school by crossing the road and reaching their place of safety in a ditch in Bell Close. They could do it in two minutes. The staff of both schools combined to keep one or other of the schools open throughout the summer holidays. In September sports were held in aid of the Witheridge Spitfire Fund. By this time 32 evacuees had gone home and the roll was down to 155. The government ordered that summer time should persist through the winter, so school hours were 9.45a.m. to 12.30p.m. and 1.45p.m. to 4.00p.m. In April the school prepared to receive evacuees from Bristol, who came in October. In spite of this by January 1942 numbers were down to 137, of whom 77 were local. The log-book noted two events in June: a boy passed the County Scholarship Exam and senior boys carried hay in the churchyard to form a winter store for the school rabbits.

There was little in the log-book for 1943, except a visit from a former pupil (Mrs Burgess, née Mansfield), secretary to the County Bee-keepers Association, to present the school with a nucleus of bees, with which they quickly won the county bee-keeping competition. By 1944 the roll had sunk to 91, of whom only 21 were evacuees. In December the wire-netting air-raid defences were removed from the windows and arrangements were made to bring hot dinners to the children. In 1945 Victory in Europe Day brought the school a two-day holiday, but Victory in Japan Day seems to have passed unnoticed. The following year visits to Ambrosia started again and the school was again successful in the bee-keeping competition.

Early 1947 brought some of the severest weather in living memory to Witheridge, and although school was only closed for a few days, school buses did not run from 27 January to early March. At one time coal and coke ran out so the stoves had to run on wood and coal dust until supplies arrived. In July the school was again second in the bee-keeping competition and the junior team came equal first with Burlescombe in their class. In the same year Mr Dryer retired. A former pupil, Leslie Bourne, remembered him as hard but fair, a man 'who put discipline back into the school'. Ray Grant recalled his quick temper, and that he used to say to a boy 'come back to me in an hour's time when I've cooled down and I'll cane you then.' He had brought in new ideas such as houses, teams, captains and prefects. He extended the school's sports to rugby, cricket, ball catching and beanbags. In woodwork the boys made wooden stools, for which the girls wove seats with strips of material. The finished product was displayed at the Flower Show and sold to the public by boys who went around the village on Saturday mornings.

When Bernard Johnson became head in 1947 there were 75 pupils on the roll. After his first 12 months 30 pupils aged 11–14 were transferred to Chulmleigh School as the 11+ selection system had begun. The school became a two-teacher school and Mrs Churchill retired in 1949 after more than 20 years teaching. Mr Johnson was only in post for three years, but he at last saw the 'School Dining Centre' opened in the Church Rooms after so many years of trying. It was very popular and nearly all the children had their dinners there, walking up from school in a crocodile of twos, each pair holding hands. The playground saw its fair share of chipped teeth, grazed knees and cut foreheads, but physical training was provided in the big upstairs room of the Angel Hotel. In 1950 Mr Johnson left.

In September 1950 Frank Sellars became the last head of the old National School. On average 10–15

The National School, 1948. Left to right, back row: *Shirley Phillips, Laura Cole, Dorothy Davey, Gladys Somerwill, Priscilla Somerwill, Jean Manley;* third row: *Dave Leach, Bobby Buchanan, Jennifer Churchill, Frances Bowden, Mary Payne, Miriam Reed, Bill Chapple, George Piper;* second row: *Gerald Manning, Peter Cole, Roger Vernon, ? Pearce, Ken Somerwill;* on floor: *?, John Bryant, Alan Southcott, Mervyn Kerslake, Bob Cole, George Aplin.*

The National School, 1952. Left to right, back row: *Frank Sellars (head), ?, Fred Davey, Ronald Piper, Denis Bawden, Trevor Champion, Miss Alford (teacher);* third row: *Janet Buckingham, Sally Cummings, Margaret Mills, Derek Cole, Robin Woollacott, Denis Buckingham, Fred Woollacott, Myra Buckingham, Margery Hosegood, Joy Tucker, Pearl Woollacott;* second row: *Cora and Julie Southcott, Thelma Cole, Jennifer Reed, Margery Tucker, Joyce Chapple;* front row: *Colin Baker, Ron Ayre, Andrew Sellars, Jill Hayes, Jennifer Sowden, Ken Somerwill, Mervyn Leach.*

pupils left each year, of whom a couple passed the 11+ and went on to Grammar School. Total numbers rose from 57 in 1950 to 77 in 1961. Mains water reached the school during this period, the two playgrounds were combined, there were outbreaks of measles, chickenpox and flu, and in the mid-1950s the first anti-polio injections were recorded. In 1953 Mr Sellars built his own house at the top of the village, Orford House was let, and the garden by the school was sold and a bungalow built on the site.

Mr Sellars was keen on taking the seniors to films such as 'Treasure Island', 'Tom Brown's Schooldays' and 'Ivanhoe' at the Tivoli cinema in Tiverton. Nature walks began in July 1951. Mr Maire showed 25 children around Witheridge Mill while grinding was in progress. In May 1956 29 children were taken to Barnstaple where they had 'a splendid view of the Queen and Duke from the stands in the Pannier market.' Before this in 1953 the school was closed for coronation week and village activities included 'a Television Show for the children in the Church Rooms.' Liaison with Chulmleigh School was established and the Chulmleigh head came over each year to discuss the school-leavers with Mr Sellers, and an open day at Chulmleigh was arranged for them. Also, the two Witheridge schools began to share events. In the severe winter of 1963 the school did not reopen until 28 January.

In July 1965 there was a retirement presentation to Mr Sellars in token of his 15 years as head. He was the last in a line that stretched back to 1799, for the new head, Mr J.A.H. Parnell, was head of the combined schools, which became known as The Witheridge Voluntary Primary (Controlled) School. The old building was finally vacated in April 1966, 120 years after it had been built.

THE COUNCIL SCHOOL, 1947–65

Difficult times followed the death of Mr Ollerenshaw of the British School. Over the next 18 years there were four headmasters and several periods when there was only a supply head in charge. Some continuity was provided by Miss Tattershall, who filled the post of assistant teacher for ten years. In 1947 there was a roll of 67 and 74 in 1948, but after the 11–14s started to attend Chulmleigh the roll fell to 52 in 1956, 40 in 1958 and 30 in 1963. As numbers fell, the schools co-operated more. They joined together to take groups to Chulmleigh for the Area Music Festival and for TB testing. They even shared teachers in emergencies.

After Mr Ollerenshaw there were four supply teachers in eight months, until Mr W.F. Symes became head in 1947. In December 1951 he left in order to teach at the North Molton CP School. Two supply teachers covered the next nine months, until in September 1952 Mr W.E. Deacon became head. He lasted until 1956, when Mr Baldey took over. He stayed until his replacement in 1964 by Mr J.A.H.

Parnell, who was initially a supply teacher before becoming head of the new combined school. None of the heads from 1947 to 1963 recorded much of interest in relation to teaching. The 11+ exam was always noted, together with those pupils heading for Grammar School or Secondary Modern. HMI visits are recorded, but without details.

Severe winters in 1947 and 1963 caused problems, and the school closed for periods. Buses could not run, the wc pans and water-supply froze, and colds and measles took their toll. On the plus side BBC School broadcasts were utilised and visits to Witheridge Fire Station and the church tower took place. There were annual trips to the County Show, and the seniors went to the milk factory at Lapford and Heathcoats in Tiverton. In 1950 a party made an educational visit to Plymouth by 'road, rail and steamer', as the log-book records it. In May 1956 32 children and two teachers went to the Barnstaple Pannier Market to welcome the Queen.

A feature of the period 1947–63 was the growing involvement of the County Council as Education Authority. Hardly a week went by without an official visit from people such as County Inspectors, Divisional Education Officers, the Horticulture Advisor, the Livestock Advisor, the Sanitary Inspector, the Youth Organiser, the Clerk of the Works, the psychologist, the Needlework Organiser, the nurse, the dentist, the oculist. In January 1964 three different officials on three different occasions inspected the school furniture, and each time condemned it for being riddled with woodworm.

School dinners began in 1947 and were at once popular; in 1949 a total of 54 out of 62 pupils made use of them. Other innovations took longer. As late as 1948 the County Council was still wondering whether to install flushing toilets, and the buckets were still being carried up the road for disposal.

There is no reference in the school log-book to reorganisation until 1963, when the *Tiverton Gazette* referred to the proposed amalgamation of the two schools. Meetings were held between the managers of the two schools and the decision was taken to merge the schools from 1 September, with Mr Parnell as head.

Women's Institute outing to Heathcoats factory, Tiverton.

THE COMBINED SCHOOLS

For two terms while the new school was being built, all the infants were taught in the British School and all the juniors in the National. The former remained for use by the infants and a path was constructed to connect it with the new building. Mr Parnell remembered the National School in 1965 as damp and cold, with grass growing out of the skirting boards. The toilets were across the playground and not in good shape. Mr Parnell opened the doors of a big cupboard behind the teacher's desk and found it full of rubbish, dust and cobwebs, so he shut it quickly! When he told the previous head, Mr Sellars, of this, Mr Sellars said he had done exactly the same thing 15 years previously. The schools dovetailed quite well with books, deficiencies in one being made up by the other. The Education Authority had condemned all the National School's furniture to be burnt, but it was in good enough order for the chairs to be sold for half a crown, and the desks for 5s.

After nearly 40 years of talking about reorganisation, proposals and counterproposals, there was one school in Witheridge. The old National School took on new life in the hands of Mole Valley Farmers, and in 2003 the British School serves the community as the base for the local GP practice.

THE MITRE CLUB

Outside West Street cottages, in celebration of George V's silver jubilee in 1935. The cottages were demolished in 1947.

In September 1944 John Benson gave the Mitre, Mitre Cottage, farm buildings and 29 acres of land to trustees, Revd Castlehow and Ernest Hutchings, so that they could establish a charitable trust to provide social and recreational facilities for the inhabitants of Witheridge and its immediate neighbourhood. This was the start of the process that led to the Parish Hall. The first committee consisted of:

Mr H.J.F. Partridge   Parish Council
Mr J. Woollacott   Parish Council

Mr E.J. Hutchings JP — Parish Council
Revd J.A.S. Castlehow — Parochial Church Council
Mr C. Maire — Congregational Church
Mr A.L. Knight — Methodist Church
Mr J.H. Dryer — National School
Alderman Lake JP — Council School
Mr G. Palmer — British Legion (local branch)
Mr E.J. Darch — Boy Scouts (local troop)

Mr R. Vicary — Air Training Corps
Miss Christine Selley — Girls Training Corps
Mr J. Adams — Young Farmers' Club (local)
Mr R. Cox — Farmers' Union (local)
Miss Constance Selley — Women's Institute
Miss A. Trawin — Local Nursing Association
Mr H.J. Leach — Bowling Club
Mrs Sillifant — Tennis Club

Above: *Coronation of King George VI, 1937.*
Andy Mitchell, Ruby Buchanan.

Left: *Outside the Mitre, celebrating*
George V's silver jubilee, 1935.

Above: *The Square during the coronation in 1937.*

Right: *Celebrating George V's jubilee*
with a bonfire in 1935.

MRS BETTY ALLEYNE (NÉE WAY) OF 17 FORE STREET, WITHERIDGE

Based on memories recalled on 12 May 1999.

Betty's grandfather was Samuel James Way, referred to here as James. He came to Witheridge from Morchard Bishop before 1878, when he is mentioned in the *Devon Directory* as a glazier. By 1880 he had established himself as glazier, builder and under-taker in the house at the right-hand end of the row of houses that ran from the churchyard. He had not been there long before a fire broke out in this block of buildings and completely destroyed it. James Way rebuilt the block in the style that is still seen in 2003. He made sure that his house, nearest the Vicarage wall, was designed to be as convenient a house for a builder as possible. For example, there was no garden at the back, but rather a cobbled area fronted a store, with a loft above it where coffin boards, deals and ladders were kept (the ladders were stored on special hangers so that they could be let down to the ground when needed). The workshop was on this floor too. Downstairs in the store were roofing slates, a handcart for local jobs, and a hand-turned grindstone, which the village butchers used for sharpening their knives.

Betty remembered her grandfather's white pony, Polly, was kept in the field called Upper Lime Close, now known as Parish Hall Field, where there was a shed for the cart. This field became known as James Way's Field. Fred Bowden, Percy Bowden's father, was James' mason, and one of his jobs was to turn powdered lime into putty lime by adding water to a cauldron kept at the back of the house. The resulting paste was shovelled out and sold by weight. People bought the putty lime for whitewashing their walls. James Way had another use for it. Twice a year he would mix up a certain proportion of lime and water and make his family drink it; it was said to purify the blood. Betty recalls that the flavour was horrible. Also outside was a pit for sea sand, used for mortar.

Upstairs, at the back of the house, the workshop also had two long benches, a full set of planes and other carpentry tools, and a container for glass, which would be cut by a diamond. Betty kept her father's glass-cutting diamond. Above the workshop a kind of garret ran from the back right through to the front of the house. Here paint was kept, along with wood mouldings for doors and picture frames, and the pony food. Betty recalled the enormous deal wardrobe that James made for himself and his wife.

Her grandfather was very fond of attending sales. It was his habit to wait until the end, and then buy mixed lots of what was left and bring them home. He had a special skill at mending leather pump suckers, when they became worn and no longer airtight. He was also skilled at sharpening saws. He employed Arthur Brent as a carpenter (Arthur's mother was a Cockney, with a fund of Cockney stories).

James was a great Congregational Chapel man, and ensured that his granddaughter attended not only the Chapel, but also the Chapel School (the British School) which he himself had built in 1898. His jacket usually held pocketfuls of the small white Bassett's peppermints, which he used to give to adults as well as children. James' wife was a great herbalist, and ordered goods from the Heath & Heather catalogue.

James was also the caretaker at Witheridge's waterworks for the South Molton Rural District

Above: *Anne Dryer holding Topsy. Margaret Baker is on board, with Betty Way looking over the horse's mane and Andy Mitchell on the window-sill, No. 10 The Square.*

Left: *Mrs Irene Way, Betty Way and Lance Corporal Swan of the Manchester Regiment.*

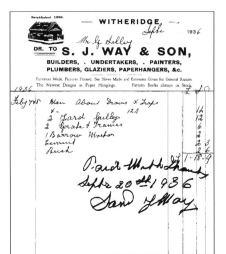

Mr Williams and his chemist's shop, which was the last chemist in the village.

Council. Twice a day he would open the trapdoor of the Witheridge Reservoir (at the corner of today's sports field by the entrance to Lakelands) and with a long stick measure the water-level. Depending on what depth he found he might have to turn off one or more of the stopcocks further down the village, so that all properties would get a share of the water. Water shortages were for very many years a feature of Witheridge life; dry summers and the introduction of baths and flushing toilets made things worse in the 1930s. Places like Ebrington's Row, Ditchetts, and Well Cottage in The Square had their own wells, but they were not enough. Eventually a source beyond Merryside towards Woodford was found and a pump installed. This was cared for by Betty's father; it filled the reservoir and the water tower at Merryside.

Betty's father, Sam Way, worked with his father. He was in the Devon Yeomanry early in the First World War but transferred to the Royal Flying Corps. On his return home he brought with him his leather and fur flying helmet, which Betty enjoyed wearing. He had been stationed on the East Coast, where he met his wife who came from Essex. After the war he worked for an estate agent in London and as a result of his ability to turn his hand to anything he was nicknamed 'Friday', from the story of Robinson Crusoe. When Betty's grandmother died, the family returned to Witheridge and the house where James still lived.

In the Second World War direction of labour was brought in, and the Way family had to leave Witheridge again. Betty's father was sent to Cirencester on essential government building work. Her mother was directed to Smiths Sectric Timers near Cheltenham to work on watches for the Admiralty. At the start of the war Betty was working for Rodney Culhene at the Village Stores and Post Office; work in a food shop was at first classed as a reserved occupation, but before long she too was directed to Smiths Sectric Timers, where she worked on instruments for Halifax bombers, such as altimeters and automatic pilot equipment.

The Ways were released from war work in 1946 and came home. Sam had his building work as well as the South Molton RDC contract for refuse collection in Witheridge. This was done by horse and cart, the waste being dumped near Witheridge Mill. Betty returned to Mrs Culhene's Village Stores and Post Office.

In the 1950s Sam died, and a move was made to Leigh House, on the corner of The Square opposite 15 West Street. It was owned by Miss Annie Trawin, who lived on the ground floor. Betty and her mother occupied the two upper floors. Water for cooking and washing had to be carried up by bucket, but there was a toilet on the first floor fed from a tank filled with rainwater piped from the roof gutters.

The following excerpt was taken from the *Mid Devon Gazette*, 19 November 1996:

A presentation was made to Mrs Betty Alleyne [Betty was married in the 1960s] *who has retired after 27 years service as clerk to Witheridge Parish Council at a coffee morning organised by the Twinning Association. Mrs Alleyne had already been presented with a clock by councillors. Peggy Miles, a former Chairman, said that the parishioners wished to acknowledge her remarkable achievement. She treated everybody with utmost*

Jack Knight's confirmation in September 1929 in the grounds of Hawley Hospital, Barnstaple.

*Outside Black Dog: Mrs Gold, Ena Clark,
Mrs Ephraim Clark, Lena Clark, Bill Gold.*

*Mr and Mrs Mansfield listening to the wireless
in the garden of Cannington Cottage.*

courtesy and had been an exemplary and loyal servant throughout her career. She had also assisted the Women's Institute, the Tennis Club, the Drama Group, the Day Centre, the Church and Choir, St John's Fair, the British Legion Poppy Appeal, Cancer Research and Twinning. Miss Miles then presented Mrs Alleyne with a cheque for £100 and a specially designed sampler. Mrs Alleyne then thanked everyone for the surprise.

WITHERIDGE CHILDREN'S CARNIVAL

Taken from the *Tiverton Gazette*, 26 July 1932.

Thursday was children's day in Witheridge when a large proportion of the 200 odd scholars of the two schools in the town held a carnival in aid of the funds of the Witheridge and Thelbridge Children's Playing Field; an appreciated amenity in the district rendered possible by the gift of £100 in memory of her father by Miss Mansfield, whose death recently evoked widespread regret. The gift was for the acquisition of the land; a grant from the Carnegie Trustees and the results of local subscription enabled the playing field to materialise.

In previous years the anniversary of the opening three years ago was celebrated by maypole displays, singing, entertainments, etc., arranged by the children. This year an innovation in the form of a carnival was introduced; the experiment proved a complete success.

Assembling in The Square, competitors were sorted out from parents, friends and spectators under the stewardship of the Committee. The truth of the statement that a carnival is essentially a children's time was shown by the animation of the host of little competitors rigged out in costumes ranging from weird and wonderful through the beautiful to the comic. Order having reasonably been obtained, a procession headed by a radiogram provided by Mr J. Knight and mounted on Mr C. Maire's car driven by Mr L. Knight marched to the Playing Field.

Among the prize-winners were:
Decorated pram: under 6, Bryan Hitchcock (Fairyland).
Walking: under 6, Jack Ayre (Old King Cole).
Nursery Rhymes: 6 to 8, Josephine Baker (Bo-Peep).
Comic Costume: 6 to 8, M. Keith (Queen of Sheba).
Floral Costume: 8 to 11, Loveday Stoneman (Summer),
   Rita Selley (Rambler Rose).
Comic: 8 to 11, Leslie Bourne (Irish Sweep).
Decorated Handcart: Billie Knight (Coster).
Comic Costume: Don Whittock (Minstrel).
Comic: Marjorie Southcott (Ruination).

On the field were numerous sports events for the children and a Punch and Judy from Bristol entertained the young audience.

*Celebrations for the coronation in 1937. Stan Ford and
George Knight before the married-men-versus-singles
football match. George scored the goal that won the game.*

Left to right: *Scouts of the 1930s: Paul Williams,
Revd Castlehow, Bill Williams and Derek Nott.*

Scouts at Mamhead in the early 1930s, including Percy Holloway, Les Bourne, Bill Williams, Percy Brewer, George Knight.

Bradford Tracy House.

Hay sweep at Leat Farm in the 1930s. Left to right: Bert Blackford, Winston Chapple, George Blackford, Bill Snow.

West Country Scout Jamboree at Bath, 1932. Left to right, back row: ?, Stanley Ford, Bill Hutchings, ?, Donald Whittock, ?, Revd Castlehow; front row: Bertie Bourne, Bill Williams, George Knight, Percy Brewer, ?.

Scouts in France, 1939. Those featured in the picture include: E. and W. Darch, Revd Castlehow, Bill Williams, Bill Dyer and Paul Williams.

Right above: Higher Queen Dart, 1926.

Right: Jim and Gladys Greenway and June at Bradford with their Morris MT 5825.

Nora and Winston Chapple at Leat Farm, 1920s.

The car, XF 6893, is probably a Bean belonging to local farmer John Reed. William Roberts is on the left, with his son, Bert, on the right in a hat.

AN ARTICLE TAKEN FROM THE SOUTH MOLTON GAZETTE

11 April 1939

Considerable interest was taken in a crooning competition, which was held at The Angel on Tuesday. The spacious ballroom resembled a radio studio during an amateurs' hour. There were several entrants who accepted the band's invitation to 'mike' a name (or noise) for themselves. A Witheridge entrant, Mr Les Bourne, came second with 'Mother Nature's Lullaby'.

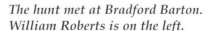

The hunt met at Bradford Barton. William Roberts is on the left.

WITHERIDGE YOUNG FARMERS' CLUB

The Early Years

The following includes extracts from the *South Molton Gazette*.

On 13 April 1933, under the heading 'Young Farmers Club for Witheridge' was a report that an advisory committee had been set up, and 16 people had said they would join the new club. Any young person aged 10–21 was eligible. The first meeting was held at the Church Rooms on 8 May, at which point leaders were appointed and 42 members enrolled.

On 25 May 1933 the Hon. Mrs Butler distributed calves to the YFC. Each member looked after a calf for 12 months, after which time the animal was judged. By this time there were 12 clubs in Devon.

On 28 September 1933 another YFC Stock Judging Competition took place:

Witheridge is to be congratulated upon the membership of its YFC, their keenness is unrivalled, as was shown on Friday when they met at West Yeo Farm, kindly placed at their disposal by Mr and Mrs Woollacott... ages range from 10 to 21... tea at West Yeo... list award winners... the Club is the largest in Devon... the event closed with cheers for Mr and Mrs Woollacott.

An inter-club social was held at the Angel Hotel on 7 November 1935. Music was provided by Mr J. Knight's radiogram and the local Rhythm Songsters Dance Band.

Archie Beer at a ploughing match.

A Young Farmers' Club visit to Avonmouth.

Ploughing match at Essebeare, 1950s.
Jack Luxton is on Ralph Tarr's Standard Fordson.

Judging mangolds at a ploughing match in the early 1950s.
Left to right: S. Hayes, J. Woollacott, a judge, J. Adams,
a judge, Stephen Selley, Toz Gibson, Harold Winter.

MR FRED RIPPON

Based on memories recalled in 2001–02.

In 1938 Fred started working at Witheridge garage. Bill Cox had taken the garage over from Doble's. He stayed through 1945, when Batten and Thorne took over. They were succeeded by Mr Humphries, followed by Mr and Mrs James.

In the 1930s the most common cars were Fords, Austins, Morrises and Standards. There was also a Hispano Suiza at Knowstone Manor and a Daimler Tourer, whose brakes Fred relined by cutting off a length of brake lining and drilling holes in it.

West Yeo had an Austin A70 in the 1960s. In the 1930s and 1940s Austin 10s were popular, and the Austin Heavy Twelve Four used to be fitted with a hay sweep and tended to boil when a load of hay blocked the air from the radiator. By 1939 two farmers owned old London Beardmore taxis.

Fred recalls Ernest Cutcliffe walking up from Coombe in his 'plus-twos' to have a whisky in the Angel with Ernie Hutchings – they were two of the few who drank whisky. Fred serviced Ernest's Triumph 2000. Sarah Cutcliffe brought her car in and worked on it herself.

Dick Cox owned a Riley, and Notts had a Bristol, which Fred believes they still have. Cedric Nott had a sports car; his father Archie had an Austin 12, followed by a Rover.

When Fred started work at the garage he told Bill Cox that he did not want to repair motor bikes, and he never did. Bill was a great wholesale/retail bicycle man – he sold three-speed Raleighs with lighting driven by the front wheel. (This sparked Fred's memories of the Ford Popular whose wiper worked off the exhaust and stopped when you went up hill.) The garage shop also sold dynamo-hub Raleighs and the cheaper Hercules. Bike accessories included bicycle clips. A few ladies' bicycles were also sold.

Among those who worked at the garage was Gibbs, who joined the Army. Bill Mann was the expert on Fordson tractors: he knew that if you had the spade-lug version you could buy curved pieces of wood to attach between the spade lugs for driving on the road, to save buying a separate set of wheels. Harvey Boundy at Rowden had one and drove it once with salt water in the tubes. Fordsons were usually driven standing up but in the 1950s the introduction of the Ferguson tractor changed all that.

Repairs of farm implements were usually done by the blacksmith. The garage had three pumps: one for paraffin and two for petrol (the tanks held 1,000 gallons). Oil was either Pratts or ROP (Russian Oil Product). The Angel Hotel had a petrol pump, Drayford Garage had two, Nomansland pub had one, as did the Gidleigh Arms, Bradfords at Black Dog, Alf Pincombe at Rackenford, Tidballs and Tom

Above: *The staghounds met in The Square, 9 September 1931.*

Above right: *Fore Street with Doble's Garage and Anstey's Court.*

Bill Rice on his OK Supreme in the 1930s.

Mr William Partridge, Mrs Elsie Partridge and Mr Herbert Partridge in the 1930s.

Pike at Three Hammers. There was also one at Thelbridge.

Bert Matthews of Rackenford had an Austin 7, until he met a milk lorry in a narrow lane and 'that was the end of the Austin 7'. On his veterinary visits Bert had the habit of starting his consultation by pointing at the sick animal and saying 'He'm going to die, Mister.' One Christmas time Bert backed his Morris 12 into a hedge and punctured the tank. He sent for Fred, who went out with his tools and a couple of gallons of petrol, to mend it. Mrs Matthews gave him tea and a pound note. Bert came back and said 'You're a ripping good chap, come in.' Bert cut a big Christmas cake in half, and gave half to Fred to take home to his wife and son (who was three months old at the time). He also gave him a pound note. Fred said, 'the missus has already paid', but Bert says 'Never mind that, that's nothing to do with me.'

In response to the cry 'Dr Morton's in the ditch again', Fred used to have to go out with the Landrover and pull him out. He remembers the time when the doctor's Triumph Herald was being repaired, he

managed to drive his hire car out of the Firs into Bill Chapple's wall and smash it up.

Some locals were reluctant to adopt the motor car, and preferred to use taxis to go to market or out on the moor to follow the hunt. For example, it was not until 1955 that West Yeo owned a car – a black Austin from Lock's of North Molton, registration number MXL 740.

Fred recalls the office in The Square being the Nott's Coombe Quarry office, occupied by Bill Vernon, before it was used by Devon General.

During the Second World War, car headlamp glasses had to be replaced by masks and low-powered bulbs and the edges of the mudguards had to be painted white. About this time most cars had no brake lights, and rules were introduced that demanded that brake-light kits had to be fitted, with precise instructions on height from the road and distance apart. Petrol was rationed, but a number of people seemed to get by without using coupons at all. Some farmers used to carry a piece of machinery in their cars in case they were stopped, so they could say their journey was essential war work. Cox, the garage proprietor, used to put a five-gallon drum of oil in his car if he was going out for social reasons. Eggs, butter and rabbits were supplied to the police station to ensure a blind eye was turned.

Originally, 'dipped lights' meant cutting out the offside headlight, but later both had to be dipped. This meant all lights had to be rewired.

One afternoon Charlie Bock at Grendon brought his rotovator to the garage for a new chain. In spite of an offer of £5 Bill Mann refused the work, as it was 5 o'clock, so Fred did the job and got the £5.

Three lorries used to bring prisoners out from Exeter to the Prison Farm every morning about 9a.m. A 'milking van' would come at 6.30a.m. with a few prisoners to do the milking. Once, near Christmas, one of the lorries stopped at the garage on its way home at 5p.m. with a blocked filter. Fred cleared the filter and off they went. A short time later there was a phone call from Withleigh where the lorry had broken down again. When Fred got there he heard carols being sung beautifully by the prisoners. The breakdowns were caused by someone putting mud in the fuel tank.

The garage shop was also a tobacconist. It sold wholesale tobacco as well as retail and Bill Cox did his round once a fortnight delivering orders and taking new ones. He went out past Bradford to the shop and the Stag at Rackenford and to the baker, Wilf Crocker. From there it was on to the Stores at Gibbet, followed by Nomansland, with Bob Drew at the Stores and Post Office, and Gordon Greenslade in the pub. Puddington Post Office was the next stop, followed by Black Dog pub and the pub at Thelbridge Cross. From there it was down to Drayford and the Stucley Arms at West Worlington. The last call was the Gidleigh Arms. In Witheridge Bill Cox supplied Churchill's bakery, Jim Buckingham's shop, the Post Office, Bill Vernon's, Percy Holloway's grocery shop, Jack Stone in the Hare and Hounds, and Bill and Ruby Buchanan in the Angel Hotel.

There was a carnival photograph of an Austin 12 Tourer, driven by Bill Cox and converted to an aeroplane, with a propeller made by Bill Gold; Fred Rippon and Ted King completed the crew. Ted King was handyman to Dr Price. If a farmer sent for Dr Price and he knew it would be down a long rough lane, Dr Price would drive his car to the start of the lane, accompanied by Ted King on horseback. Dr Price would then ride the horse down the farm lane,

make his call, ride back up, get in his car and drive home, leaving Ted to ride the horse back. Many of the longer farm lanes were rough, such as North Coombe, Malson, Wilson and Grendons.

In the 1960s the garage had a small breakdown truck and a Bedford van. Frankie Kingdom had a Ford 8, while Marie Gloyn and Mrs Culhene at the Post Office had a van and Percy Holloway had an Austin. In earlier days Whitfields the bakers in West Street had a horse and cart, driven by Frankie Kingdom, who once tipped it over at Worlington. Touts the butcher's had several vehicles. One day Frank Gowan was delivering for Touts in Puddington when the engine stopped. A phone call was made to the garage, and Fred said he would be right there and asked Frank to open the bonnet. When Fred arrived Frank still hadn't worked out how to open the bonnet.

Frank Holmes at the Gidleigh Arms kept a Morris Cowley on blocks in a shed during the winter. Each spring Fred would go up there, put its wheels on, let it down onto the ground and see that it was running. In the summer it was used about the fields, sometimes with a hay sweep fitted. In the autumn Fred would go out again, put it up on blocks and take its wheels off for the winter.

Bill Buchanan put a petrol tank and pump in the yard of the Angel Hotel to catch the bar trade after the garage had closed for the day.

In the late 1930s Cummings Bowden and Arthur Buckingham worked in the bus depot next door to the garage. In the garage was a single-post raised ramp, but no pit. There were drills and grinders, and over the office was the tyre department. Avon was the only make of tyre stocked; Avon Dualtread was the top of the range. Beside the office was the store. There was an air line out by the pumps, but it was taken in at night. To take an engine out a tripod was fixed up, or it was lifted out manually. There were no regular car services then and tyres were changed when they were bald. There was a warning picture above the bench, showing a woman and two children at a table with an empty chair; the caption read, 'that chair would have been filled if only he'd replaced his worn tyres.' Spare wheels were mounted on the running board (with a petrol can bolted on) or at the back.

When Fred was at Stag's Head, Filleigh, he sometimes saw Henry Williamson, author of *Tarka The Otter*, who was a Fortescue tenant at Shillingford. He drove an Alvis Tourer.

Hay sweeps were fitted to the fronts of cars. Mr Beer at Stourton fitted them to his two second-hand Beardmore London taxis; others favoured cars like the Austin Heavy 12. The chassis of cars were immensely strong in those days.

The village Exe Valley Electricity Company installed electricity at the garage in 1937, the same year that a vehicle ramp was put in, powered by oil and compressed air. Once, when Fred was working under a car, the ramp began jerking downwards, and it was found that the seals were leaking so they were replaced and refilled with 30 gallons of liquid.

Rivals to the garage included Bill Radford at Nomansland and the bus garage next to Cox's which did some car work. Once Cox told Fred to go down to Nott's depot to fix a lorry's gears. It was actually Frank Lawrence's job but he agreed Fred could go, tipping him off that the gearbox in question would only come off if it was put in second gear.

One day a Coombe Quarry lorry stopped outside the baker's for a loaf. Unknown to the driver Fred Davey's young son had crawled underneath, and when it moved off he was killed.

Snow & the Big Freeze, 1963

Many bought and fitted snow chains, but John Malseed, the vet, went for snow tyres. It was found that in extremely low temperatures diesel could freeze. Once Fred went out to Mr Ashelford's whose Bedford lorry's diesel tank had frozen. His solution was put a straw bale under the tank and set light to it. This worked and did no harm, as diesel on its own does not burn. Swift's lorry froze solid at Newbridge. There was very little antifreeze about then.

The roads were treacherous, but Courtney Thorne drove his Mini back from South Molton without mishap. Bill Hill of Foxdon also drove back from South Molton, but when he reached the garage at Witheridge and tried to back into the yard, he found he had no steering as the track rod was missing. Fred went out as far as Meshaw but could not find it. Eventually a Nott's lorry picked it up on Alswear Straight. How Bill Hill had steered his vehicle from Alswear to Witheridge with no track rod remained a mystery.

On a visit to Ashelford's Fred found the road blocked with snow. He drove through Hayes' fields to get round the blockage – easy because the wind had swept the fields clear of snow and they shone like mirrors.

Bill Buchanan of the Angel Hotel got his car stuck at Stretchdown. By the time he had walked down to Fred at the garage and back up again, the snow had drifted and the car was no longer visible.

The man from Morchard Bishop who brought the daily papers used to mix oil with water in his car's tank to stop it freezing.

Mr Les Bourne: 'The Start of a Journey'
No. 5621060 Bourne LG,
2nd Battalion Leics Regt
Memories of 1939–45.

Private L. Bourne in the Territorials, 1939.

Along with 22 other lads from Witheridge I joined the Territorial Army in 1938. We were signed on in the big room at the Angel, quite a few of us were just 17 so had to get our parents' agreement. I well remember Joe Churchill telling the officer who was in charge of the proceedings that it was he who was the instigator of getting us to join, and that he was entitled to half a crown for doing so. I don't know whether Joe ever got his cider money, that was half a crown for each person. From then on it was drill parades at South Molton Drill Hall, picked up in The Square each Thursday evening and taken by bus. In due course we were given a uniform – some fitted, some didn't. We had to wait quite a while for Army boots; mine were a pair of black ones, which were termed as Best Boots back then. We did get a rifle each and the usual infantry equipment, which we had to blanco and polish the brasses, which in itself was some effort, considering it was ex-1914–18.

The next big event was in August 1939 – a fortnight's camp at Corfe Castle, where we got to fire our rifles and do some infantry training, and a real must was learning how to salute officers. We all returned to work little knowing what would be coming 4 September 1939. We all got our calling up papers the Friday before the 4th, we were all told to gather in The Square on the Friday evening, where the officer in charge would make sure everyone was on parade, and our bus [on the] South Molton Drill Hall. That was one order that was not carried out. Instead we all gathered in the Angel and there we all stayed until closing time, the officer had to have bed and breakfast at the Angel and we embussed the Saturday morning. The officer's name was Lt Gregory Jones and he told us we hadn't made a very good start at obeying orders, but he couldn't have made it himself because Mrs Buchanan had a job to wake him next morning. After picking up our kit we then went on to Torrington where we were billeted but to different families. Having stayed there three weeks the whole Battalion went on to Plumer Barracks, Plymouth. That was rather a rude awakening with the first haircut, which we had to pay for, and where we started standing to attention to anyone with one stripe and above. We weren't allowed into Plymouth for three or four weeks,

133

Plumber Barracks, Plymouth, September 1939.
Left to right, back row: *E. Hartknoll, S. Orman,*
S. Cole, S. Ford, P. Chapple, A. Bourne, J. Ford,
E. Bristow, S. Cockram, C. Bristow; middle row:
F. Gibbs, A. Stenner, S. Hurst, CSM Pike, Second Lt G.
Jones, Sgt Andrews, A. Stenner, C. Coleman; front row:
A. Tucker, E. Hunt, L. Bourne, O. Mudd. There are five
pairs of brothers here – Bournes, Stenners, Fords, Hunts,
and Bristows. R. Grant and two others were in
hospital with German measles.

not reckoned to be smart enough, and when we did go that was an eye-opener for young lads from Witheridge who were keen to explore the bright lights of Union Street. We had then started getting paid 14s. a week, of which we only got 10s. We were told that 4s. had to go into a credit account to help pay for any barrack room damage there might be. Out of the 10s. we had to pay for blanco for cleaning equipment, Brasso, all soap, toothpaste, boot polish, haircuts and on top of that you were told that you were on duty 24 hours and any leave was a privilege. I don't think there were many people in this country at that time who were working just for a penny an hour, which was what the British soldier was getting.

There was a short spell at Exmouth after Plymouth and we were then sent to Seaton – just my company – it was a holiday camp turned into a POW camp for German seamen. The estuary of the river was alongside the camp and it was so cold, and then we didn't all have Army greatcoats, so the lads doing the first two hours on were lucky as they started with a dry coat, the next lot had to wear the coats the first lot had taken off. Most times they were really sodden – all part of Britain being ready for war.

After Seaton the Battalion was put on a train and the rumour was that the next stop would be France, but Dunkirk happened and we finished up at Richmond in Yorkshire. My company was sent to an aerodrome called Lindholme, where they flew Hampden bombers; we got there 2.30 in the morning and were given the best food we had had for ages. The RAF lads were glad to see us, because it meant they had someone to guard the bombers. We got to know all the air crews, saw them take off and kept the cocoa hot for when they came

back. Some never did, and the rear gunners would be shot to bits.

The next move took us down to Sussex, a place called Pett Level; invasion was on the cards, so the first job we did was to dig foxholes in the sides of the cliff, which we manned every night. By day we laid landmines along the beach. The Germans sent spotter planes over almost every day, and of course blew the mines up twice. Another move took us over to Essex, a place called Bradwell on the river Blackwater. What a dump! Another so-called invasion site. That didn't last too long because that's where the Battalion had to start sending drafts to other Regiments. We couldn't understand why we couldn't be kept together and it was only after the war that I was told the reason why. At the first reunion dinner I attended our first CO was there and he told me that there were too many lads from the same village in one unit and we had to be split up.

It was there I left the 6th Devons and joined the 4th Devons for Gib, the last place I wanted to be. That lasted for 12 months and then quite a few of us moved on to India, landing at Bombay and going to a large transit camp where we were put into different age groups, the youngest being told we were going to join the Chindits. By the way, the camp was called Doolali. I'd often heard the name used for someone who was reckoned to have had too much sun, never thought I'd ever go there. The next destination was to a jungle camp in the State of Bhopal, central India. There we were made to hand in all Khaki Drill clothing, anything white, and issued with everything green, all spit and polish obliterated, brasses painted green, boots dulled, nothing to shine at all. The training was really tough and we had to get used to dealing with mules, loading and unloading. Some of them were big South African mountain mules, kick a gnat's eye out, but we grew to respect them when the going got for real. We were under canvas, sleeping on things called charpoys, wooden frames with four legs and rope strung across. Every day our tents got turned over by a group of monkeys, eating everything in sight. No one was allowed to miss training to look after the empty tents. It was there I met Donald Southcott. He had to be flown out of Burma, having had malaria so many times.

The time came when we were sent to the different battalions that made up the Chindits. I was sent to the 2nd Battalion of the Leicestershire Regt, and from then on it was the long slog through that stinking place called Burma. Operating behind enemy lines is somewhat different than having them in front; there were no big weapons to back us up, and no tanks. My weapon was an American carbine, lighter than a rifle, a 15-round repeater. We had nowhere to sleep at night other than the trees and plenty of other things to cope with – malaria, jungle sores, dysentery, leeches, ticks and very big ants that bit like hell. When full the pack weighed 80lbs, and each had to carry five days' rations, which consisted of 15 packets of USA K rations, plus our arms, plus four mags of extra ammo for the Bren gunner (each mag held 50 rounds). When I joined the Chindits quite a few of the lads were from around the Loughborough area. I was a sergeant at the time and the first lad I spoke to wanted to know where I came from. I replied 'Devon'. He then said, 'I thought you might'. His brother had married a Devon girl from Black Dog, and was Frank Gowan's brother Stan.

There were times I wondered what we were doing in such a godforsaken place, just hoping we would make the next supply drop which landed in the trees. We got to know each other so well – some didn't make it. We had a wonderful officer, Captain May, one of the Bryant and May match family, my idea of what an officer should be.

Looking back after all these years I still think it was a bonus that I made it; many didn't. Besides being shot, malaria, jungle sores, and dysentery took their toll. I must mention that two of my schoolmates who were called up with me were killed in Burma. They were Freddie Hartnell in the King's Liverpools, and Percy Chapple in the 1st Devons. I was glad when my demob came up. Number 28 group, we came home on the SS Carthage, landing at Southampton and to Leamington Spa for demob. I had to walk home from Tiverton and something that I always remembered was meeting Mrs Tidball coming out from Higher Chapel graveyard; she gave me a hug and said, 'I'm so glad to see you have come home.' Her own two sons had been killed.

At my demob I was given £60 as my final payment after six years' service. Starting back to work for E. Hutchings was very strange, as I still had two years left to do to finish my time, before I was a full-blown carpenter, and those I had to do before I was given my certificate. My pay in 1939 had been 16s. a week, but my first week's pay for Hutchings was 32s. I was also presented with a bill for £45 for

Those killed during the Second World War 1939–45	
Walter Roy Tidball	R.A.F.
Frederick Leonard Tidball	R.A.F.
Percy Albert George Chapple	Devon Regiment
Frederick John Hartnell	Devon Regiment
Dorothy Jean Keith	A.T.S.

accumulated Income Tax on my Army pay (British gratitude for services rendered). I then decided that no way was I going to continue working for that sort of money, but was told that although I still had two years to serve I would be allowed full rate of pay.

There was no football in Witheridge at that time and I wondered where to get a game. Raymond Grant and Bim Leach were prone to having some Saturday nights in the Black Horse in Tiverton, which happened to be Tiverton Town Football Club's watering hole. The landlord was the club secretary. Ray heard him say that they could do with a good centre forward. Ray got the form and signed me on, telling me when he came to work on the Monday morning that I had the honour of being the first lad from Witheridge to play for the county.

ARP SPECIAL CONSTABLES

Mr Perce Coles was the special constable in charge of blackouts; he was described as 'lurking about to catch people'. Emily Williams was once caught showing light, and was indignant. For a long time the church was not blacked out, and evening service was held in the Church Rooms. The ARP post was at Merryside and members wore navy-blue serge coats.

Emily recalls three or four bombs in a field down towards Worlington. One German plane came down near Black Dog after a dogfight; crowds had stood watching and drove out to see it. She remembers no plane coming down at Bradford.

The Americans were in a camp at Cruwys Morchard for a time. Three times one of their transporters knocked the corner of the shop and house at the end of the cob-and-thatch row in Fore Street (since cleared when the road was widened) opposite Mill Park. On one occasion the bed hung out after

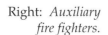

Len and Roy Tidball (above), Witheridge boys. They served as air crew (left) with Bomber Command and died in action 8 November 1942 and 26 July 1943 respectively.

Right: *Auxiliary fire fighters.*

Auxiliary fire service. In the Second World War there was a locally manned service. Alan Vernon ran errands for them, including collecting grass to make smoke for training. They practiced at Higher Park, a deserted building lent to them by Jim Woollacott. On one occasion they overdid it and the building caught fire. Fred Leach was upstairs plying the hose. Soon the fire subsided but there was no sign of Fred. He had fallen through the floor but, as he had held onto the hose and the men had continued to pump, he was soaked to the skin and none too pleased!

Home Guard non-commissioned officers, 1940.

Girls Training Corps, Church Parade, 1943. Left to right, back row: Margaret Squire, Sylvia Leach, ? Alford, Marjorie Morrish, ? Meacham, Lorna Pearce, Margaret Trick, Betty Kingdom; middle row: Nora Searle, Hilda Rowcliffe, Gwyneth Guscott, Eddie Billingshurst, Joan Rowcliffe, Betty Rolle, Olive Vicary; front row: Orpah Mills, Mrs Mitchell, Christine Selley.

Right: *Bill Darch, aged 13, delivering milk for W.S. Selley.*

Below: *Royal Army Medical Corps in The Square, c.1940.*

the impact. The Americans patronised the Angel, 'beer in one hand, whisky in the other', and the hedge banks between Witheridge and Cruwys Morchard were said to be littered with their beer bottles. One evening Emily's husband went into the Angel and was told he was late; it was inferred that the Americans' custom was preferred to his so he walked out and didn't use the Angel again for some time. Emily recalls no village girls marrying Americans, although at least three land girls married locally and settled here.

SPORTS AT WITHERIDGE, 1941

To mark the first anniversary of the coming to Witheridge of evacuee children, the two Witheridge schools combined to hold a successful sports day. Senior and junior events were held in a field lent by Mr S. Selley, while infants enjoyed games in one of the playgrounds. More than 300 children contested the several events. For the older children Mr L. Ollerenshaw (headmaster of the British School) was starter. He was assisted by Mr Gates and Miss Rowland. Mr J.H. Dryer (headmaster of the National School), Mrs Churchill and Mr Thomas combined the duties of ushers and judges. The infants were under the charge of the Misses' Hall, Alford and Howells. The afternoon ended with a display of folk dancing by senior boys and girls of both schools. Spectators joined in towards the end.

Sports Day Results, 1941

Race	First	Second	Third
Skipping, Junior Girls:	C. Martin	D. Skidmore	M. Fribbens
Skipping, Senior Girls:	J. Brent	T. Skidmore	V. ?
Relay, Junior Boys:	J. Baker B. Gladman W. Rowcliffe A. Playford	P. Squire C.Tudball F. Blackford R. Taylor	
Relay, Junior Girls:	D. Watts G. Allingham M. Cockram S. Holland	M. Fribbens B. Burnett S. Elbourne M. Urquhart	
Relay, Senior Boys:	R. Mack D. Mack G. Buggs E. Edwards	D. Williamson E. Toms R. Reed R. Petty	
Relay, Senior Girls:	M. Gearing M. Conibeer O. Boundy W. Russel	M. Grant J. Rowcliffe E. Grant M. Gloyn	
Wheelbarrow, Senior Boys:	J. Buggs & N. Cole	D. Montreath & A. Davies	R. Mack & R. Leonard
Wheelbarrow, Junior Boys:	C. Gearing & M. Hill	J. Samways & D. Grant	G. Pyne & J. Chapple
Blindfold Race:	C. Russet & E. Edwards	K. Williamson & M. Criddle	H. Rowcliffe & A. ???
Stilt Race:	J. Burnett	E. Toms	E. Howard

Hoop Relay, Junior Girls: F. Selley, E. Rowcliffe, S. Wood, R. Avery, F. Davey, P. Brasse, D. Skidmore, A. Gearing

Hoop Relay, Junior Boys: D. Bond, J. Williams, D. Grant, H. Heelas, W. Rowcliffe, J. Pearsons, H. Rowcliffe, J. Samways

Hoop Relay, Senior Girls: E. Skidmore, J. Chapman, M. Tanner, D. Hill, M. Criddle, P. Ford, J. Nott, S. Bourne

Hoop Relay, Senior Boys: R. Partridge, R. Rowcliffe, J. Burnett, F. Widdowson, W. Sullivan, R. Lewis, K. Gibbs

Tunnel Ball & Overhead Ball, Junior Girls: J. Baker, P. Baker, A. Beattie, A. Playford, T. Green, K. Smith, R. Gladman, B. Gladman

Tunnel Ball & Overhead Ball, Junior Boys: E. Clarke, E. Burt, F. Holloway, I. Vaughan, K. Pope, D. Davies, J. Miles, S. Murphy

Tunnel Ball & Overhead Ball, Senior Girls: J. Brent, S. Darch, M. Gorrod, B. Rolle, V. Montreath, S. Govier, E. Grant, I. Dart

Tunnel Ball, Senior Boys: H. Rowcliffe, R. Rowcliffe, J. Burnett, E. Howard, K. Muxworthy, R. Williamson, J. Dalladay

Overhead Ball, Senior Boys: Tie between the previous team and R. Leonard, T. Murphy, J. Davies, C. Russet, A. Cockram, L. Simkins, B. Hitchcock, E. Playford

WAR DONATIONS BY THE WITHERIDGE WOMEN'S UNIONIST ASSOCIATION

1941	Red Cross Fund	£10
1941	Auxiliary Hospitals	£10
1941	War Weapons Week	£2.5s.
1942	Red Cross Funds	£5
1943	Mrs Churchill's Aid to Russia Fund	£3
1943	Duke of Gloucester's Red Cross Fund	£5
1944	Duke of Gloucester's Red Cross Fund	£8
1945	Earl Haig's Fund	£8

WALLY SULLIVAN

Wartime memories of an evacuee.

Winston Kelland Robert Maunder died on Saturday 11 December 1999. Freda and Peter Tout telephoned me the same day, and I travelled down for his cremation on Friday 17 December 1999. Peter and Freda kindly invited me to stay the previous night, and the following day all three of us went to Exeter for the funeral. It was during my stay with them that we reminisced about the war years, during which time I lived in Witheridge. Peter and Freda presented me with a copy of Witheridge Memories *and very kindly suggested that I should add my memories to them.*

Well, I am no writer; in fact, I don't think I have ever written anything other than a few letters and reports in my life. So perhaps you will kindly keep this in mind.

Somewhere along the line I have to find a starting point such as my date of birth, where I came from, and how I arrived in Witheridge as an evacuee, and so on. Mind you, it is such a long time ago that I don't suppose many will remember me. Even so, some may, so I had better start somewhere.

Reading Witheridge Memories *awakened many of my own memories; although some of the tales and people were well before my time, or beyond my experience, some of them were not, and I remember them well. I had hoped not to be influenced by reading these accounts, but one of them did affect me very much, and I only hope the author will not mind my quoting her. The account by Margaret Gillard (née Baker) was so touching:*

Why do I have to go back? Why is it that every so often the urge comes upon me to return to Witheridge – the ugly (well maybe not) North Devon village where I was born and brought up? Something in me changes as I near the village. There is an excitement, but also a feeling of inner peace. I have the feeling of 'shedding a load'. I don't know if it is just 'escapism' – the safety I feel of returning to my childhood.

Now I know I wasn't born there, but there is always a feeling of returning to my childhood. I have to say that my years in Witheridge were very influential in my life. Much of my happiness was attributable to many of the village people of the time, but none more than Winston Maunder.

My own memories of Witheridge may not be in the right chronological order, and my memory of the geographical layout of the village may be somewhat hazy. Not the physical layout of the place, for that is as vivid as ever it was, but I may go a bit awry with some of the names of places and I may get some of the people's names wrong as well!

I was born on 2 November 1929 in Lambeth, a borough of London. My father was a professional soldier, and my mother a housewife, as most women were in those days. Not that she had much choice really, because I was the last child of a family of eight, and the eldest, my sister Mary, was 20 years older than me.

In 1939, as war was looming, the powers that be decided that all schoolchildren and all mothers with young babies should be evacuated to places of safety away from the cities that were expected to be bombed. I was approaching ten years of age, and it was decided, after much soul searching, that I should be evacuated with my school, as the teachers would be with us to keep us safe.

On Friday 1 September we all assembled at our school and were entertained at Waterloo railway station en-route for our 'place of safety', as yet unknown. It had to be kept secret apparently, because of fear that the train would be bombed. When we arrived, the teachers had postcards already written that we had to send to our families to

Witheridge war memorial.

National Service in the Devonshire Regiment, 1951.
Gordie Pyne (back left) with Fred Tanner (back right).

Left to right, back row: *Joyce Arrighi, Enid Grant, Iris Barnes;* middle of front row: *Joan Brent. Joyce, Enid and Iris were evacuees.*

Enid and Peter Yeoman – bed and breakfast at Hope House, March 2000. This was evacuee Enid's first visit to Witheridge since 1945.

The launch of Witheridge Memories *in the mid-1990s.* Left to right: *Peter and Freda Tout with John Usmar.*

inform them that we had safely arrived at Swanage, Dorset. I won't go into the details of schooling, billeting and homesickness, but it was all rather unpleasant.

It so happened that the family I was sent to with another London boy, took a shine to him, but tended to ignore me. I was not really aware of this, but I did know I was unhappy. The following Good Friday, my eldest sister and her husband came to visit me by train and returning to London the next day my sister reported my unhappiness to my parents, and with their consent promptly returned to Swanage the following Monday and took me home.

I was delighted to be home, but the snag was that the very thing I had been evacuated from, i.e. the Blitz, had started in earnest. So, with my family, I endured the bombing. Not that it was too much of an endurance, for at times I thought it was quite good fun. But there were other times when it was scary.

My father had just recently died, and the elders of the family felt they could cope better if the recently widowed mother, disabled sister and me, a small boy, could be evacuated to somewhere safe. This was virtually at the end of the Blitz, and before the V1 and V2 attacks. It was after the Germans had set fire to the City of London, and the shelter next to us had received a direct hit. That was a night! The whole sky was glowing red. We had to leave our shelter and cross the green to a reinforced ground-floor flat. This was the only time I experienced shrapnel 'pinging' around. Not that I was too worried, as I was carrying blankets, pillows and that sort of thing, and misguidedly thought I was well protected. Not so my poor family, they were older than I and realised the danger. This, I suppose, was the last straw for them, so they arranged for my mother, sister and I to be evacuated to Witheridge.

We arrived at Tiverton by train, and although to me this was an adventure, to my poor mother and sister, it must have been quite miserable. Here they were, one elderly (well, late forties – to me it seemed quite elderly!) and recently widowed, and the other disabled. Not knowing where on earth they were going, or what they were getting into.

From Tiverton we took a taxi to Stretchdown, and were welcomed by the occupant of a bungalow, a Miss Lukins. She was very kind and nice to us all, and after a very short while we all settled in.

Of course, I had to go to school in Witheridge, and I don't know how it happened, but I somehow ended up at the National School, or Church School as I think it was sometimes called, which was run by a headmaster named Mr Dryer. There was another male teacher whose name escapes me, but I seem to remember he was always smart, tall and quite good looking. A rather slim lady who wore tortoiseshell spectacles ran the infants' class, and finally there was Mrs Churchill, who played the piano for assembly, music and singing.

Meanwhile back at Stretchdown, life was becoming a little tiresome for me, as the only other boy available to play with was one named Kenneth Gibbs who lived next door. Most evenings, after school, and weather permitting, we walked back into Witheridge to play with friends. This meant during normal school days walking to school, walking back again for lunch (my mother flatly refused to allow me to take sandwiches like most children), back to school after lunch, back home again after school for tea; back to Witheridge to play, and back to the bungalow before dark. What a chore all that walking was. Still I suppose it was good for me. I can't think for the life of me why I like walking now!

Still, unknown to me, it transpired that three women and one small boy in a small bungalow was too much. I was alright, because Miss Lukins took to me and treated me well, but apparently the three women didn't quite get along. Also, unknown to me, my mother had metaphorically cried upon the shoulder of Mrs Baker at the Angel pub, and I think she took pity upon us. She very kindly offered us her cottage to rent fully furnished, which was next door to her son Leslie's black-smith's shop. The rent was, as I understand, 13s. per week, which was very good even for those days. Yet my mother had only 10s. a week widow's pension, so could not afford it. Yet again, Mrs Baker came to the rescue and offered my mum a few hours cleaning at the pub to make up the rent. Shortly after this, we three moved into the cottage. Incidentally, whenever I happened to be around Stretchdown, Miss Lukins was always very nice to me. My mother and sister never travelled to Stretchdown, and as far as I know Miss Lukins never travelled into Witheridge, so they never met again. Nevertheless, everything remained quite friendly.

Whilst at school we were allowed to do so many hours helping with agriculture. I seem to remember going potato picking when my hands became so frozen and bent that I was unable to straighten my fingers. That didn't matter really because we got paid 2s.6d. a day, and to this day I can still taste the food we were given. Especially the home-made bread and jam and the home-made cream. Cor!!

I can also remember my paper rounds and working for Mr and Mrs Kessal (I think that is how they spelled their name). Later the shop was taken over by Mrs Burr and her mother, Mrs Schooling, and I still delivered newspapers for them – after school hours, of course.

When the time arrived for me to leave school, aged 14, I went to work for Mrs Burr full time. I still dealt with newspapers, but it was not this that got me down; it was more the selling of things, especially some things. One day, whilst helping Winston Maunder do something or other, I can't remember what, he said to me 'How much do you earn working at the shop?' I remember thinking that he had a cheek asking me such a question. Nevertheless I told him that I earned a pound a week. He said 'If you would like to come and work for me I will pay you £1.10s.0d' Wow! That was a pay rise of 50 per cent, which I had never experienced before (or since). Had he offered me less, I would still have taken it. Mind you, he never knew that until years afterwards. I stayed with Winston until I returned to London. We both worked hard, had fun, and never had a cross word. I can honestly say that those years were some of the happiest of my life.

During our time in Witheridge, my brother Harry, my sister Mary and her husband, and my sister May visited us every Bank Holiday. These were lovely times, until the time came for them to return to London. However, on one of these trips, my brother Harry decided to stay on after working a short while for Mrs Culhene at the Post Office delivering post to outlying farms. For a short while he also cycled into Tiverton each day to work for Starkey, Knight & Ford, before eventually working for Bill Vernon at the bank. I don't know what he did there. Before the end of the war though, he was conscripted into the Army and served somewhere in Europe.

My mother, sister and I stayed in Witheridge until after VE day, and then returned to our home in London. I pleaded with my mother to let me stay in Witheridge, but to no avail. She understood my desire to stay, but having four sons serving in the Army abroad, plus two daughters and a son-in-law facing the V1 and V2 rockets in London, she was not about to let me out of her sight again. She had suffered enough when she let me evacuate to Swanage in 1939.

So far I have given an outline of how I came to Witheridge, where I attended school, where and with whom I worked, and when I left. I have not yet related my memories, which are many and varied and very valuable to me. They reveal what a rich and wonderful life we lived in this wartime village. In an effort to achieve some sort of order, I will start north of the village and work my way through towards Stretchdown, where it all began.

Newbridge, I think it was called, where us lads used to swim in the Little Dart. It was somewhere near here that the school I attended had some allotments. Also near here was an old barn or shed, where a mechanic from Cox's garage was rebuilding an Austin 7 and I spent every spare moment helping him do minor jobs on the car. I was probably more of a hindrance than a help, but I thought it was great.

Coming back towards the school, and next door to the playgrounds, was another school allotment where we also had rabbit hutches, lots of them, and pinned on the wall of a hut nearby were all the prize cards we had won at various shows. I well remember we bred Flemish Giants, Blue Beverans, Olde English, Dutch and Chocolate Havanas. These were all cared for by us pupils under the careful supervision of Mr Dryer. What a versatile man he was, for he also taught us bee-keeping, and we won prizes for that as well.

Next to this were the school playgrounds and the small school. What an honour it was to be given the task of cleaning out the rabbit hutches, collecting sawdust from Mr Hutchinson's sawpit, tending the bee colonies, and gardening. I know it doesn't sound like it, but it was wonderful stuff for young boys. I have often wondered if Mr Dryer realised how much we enjoyed doing these things. Perhaps he did.

Next door, and still going south, was Les Baker's blacksmith's workshop, and I spent many hours watching him at work. I expect he got fed up to the back teeth seeing me just hanging around.

Next came Mrs Baker's cottage that we occupied. It had a water tap outside the front door in the street, and it was my job to keep the cottage water-supply going by regularly filling a small milk churn. It was also my task to keep a supply of water for the outside toilet, which was down the bottom of a very large garden. In the terraced cottage next door lived Mr and Mrs Kingdom who regularly supplied us with fresh vegetables and now and again a brace of rabbits with the odd chicken from time to time. Then came Percy Bowden's tailors shop, and next to that Masters, the butchers.

Mr Masters had a Vauxhall saloon motor car with a fluted bonnet, and a van for delivering meat. Sid Ware worked for him at the time, and sometimes I would ride with him when he was delivering around various places. I used to wonder how anyone could drive in such blackout conditions, with tiny headlamps giving very little light ahead, and which, by regulation, were hooded.

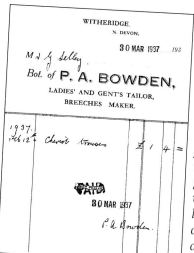

Opposite the row of buildings I have just mentioned was the church and the graveyard. The church was run by the Revd Castlehow, who was also our local Scoutmaster. From time to time he would come to the school to take a class for religion. He had two London evacuees staying with him also. One was Charles Burnett, and the other Joe Dalladay. Joe went home to London for a while, but shortly afterwards returned to the Vicarage, having lost a leg during a bombing raid. It didn't stop him playing with us mind you!

Just by the churchyard wall, and almost touching the paper shop, was a telephone box, where every evening my mother would telephone our family in London; I think it cost 2d. because it was pre-arranged that as soon as the money expired, they would phone back. I used to go with Mum sometimes, but often I would be doing something else.

Then there was the paper shop where I used to work, and next door to that was Lloyds Bank, which was managed by Bill Vernon. He was married to Olive (née Baker). Olive and Bill had two children, Alan and Roger. Alan was about my age, and on wet days I would enjoy playing in

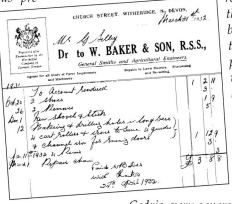

the attic of his house with his wonderful train and Meccano layout. I had never seen the like of this before. When the days were fine, the lure of playing with my friends out in the village was too great, and Alan's marvellous layout was quickly forgotten.

It was along here that Mr and Mrs Mitchell lived (I think that was their name) and they cared for Andy, who I think was Mr Mitchell's brother. He was handicapped, and would pace up and down in front of these houses nearly every day. Dear old Andy, he was such a nice fellow and I can quite picture him even now. Mrs Mitchell was a nurse, or had been I think, and she used to teach us Scouts first aid.

Also in this row of houses lived Mr Dryer and his family, and the Way family. It was to Mrs Way's house we had to go when the school dentist, who arrived in his Jaguar car from near Thelbridge, used her living-room as a surgery. I think Mrs Way had a daughter named Betty.

Back across The Square to the police house, occupied by Sergeant Palmer, and I am not too sure, but I think there was also a Special Constable name Percy Cole. Sergeant Palmer was a very big man; I was always somewhat in awe of him. On one occasion Winston Maunder allowed me to take the 12-bore shotgun to bag a brace of rabbits for my mother's table. Winston had some fields just past the school, and it meant that I had to pass the police station to get there, it was quite nerve racking with a 12-bore shotgun, dismantled lock, stock and barrel and wrapped in an old sack. If Sergeant Palmer had been outside as I cycled past, I'm sure I would have had the most guilty look about me.

I recall one occasion when he was required to deal with some of us boys in his capacity as a policeman. It happened when some of my friends and I, evacuees and locals, decided to split into two 'armies' and fight a 'war' across 'no man's land'. Using a field behind the Mitre, owned by Jack Mills, we lads in our enthusiasm to do 'battle', damaged quite a bit of Jack's hedge. The trouble was, he caught us in the act – red-handed, so to speak – and marched us down to Sergeant Palmer. He read the riot act to us, of course, and threatened us with all sorts of terrible things, but in the end told us that we all had to return to the police station later that afternoon with our savings to pay for the damage. We all returned at the appointed time, but the trouble was most of us didn't have any money, and we were too scared to mention it to our parents. However, there was one boy who did have savings, and that was Cedric Tudball.

Cedric, very generously, but tentatively, offered to pay for us all. Anything to escape prison we all thought, so we gratefully accepted his offer. It was not needed though, as both Jack Mills and Sergeant Palmer had relented and we were let off. Heaven only knows, Cedric would not have had enough in that little savings book to pay for the damage we had done. To this day I'm not quite sure if they relented because of prior arrangement, Cedric's naïve generosity, or the look of fear on our faces.

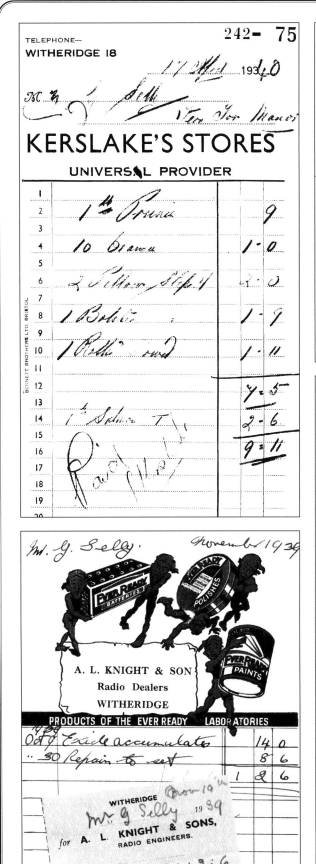

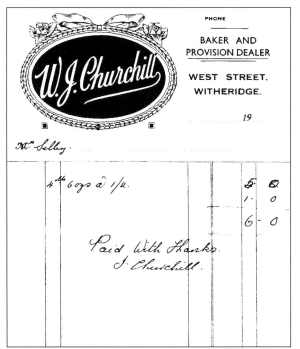

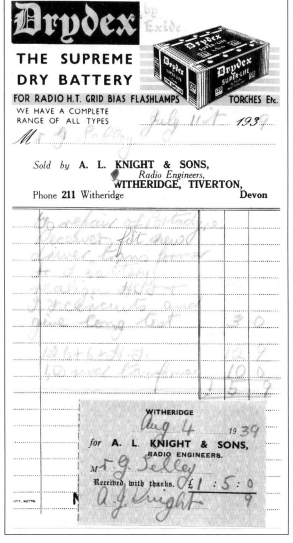

Sergeant Palmer had a daughter who was very good at tennis, and often played at the village tennis club. She was a long way above our standard.

Just behind the police station was Bill Gold's wheelwright workshop. Another craftsman I used to watch with much admiration.

Then, in the middle of The Square was the home of Mr and Mrs Joe Churchill. Joe used to maintain the church clock, did a little saddlery, and cut hair from time to time. He also drank quite a lot. One Saturday afternoon, much to my regret, I asked him to cut my hair. Joe readily agreed, and proceeded to cut my hair with what appeared to be sheep shears. He cut one side of my hair, and reaching beneath his bench, withdrew a bottle and took a couple of swigs. He then told me that he had run out of cider, and would not be long, as he was just going to get a refill. I waited for hours, until he eventually returned quite sozzled. It was not possible for him to finish cutting my hair, so I had to leave it cut just down one side. That is how it had to remain until he was sober, which I think was just before school the following Monday morning!

Finally, in The Square, was the Angel public house. This seemed to be the social centre of the village, particularly for the soldiers posted to the area. Mrs Baker was there, of course, as was her daughter Ruby Buchanan and her son Bobby (I think that was his name). Mr Buchanan, I am quite sure, was away serving with the RAF. It was to the Angel that Ralph Tarr would sometimes come on a Saturday night on horseback and tether his horse in the yard of the pub whilst he imbibed. Mind you, at the end of the evening his imbibing would prevent him mounting his horse to go home. So we lads would help Ralph up onto his horse, lead the horse out of the yard, point the beast in the right direction, and he would take Ralph home. It never failed, so far as I know. I wonder if Ralph ever knew we did that. I never thought to ask. The room above the Angel was the only room in the village big enough to hold dances. The usual thing was to have a whist drive first, then move back the tables for dancing. It was only a three-piece band, and I don't seem to remember much about it, as I was a bit of a wallflower when it came to dancing. But I do remember that one of the village bakers, Frank Kingdom I think, played the drums.

Talking of bakers brings to mind Churchill's bakery, just downhill from Partridge's shoe shop. My mother used to get me to take our Sunday lunch around for him to bake, and when I returned later to collect the cooked lunch, it smelled so good, I could have eaten it on the way home.

Near this bakery lived the Fords. I remember Peggy Ford and I seem to remember that a Czechoslovakian soldier stayed there, or was visiting there. He was the chauffeur to the exiled Czech President Benes. I also think that Stella Bourne lived somewhere near here.

Follow me back to Partridge's shoe shop. We lads used to call him 'Sprigwalloper', but not to his face of course. We used to sing a little ditty about him:

Come to the Anniversary
Hear old Sprigwallop si-ing
Songs and recitations,
Come and jo-in in.

I can't write the music I'm afraid, but I could still sing it for you, if you wanted.

By the side of Partridge's shop was a lane that took you past a small hall, where we sometimes held whist drives, and regularly held our Scout meetings under the ever-watchful eye of our Scout leader, the Revd Castlehow. Just a little further down, and on the right, lived Percy Bowden the tailor, and just a little further still were some cottages that caught fire once, and where Winston and I climbed through a downstairs window and handed to people outside furniture and other things that it was possible to save. There was fear at the time that sparks from the fire would pass over Churchill's bakery and set fire to cottages in that road. I don't think it happened though.

Going further down the lane we come to a terraced row of cottages at the bottom. I have forgotten the name of them, but the first cottage was occupied by Mr and Mrs Leach and their daughters Sylvia and Sheila. Sylvia was a bit older than me, but Sheila was about my age, and one of my peers. Further along the row of cottages was [a cottage] that was occupied by the Chapple family; one of their sons was killed during the war whilst serving in the Army.

Past the front of these cottages you came to a footpath and if you turned left and walked up the hill, it brought you out to the road at the side of the Post Office and general store run by Mrs Culhene. Just a little further to the left was the electrical and radio shop, I think it was called Knight's. Mrs Culhene, an unusual name I always thought, reminds me always of the 'Savings Weeks' we held during the war, and it was through her kind offices that we were allowed to display the model aircraft we had made. It was mainly Alan Vernon and I that made these models, I think. We always had them suspended on threads of cotton in such a way that it appeared that the enemy aircraft were being shot down by our allied aircraft. It seemed the right thing to do somehow.

Further along on the right lived Mrs Tudball, the midwife, and her son Cedric. He was definitely one of

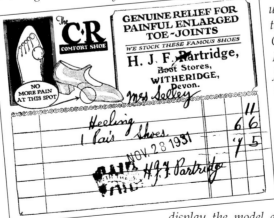

my friends, but always seemed to be getting me into trouble. Not for anything that he did, for he never really did any wrong. It was more what he said. He always seemed to say the wrong thing to adults, when I was with him, and sometimes they were not too pleased.

Opposite was the chemist's shop, but I cannot recall the name of the chemist.

Just a little further along was the Selley dairy and farm. I can remember Mr and Mrs Selley very well, as I do Rita, Freda and Stan, but I cannot easily recall Eric or Thelma. I knew them though.

Further along, and still on the same side of the road was Kerslake's shop. Mr Kerslake always seemed to be standing at the front door of his shop wearing hobnail boots, leather leggings, and corduroy breeches.

Almost opposite was Kingdom's bakery as I recall, and I think this area is called Trafalgar Square. I'm not too sure about this. I do know that Mr and Mrs Tidball lived in The Square. Mr Tidball ran Greenslade's Tours and Bus Company in the village. They had twin sons. Both of them, I think, were bomber pilots and they were both killed during the war within a very short time of each other. Poor Mr and Mrs Tidball, I can still picture her going regularly to the chapel cemetery near the bus garage.

Also in Trafalgar Square was a Mrs Monteith and her son Douglas. He was about my age and one of my friends. As we were leaving to go home at the end of the war, he and I took, what we thought at the time to be a solemn oath: that wherever we happened to be we would keep in touch and meet now and again. We haven't seen hide or hair of each other since.

Take the left-hand fork in the road from Trafalgar Square towards Rackenford, and on the right was Winston Maunder's farm and dairy. This is where I worked for Winston, and there are countless memories that I could recall from there. However I will not bore you with them, except to say that I often call them to mind. Incidentally I should mention Mrs Olive Sillifant. She was Winston's part-time housekeeper, and jolly good fun she was too. I think her husband was a carpenter who worked for the village builder, a Mr Hutchings. I am quite sure they came from Croydon, Surrey, as I seem to remember visiting her and her husband after the war.

Coming back towards Trafalgar Square, and turning left into a lane just before Winston's farm and dairy, was where the Pyne family lived. Now I don't remember Mr and Mrs Pyne, but I certainly remember Gordon and Kathy, both about my age, and good friends too. Further along this lane lived the Vanstones.

If you came out of the lane and turned left you came to Hutchings builders yard. It was from there, in the sawdust pit under the circular saw, we collected sawdust required for cleaning out the school rabbit hutches. One day, Raymond Reed and I were deputed for this very task, and silly as it may seem now, Raymond and I were throwing sawdust at each other, whilst in the pit under the teeth of the saw. Trying to avoid my aim, he jumped up and struck the crown of his cranium against the teeth of the saw. Well, blood seemed to be everywhere, and in sheer panic, I placed him into the wheelbarrow we were using to collect the sawdust, and took him all the way back to our school to Mr Dryer. He was quite conscious mind you, and did not seem at all worried about the situation. I was though. It would, of course, have been much simpler had I taken him to Dr Price's surgery, which was much nearer than our school, but I didn't think of that. Still it didn't matter as Mr Dryer took charge, and Raymond got better. Unfortunately for Raymond, he had his head swathed in bandages for some time afterwards.

Ivan Vanstone and Bolster outside Bow Cottage, 1950s.

Further along on the right-hand side of the road was Greenslade's store, nothing to do with Greenslade's Tours I believe, but it was at this very point that the road was at its narrowest. I don't suppose when the building was erected it was ever envisaged that such huge beasts of the road as military tank transporters would pass this way, but during the war they did. Well I think I can say with all honesty that every time one of these vehicles went past, a large part of the shop went with it. Being made of cob it seemed to come down quite easily, but as I understand it, it was also repaired quite easily too. So that was alright I suppose.

Then came Cox's garage which was run by Mr and Mrs Cox. They were always very nice to me when I delivered their daily newspapers. They were even nice when I collected the money at the end of each week.

Almost opposite was Dr Price's surgery. Mrs Price was a Roman Catholic and used to take my mother and me, on the odd occasion that petrol rationing permitted, to Tiverton or South Molton to Sunday Mass. I have often wondered if, the frequent times Dr Price did his rounds on horseback, whether this was designed specifically for this purpose. Dr Price treated me on two occasions that I recall. Once when I broke my nose playing tennis, and the other, when I cut my ankle with an axe at Scout camp. I should never admit this I know, but it was quite ironic that only the day before I had won my woodcutter badge before the Revd Castlehow!

Pass the Chapel and its graveyard as well as the lane leading to the tennis and bowling club, and keep going up the hill towards Stretchdown. On the right was a row of council-houses. Behind them was the recreation ground. It was not a very well equipped ground as I recall, but I do remember playing football there with Winston Maunder and others. He was no mean footballer either. I can also remember helping Stan Selley to clear a patch of ground for a cricket pitch. We hoped it would be good enough to play upon, but it wasn't really. Even if you bowled a good line and length, which was rare, the ball still seemed to have a mind of its own, and seemed to go anywhere. Still we had lots of fun.

I seem to remember that somewhere near here was a post of the Royal Observer Corps. This was manned by Sergeant Palmer and others, and they used to allow me to attend the post as a 'visitor' and watch them at work. I was good at aircraft recognition, which I learned as a member of the local Air Training Corps. I could recognise aircraft almost immediately, and I suppose the ROC members appreciated that.

Just a little further towards Stretchdown there was a triangle in the middle of the forked roads, and I think there used to be a blacksmiths there. Well, my memory of that place is linked to a field just across the Tiverton road. I was returning to Witheridge from the direction of Thelbridge. I was on my bike having just delivered some milk. It was broad daylight, and overhead was a light military aircraft, possibly an Auster or a Westland Lysander (the latter, I think). It was gradually descending towards this field with its engine coughing and spluttering, and before I realised what was happening, it crashed into the field. Nobody else was about so I dashed across to the site of the crash. The aircraft was about in the middle of the field and was tipped onto its nose. This had caused the propeller and engine cowling to be bent out of shape, and as I arrived the pilot climbed out of the cockpit. I knew enough about the insignia of the military to know that this was an Army officer. He asked me if I was British, and then asked, 'Can you be trusted?' 'Yes Sir' I said, full of pride. He then told me that he was on a top-secret mission, and would I look after the aircraft while he made a top secret and urgent telephone call. Well, talk about Dick Barton, I was as proud as a louse, and readily agreed. I was so vigilant; I don't suppose a fly could have got near that aircraft without me noticing. Upon his return he said, 'Well done lad. Thank you', and I left. Shortly afterwards an aircraft transporter arrived and took it way. It was neither top secret nor urgent, of course, but I thought it was at the time. I daresay he had a good laugh when he returned to the officers' mess.

There you are then; my memories of my years in Witheridge. My years there and the memories I have stirred up are very precious to me still, and will never be forgotten. I particularly remember Winston Maunder, my employer, my mentor, and above all my friend.

Please forgive my rambling on so, but in a way it just goes to show the effect Witheridge had upon me. My time in Witheridge was during my formative years, for which I shall be eternally grateful.

I have often thought how nice it would be to have a reunion; a wind-back-the-clock type of reunion, where it would be possible to meet old friends and chat for days. But I suppose that will have to wait until we are all 'evacuated' to a 'place of safety' in the sky. As Vera Lynn used to sing during the war, 'We'll meet again...'

An Article Taken from the South Molton Gazette

31 August 1945
Witheridge was gaily bedecked with flags for VJ Day. A United Service was held in The Square. Fireworks were discharged and sumptuous teas were provided. Sports were held in a field kindly lent by Mr A. Tucker. A dance raised £8 for the Welcome Home Fund. For the free Victory tea for the whole parish all provisions were given. The profit on the two days events was £55.5s.7d.

An Article Taken from the Tiverton Gazette

22 February 1955
Death-watch beetle in belfry timbers. Witheridge discovery by workmen dismantling bells.
Ravages of the death-watch beetle in the belfry flooring timbers of Witheridge Parish Church were revealed when workmen, who yesterday completed the dismantling of the peal of eight bells, had to enlarge a trapdoor. The discovery was made when Mr J. Walker, a bell-hanger employed by the well-known firm of Taylors of Loughborough, began to cut a hole in the belfry flooring to lower the bells through to the floor of the church below.

As the hole was enlarged Mr Walker, assisted by Mr Jack Leach, of 10 Pullens Row, Witheridge, found that the timbers of two of the joists supporting the floor crumbled to dust at a touch. They reported the matter to the Vicar (the Revd J.A.S. Castlehow) who immediately inspected the decayed woodwork.

'No one can say what has been holding the beams up', Mr Walker told a Gazette reporter. 'The ringers have been certainly risking their necks'.

So, in addition to the £1,540 cost of dismantling, renovating and rehanging the bells, parishioners are now faced with a bill for repairs to the timbers. A fund,

Rehanging the church bells, 1955. Left to right: *Fred Blackford, Betty Way, Percy Bowden.*

A tea party after the rededication of the bells, 1955.
Those identified are: *Mr and Mrs R. Tapp and Gordon, Roger Vernon, Alan and Christine Vernon, Revd Castlehow, Jennifer Churchill, Josephine Manning, Mrs J. Leach, Mrs J. Woollacott, Mrs S. Way, Mrs C. Manning.*

started two years ago, for renovating the bells and renewing the framework stands at £1,100, the Vicar said.

Last of the six tons of bells to be moved was the 25cwt tenor, dated 1754. The others, four of 1754, one of 1800, and the remaining two of 1889, were taken out of their wooden framework during the week.

They are on their way to Loughborough for cleaning, the addition of new ringing fittings, and a new Ellacombe chiming apparatus. They will be away for about six months and will be rehoused in a new steel framework. The old one was so worn that no competition ringing

could be done owing to the strain on the ringers in overcoming the inertia of the bells, caused by sinking in their grooves. The bells were removed by means of block and pulley tackle to the church flooring and stacked side by side in the churchyard to await collection.

AN ARTICLE TAKEN FROM THE GAZETTE, C.1954

Snatched child from fire danger. Awards for Witheridge housewife and old age pensioner.
A Witheridge housewife and an old age pensioner were presented with awards from the Society for the Protection of Life from Fire at South Molton on Tuesday. Mrs Thelma Fincham, of 8 Pullens Row, received the Society's framed certificate and a cheque for five guineas for rescuing a 20-month old baby from a blazing house at Witheridge, and Mr Albert George Chapple, of 6 Pullens Row, a cheque for three guineas for helping to fight the fire.

Police Inspector W.G. Carpenter said that when fire broke out at about 10.30a.m. on Monday February 24th in 4 Pullens Row, Mrs Baker, the wife of the occupier, had left home to keep a dental appointment, leaving her ten-year-old daughter, Margaret, in charge of the 20-month old baby. The child was sleeping in her cot in the bedroom immediately over the kitchen, where clothes were drying on a clothes-horse in front of the fire.

During her absence Margaret visited her Aunt, who lived next door, and on returning found the kitchen full of smoke, and realised that the clothes had caught fire. She called Mrs Fincham who, joined by Mr Chapple, with commendable resourcefulness started rescue operations and made efforts to fight the fire before the arrival of the police and fire brigade.

After entering the kitchen and finding that the dense smoke and heat prevented her from reaching the staircase, Mrs Fincham obtained a ladder and entered the bedroom from outside. She reached the baby in the cot just as PC Elstone got to the bedroom up the stairs and the child was brought to safety.

Meanwhile, Mr Chapple, who is 69, had been carrying buckets of water and had kept the fire down in the kitchen. 'There is no doubt that his actions prevented a more serious fire, which was held in check until the arrival of the Fire Service', stated Inspector Carpenter.

The shop and row of cottages were knocked down in 1967 to widen Fore Street.

View from the tower.

Cypress House at Christmas.

West Street in the 1950s. Stan Hill's Austin 10 is in front of his shop. On the left is Partridge's shoe shop.

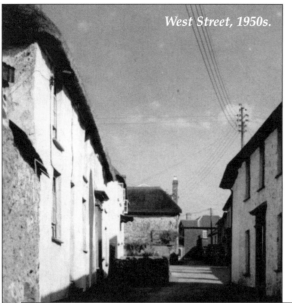

West Street, 1950s.

Above: *The garage was altered from a thatched cottage in 1931 at a cost of £50.8s.4d. To the right of the garage can be seen the wooden construction that was Gordon Keith's fish-and-chip shop. Behind the shop can be seen the thatched building which was a blacksmith's.*

Above: *Greetings card.*

Below: *Aerial view of the church and Vicarage. The original parsonage house was burnt down in the 1830s. The Benson vicars preferred to live in the Mitre, which had been built to capture the coaching and other trade brought by the 1837 turnpike, an objective that failed. The Bensons finally built a new Vicarage in the 1880s.*

Above: *The building on the left was the property of the Tiverton Roller Mills demolished in 1966 when the road was widened. It was built in 1894 as a butter factory, on a site given by Mr Maunder, of The Lawns, the house in the middle of the picture. Local names such as Elworthy, Maunder, Partridge, Selley, Smyth and Eastmond were directors. By 1897 production had reached a ton a week and a box-making machine had been installed, so butter could be dispatched in the company's own packaging. After some years the business ended, and the building became the property of Mr Charlie Maire, the miller at Witheridge Mill. The shop beside The Lawns was Percy Holloway's grocery shop.*

Chapter 6

50 YEARS OF PROGRESS

THE LAST 50 YEARS OR THEREABOUTS

In 1966 the Revd J.A.S. Castlehow died. He had been vicar of Witheridge since 1922 and had laid the foundations of Witheridge's local history, and his scholarly work covered 60 of the old foolscap pages. We are greatly indebted to him. In the late 1970s we, the authors of this volume, began to write down the memories of some of the older generation. An initial attempt at tape recording was abandoned due to persistent interjections of 'is that thing still on?' We did nothing with these memories for many years. By the mid-1980s we had begun to collect old photographs and to copy out several hundred excerpts from the *South Molton Gazette, 1857–1939.* The result of this was the publication in 1988 of *Old Witheridge.* Our collection of memories finally saw the light of day a few years later. In the year 2000 John Usmar wrote and published *80 Years of Witheridge Football Club,* and in the same year we and others put together the material for the Parish Council's *Witheridge 2000,* the photographic record of the millennium year. The final pages of this book take the form of a review of the last 50 years with an occasional look back further.

The last half of the twentieth century saw many changes. By 1950 mains water and electricity had at last been connected, and this was followed by a substantial increase in housing. The homes in Fore Street had been built just before 1939, but in 1948 the development of Butts Close began. This continued in stages, and soon incorporated the first old people's bungalows. As time went on Butts Close continued to expand up and across the top of the village.

The likelihood of tenants owning cars was at last recognised by the construction of a block of garages. Set separately in Butts Close from the main road was East Close. These included a residence for the warden.

By 1961 the population had fallen below 700, the lowest for around 200 years, but this was about to change; in the last 30 years it has risen steadily. Appletree Close took the place of Ebrington's Row, whose solid walls took a lot of knocking down. Lakelands followed, and then there was a pause before the major expansion of Brooke Road and its associated side roads. All these were given local historic names. The population soon reached 1,200. There was then a 20-year breather before 2000 when houses sprang up around the site of a long-gone farm called Broomhouse. Anstey's Court, on the old garage plot, took its name from former dwellings across the road.

The 1960s also saw the two schools come together as one, after 25 years of negotiation and over a century of rivalry.

The launch of the book Old Witheridge *in 1988. Peter and Freda Tout and John Usmar are in the centre.*

Aerial view of the village before expansion began in the 1970s.

Francis Venner reopened the school swimming-pool in the 1990s.

Cedric's tree. In memory of Cedric Tudball, who spent his early years in Witheridge and was educated at West Buckland, a tree was planted on 13 December 1997. He had been back to the village in recent years and died 15 October 1996. Left to right: Sandra Tudball (widow), Joyce Vanstone, Gordon Pyne, John Usmar (seated), Debbie Tudball (daughter), Edward Martin, Dick Alleyne. Cedric left us a story about the Scouts entitled 'After 50 years may I say sorry?':

Over these years there have been changes in the pattern of employment. There was a time when a full busload of workers would go daily to Tiverton to 'the Factory', as Heathcoats was called. Changes in farming practices have had a great influence too.

NOTES ON FARMING

In the 1950s at least 30 farms in the parish had one or more cows, and daily churns were sent to the Milk Marketing Board. The sound of the milk lorries and their rattling churns was familiar. Even dairy herds were rarely more than 30 cows. Single-suckled beef cows had to have their surplus milked by hand. Roadside milkstands varied from blocks and concrete to a few pieces of wood. In 2002 there was only one local farm selling milk. The 1950s saw builders such as the Vanstones and Hutchings kept very busy bringing shippens up to modern standards of milking hygiene. Breeds of those days were Jerseys, shorthorns, Ayrshires, Friesians, redpolls, and Devons. There was a high butterfat premium for Channel Island milk. However, dual-purpose breeds were on their way out. Many generous grants were available for hedge removal, drainage and buildings. Fields for centuries had been small, but three acres and less did not suit modern machinery. Drainage often revealed traces of old stone and alderpole systems.

Silage was still a novelty; some was made in free-standing clamps by buckrake or greencrop loader, before silage pits were introduced. Root crops were still popular. Mangolds were stored in clamps known as 'caves', and covered with straw, bracken or hedge parings or anything handy to keep the frost out. Sheep liked them and relished them even in spring. Swedes and turnips were grown. Swedes have held their own through the years, although now they are mainly grown for human consumption. Roots were labour intensive, singling and weeding being done by hand. Wheat, barley and oats were grown, and a mixture of two of these was called dredge corn.

During the summer of 1943 the Revd Castlehow left two Scouts in control of their camp at Mamhead while he took the remainder to Dawlish Warren for a swim. Unfortunately, however, a dog entered the stores tent and ate about a quarter of a large fruited slab cake that had been donated to the troop by the village baker. When disturbed, the dog ran off, leaving the crumbled remains.

The two lads, having to hide the evidence and explain the missing cake, came up with the following solution – they crumbled the remainder of the cake and tumbled the fruit and crumbs into a large jelly – they made a trifle and in doing so explained the empty cake box, and ensured that the vicar didn't know that some of the cake was missing, further to this he knew nothing of the dog, or its saliva!

The troop enjoyed the trifle and on being told the recipe, the vicar said (and I quote), 'Oh Lord – one doesn't use really rich fruitcake for trifle', whereupon Gordon Pyne and Cedric Tudball looked furtively at one another and giggled. I cannot say 'Sorry' to Jasper, but to those who ate and enjoyed our 'Dog Cake Trifle' I would apologise and at the same time wish that Gordon and myself could roll back the clock and make another one.

I have eaten and forgotten many trifles in my lifetime, but that one made in an enamel bowl I will remember, and 'to tell 'ee the truth m'dears twas a good bit of tackle'. You ask Gordie – ee'll tell 'ee!'

The 1950s saw the completion of the switch from horses to tractors. The versatile Ferguson 20 with innovative hydraulics hastened the change. A conversion kit could also be bought for the Fordson Major. Contractors and a few farmers bought the new combines, and pick-up bailers came in. Conversion of horse-drawn implements brought much work to local blacksmiths. Modern trailers began to be made in Tiverton and Exeter. Before combines all farms had a visit once or twice a year from the thresher. Threshing needed at least eight people, more if a reed comber was attached. These were drawn from nearby farms on a reciprocal basis – known as a threshing round. For example, there was one that consisted of West Yeo, Town, Dart Raffe, Lower Park, Hellinghayes and West Yeo Moor. In the morning the rick would be uncovered and work would begin. The midday meal would be provided by the farmer's wife and her daughters, and there would be plenty. Corn and weedseed would be bagged and the straw ricked, unless the reed comber was in place to ensure straight and unbroken straw for thatching. The farmer's dogs and children would be kept busy dealing with the rats and mice. Their job was made easier if the contractor had brought a roll of small mesh netting to put round the rick.

Electricity was slow to reach many farms, and several dairy farms still had to install their own power plants, such as the Lister Startermatic. Mains did not reach some before the mid-1960s. Sometimes a farm's existing water-supply did not pass muster for the Milk Marketing Board, and a dowser had to visit in order to find a purer supply.

There had been local markets at Gidleigh, Thelbridge and Witheridge, but the 1950s witnessed their demise. Marketing of livestock became more centralised and to a large extent big buyers replaced the local butcher. This period saw the start of the erection of purpose-built chicken houses, and flocks expanding from a dozen or so in every farmyard to specialised units of many thousands. Today 60,000 is not uncommon. The farmyard was the place for the Rhode Island reds, white leghorns, bantams, austrolorps and Guinea fowls – the latter were called 'gleanies' because they and other poultry were turned out to stubble fields to fatten for Christmas. Ducks, geese and turkeys were also profitable, and in general poultry was an important source of farm income.

The traditional mixed farm always had at least one pig and many cottagers used to fatten two – one to sell and one to be slaughtered for the family. Saddleback, large white and landrace were favoured.

Since 1950 the number of farm workers has declined dramatically. At one time every farm employed at least one extra person, if not two, three or more. Now there are hardly any to be seen. Much farm work is done by contractors, and very few occupants of farmhouses are dependant on their farm land. Barns and outbuildings have been converted to holiday accommodation. Some land has come under the set-aside scheme and there has been a significant rise in the number of trees being planted – not only conifers but many hardwoods as well.

The first local veterinary surgery was set up in the 1960s. Since then the premises have been expanded and the staffing levels have increased. The arrival of myxomatosis in about 1955 had a major effect. Firstly, it deprived the farmer of a useful source of income. Secondly, it reduced considerably the loss of young corn eaten by rabbits. Thirdly, it much reduced the annual damage done to hedge banks, which formerly had to be repaired every winter.

A serious blow to farming in the last 50 years was the 2001 outbreak of foot-and-mouth disease. Some farms in the parish were stricken, and it is likely that the after effects will continue to be felt for a long time.

THE GROWTH OF THE VILLAGE

In 1950 we still had two of our original pubs – the Hare and Hounds and the Angel. A Tiverton brewery kept the Angel in hand for many years, but did little for the comfort of the customers (when hiring the upstairs room in winter patrons had to be prepared for insubstantial heating and, consequently, many wore their overcoats). There was much more atmosphere in the Hare and Hounds and it was a sad day when it closed. The Mitre had been built in about 1840 to catch the passing trade brought by the then new turnpike road. Unfortunately for the Mitre, the Angel had got in first and cornered the market. About this time the original parsonage house burnt down, and the vicars preferred to live in the Mitre for 40 years until a new Vicarage was erected in the 1880s; it became a pub in the 1970s.

Soon after the Second World War Tracy Green and Venbridge Cottages were destroyed by fire, and Witheridge got its own fire brigade in 1947. Early members included Percy Brewer, Ralf Tarr, Frankie Kingdom, Stan Price, Bill Vernon, John Leach, Bill Somerwill and Stan Selley. The first fire attended was at Lower Thorne, Rackenford. The Austin fire engine towed a Coventry Climax pump. The brigade was housed in North Street behind the double glass doors. Daytime warnings were given by siren, while those that came by night were signalled by a bell that rang in every fireman's house. Fred Woollacott was at the National School in the late 1940s and remembers how the children used to rush to the windows if the siren sounded, to see the engine pass. When the siren went, John Leach would leave the horse he was shoeing in the blacksmith's next to the school and run up the road, followed by Ralf Tarr from Muxeries on his bicycle. Later new premises were built next to the school, and the firemen remain a proud feature of village life today.

The stone police house in The Square was built in the late-nineteenth century. For decades the force consisted of a sergeant and constable. Little use was made of the cells in later years; the last sergeant's wife filled them up with home-made wine! A new

Above: *Jack Stone and Nobby Clark in the Hare and Hounds. Jack was landlord and a former police sergeant.*

Right: *William Reed, landlord of the Hare and Hounds for 31 years. He then farmed Buddleswick for 38 years until his death aged 95.*

The Hare and Hounds.

The fire at the Hare and Hounds, 1995.

Above: *Sponsored knitting for the fire brigade, 1973. Left to right, back row: Kit James, Bill Gordon, Martin Champion, Terry Ford, Francis Venner, John Leach; front: Sylvia Cole, Margaret Parker, Lucy Yendell, Jill Yendell, Nora Gordon, Joyce Chapple, Maureen Champion, Joan Beer, ?, Joan Yeo.*

Right: *The fire engine in 1985. Left to right: Bill Gordon, Fred Leach, Terry Ford, Martin Champion, John Leach, Danny Leach, Ron Ayre, Merv Leach, Peter Gowan, Alan Brayley.*

Left: *John Leach dismantling the forge after it had been bought by Stoneman Brothers, 1968.*

Below: *The Square, 1950s.*

Three drivers for Greenslades, 1950s. Left to right: Alwyn Sowden, Jack Pullen, Arthur Bryant.

police house was provided near the school, but did not serve long, as reorganisation removed many local bobbies across the country.

Mr Gordon Pyne's memories begin just before the Second World War:

Before the war and rationing put a temporary closure on butchery businesses, there were a number of slaughter-men in Witheridge; among them were Sid Dart, James Hill, Cummings Bowden, Mr Bristow and Sid Ware. Not until 1954 did rationing end and slaughtering begin again at the back of Tout's the butcher's opposite the church gate. The round covered not only the parish but parts of Thelbridge as well, such as Marchweek, Woodford, and Summer.

In wartime the churchyard grass would be cut by scythe and made into hay; the rick would be on the Vicarage lawn, on a staddle or staddling of sticks and browse to keep it off the ground and dry. The Vicarage garden was renowned for its fine fruit, especially pears and Victoria plums. War encouraged rabbit keeping, and this developed into a craze for show rabbits. The Vicar kept Superfex, Percy Bowden took his Beverins to shows. At the National School were black and white Dutch rabbits and Flemish Giants, which were favoured by Arthur Bryant [these are all breeds of show rabbits]. Bee-keeping was also popular. The two fami-lies who replaced the vicar in the 1960s used to keep bees, and this enterprise led to the honey business in South Molton.

In the 1950s and '60s deliveries to the door were commonplace. Milk and eggs were taken by round by Toz Gibson, Stephen Selley and Winston Maunder. Many drank scald milk as it was cheaper and said to be better for you. If these three let their cows out at the same time The Square became not only dirty but chaotic as well. Percy Holloway delivered groceries, Touts

delivered meat, and round the farms came sellers of fish, medicines, clothes, etc.

Williams the chemist was in West Street, with big glass vessels of coloured water in the window, and the rows of brass-handled drawers.

Bill Vernon presided over the office of Nott's Quarries in The Square, until it was taken over by Devon General as a bus office. Also there was Joe Churchill in the Pound House, where he combined the skills of postman, barber, harness-maker, and cider drinker. Jack Payne at Butts Close was another barber; he also mended boots and shoes. Funerals were in the hands of Ernie Hutchings and his son Bill, until Bill Rowcliffe took over. Doug Venner ran a coach business and had two petrol pumps in the old quarry at Drayford opposite the mill. Jim Leach was in charge at Hamlin's Mill in Fore Street, and grocery shops were run by Isaac Kerslake (chairman of the British Legion), Percy Holloway and Frankie Kingdom. Witheridge Mill closed in the 1960s, Charlie Maire being the last miller.

By this time all that was left of Mr Adam's blacksmiths business in the triangle at the top of the village was a shed. George Beer had bought the black-smiths shop by the National School from Les Baker and John Leach was the last smith there.

In the early days of transport a vehicle had to do more than one job, and Arthur Bryant's lorry did just that. He'd move cattle one day and furniture the next — sometimes both on the same day.

We are grateful to Mr Pyne for his recollections.

In the 1930s Miss Benson offered the village the building known as the Mitre for use as a social centre, together with 23 acres of land. The offer was rejected, only to be offered again later and accepted.

Later still it was realised that the Mitre would not make a village hall; if only because there was no big

Unpacking for the new Parish Hall, 1964. Left to right: Graham Bristow, John Usmar, Peter Tout, Freda Knight, Freda Tout, Les Bourne.

Party in the Angel Room, 1950s. Pictured are: *Pat Winter, Christine Cole, Christine Lewis, Derek Cole, Fred Woollacott, Cora Southcott, Derek Holloway, Anne Manley, Brenda Winter, Marjorie Tucker, Janet Buckingham, Stella Cole, Roger England, Barry Rippon, John Winter, ? Rowcliffe, Una Reed, Sally and Ruby Tucker, Jean Osborne, Janet Kingdom, Gladys Leat, Margaret England, Nancy Tucker, Maria Cole, Veronica Osborne, Trudy Southcott, Ron Elston.*

Below: *The tenth anniversary of the Monday Afternoon Club, 1974. Left to right: Fred Bryant, Mrs Tom Kingdom, Betty Bryant, Mrs Bob Parkhouse, Mrs Tout, Mr and Mrs Jim Leach, Mrs Stoddard, Mr Bob Parkhouse, Mrs Charlie Crook.*

Above: *A party in the Angel Room.* Those present included: *Mr and Mrs Kerslake, Mrs F. Lawrence, Mr D. Taylor, Mrs S. Hayes, Mrs D. Williams, Mr F. Bowden, Mrs I. Mann, Mr A. Williams, Mrs Q. Woollacott, Miss R. Selley, Mrs F. Sellars, Mrs W. Maunder, Mrs W. Chapple, Mr and Mrs C. Maire, Mr B. Chapple, Mr W. Kingdom, Mr Bristow, Mrs Beer, Mr and Mrs F. Kingdom, Mrs Polly Ford, Mrs Parkhouse, Miss M. Benson, Mrs A. Bryant, Mrs A. Berry, Mrs Middleton, Miss A. Trawin, Mrs Willis, Mr W. Tidball, Miss W. Boyd, Mrs A. Hutchings, Miss L. Whitfield, Miss C. Woolway, Mrs Borden, Mrs M. Reed, Mrs Partridge, Mrs N. Beer, Mrs J. Leach, Mr J. Bryant, Mrs G. Cumes, Mrs G. Bristow.*

Presentation to Mr and Mrs Stoddard on their retirement from the Parish Council. Left to right: Bill Rowcliffe, ?, Betty Alleyne, Mr and Mrs Stoddard, Francis Venner, Les Norgrove, John Usmar, Tony Parnell.

function room. The trustees therefore sold the Mitre and all the land, with the exception of one field, known then as Way's Field, and originally as First Lime Close. The money was invested in the name of the Witheridge Parish Hall. Through the 1950s the Angel Room served as the village function room, being used for dances, plays, receptions, meetings and parties. Smaller events were held in the Church Rooms.

In the early 1960s interest in having a real parish hall began to grow, encouraged by the vicar, the Revd J.A.S. Castlehow. A committee was formed, money began to be raised, and plans were drawn up for an architect-designed building. It was soon clear that even with the grant available such a building could not be afforded. Contact was made with a firm called Devon Lady, who specialised in the modular cedar-wood system. Contracts were signed and the job was done. During this period a parish collection took place and although the response was generous, there were still a few doubters. The hall was opened in 1964 and was at once popular; soon even the doubters began to wonder how we ever managed without it.

By the 1970s it was clear that Witheridge was about to expand, so funds were raised and grants obtained and the hall was extended. A hard tennis court was an early addition, together with a storage hut, kids' play area and extended car park. Room was found for the recycling hut, where newspapers and bottles are collected. A truck calls for bulky items. The main room was and is used for meetings, badminton, short-mat bowls, drama-group productions, flower shows, fund-raising events, dances and discos – all traditional uses for a village hall.

AN ARTICLE TAKEN FROM THE TIVERTON GAZETTE, MAY 1964

*A New Parish Hall is Opened in Witheridge.
Biggest Day Since Coronation.*
A warning that the future management committee should be strong and guard against the wrong sort of

outsiders being attracted to functions there was given by Lt Col William Edds when the new Witheridge Parish Hall was opened on Monday.

Col Edds, the president of the fund-raising committee for the last eight years, said the existence of the hall was the best possible reward for those who had not only believed in it but had also been prepared to work for it. 'This effort goes back to long before I came to the village' he said. 'A parish hall of this type can be a very great asset to the community or it can be a nuisance. If it is used properly, with good administration, it can be a very great help to the young, the old and the parish in general. If on the other hand it is used to attract the wrong sort of element into the place, it could be a nuisance. One of the things we have to do is to appoint a strong committee of management who will see that the hall is used properly in the best interests of the parish and nothing else.'

The hall queen, Mrs Wendy Blackford, who raised £54, was crowned by Mrs Edds. Her attendants were Miss Rosemary Yendell (£25) and Miss Pearl Woollacott (£20). After the crowning ceremony the tape sealing the doors of the hall was cut by Mrs Blackford, and the crowd surged inside.

Guests at the opening included Mr and Mrs T.N. Allanson-Bailey and Mr and Mrs C. Allanson-Bailey (relatives of the late Mr John Benson, who gave both the ground and a substantial part of the money for the hall), Mr J. Adams (Chairman of the Parish Council), the Chairman of South Molton RDC (Mr J. Littlejohn) and his wife, and the RDC surveyor (Mr L.W. Eves and his wife).

Designed for versatility by Col Edds after consultations with the contractors, Messrs Devon Lady, the building is roomy, light and elegant, and suitable for all kinds of social events, a planned Darby and Joan Club, a table-tennis club, and even a chiropody service for pensioners. Through the entrance hall with its ancillary cloakrooms is an anteroom with bar that can be completely separated from the main refreshment counter. Behind both is generous kitchen space. With strong portable staging one end of the hall can quickly be converted for use by the local dramatic society, whose members have been among the keenest helpers.

Col Edds commented, 'It was noticeable that towards the final stages of the building we did not have to ask for help. People came along to do the decorating quite off their own bat, sometimes as early as 7a.m.'

No one was daunted by Monday's dull weather, and in any case, some forethought had provided a large marquee for the many slide shows and stalls. Outside was a children's playground with swings and slides; there were pony rides, sports, bicycle and dog races, a tug-of-war contest, clay-pigeon shoot, bingo and a grand dance.

It was indeed the parish's biggest celebration since the Coronation, but it had a practical side too. The building, its furnishings and the car park will cost in the region of £8,000, and it was hoped to start relatively free of debt. The hall stands in a field of about 2½ acres, but a portion *of the ground is to be sold. A generous surround has been retained to allow for extensions to the car park or even of the hall itself; and there is room at the back for a couple of tennis courts.*

The final accounting will be carried out during the next week or so, and a balance sheet is to be presented in about a fortnight. Anyone with views to express can attend a public meeting in about a month's time at which a management committee will be appointed and the general policy laid down.

JOHN BENSON OF FOXDON

John Benson traced his ancestry to King Edward I, who reigned from 1272 to 1307. One of the King's grandsons was Hugh de Courtenay, Second Earl of Devon. This Hugh's great-great-granddaughter, Appolonia, married Thomas Melhuish of Witheridge. Their son, Robert, married Ann Paulet, and they had a son, Thomas, who died in 1690. Thomas' grand-daughter, Grace, married a John Benson, and their son, Thomas, married Frances Melhuish, whose brother, Revd Thomas Melhuish, was vicar of Witheridge from 1745 to 1793. The Melhuishes were patrons of the living from 1643 to 1832. The first Benson vicar was John Peter (1843–76), appointed by a Melhuish descendant. The Bensons themselves became patrons, and in 1876 Mary Melhuish Benson presented Prockter Melhuish Benson. This sequence ended when in 1893 John Peter Benson was both patron and vicar. He was uncle to our John Benson.

John was born in 1877 in Dorset, the son of Revd William John Benson. He was educated at Christ's Hospital and Selwyn College, Cambridge. He attained his MA degree, but rather than take holy orders, he became a schoolmaster. In about 1906 he was taken on as a tutor to the young son of a wealthy couple, who travelled much in Europe. He held this post for eight years, and many countries were visited, including Russia. Among the rewards he received for his work was a set of Fabergé eggs, made of gold and encrusted with diamonds and other precious stones. He returned to England before the First World War, but failed the necessary medical examination for service in the Forces. He was, and remained, unmarried.

In the early 1920s he taught at Dartington Hall, and later at Canford. A legacy in 1929 allowed him to retire at the age of 52, and buy Foxdon, where he lived until the 1950s, when he had the house at the top of the village built, known then as 'Moorview'. He died here at the age of 61. His retirement had given him the chance to devote himself to his true love, namely historical studies. He was an active member of the Devonshire Association, but it was to *Devon and Cornwall Notes and Queries* that he contributed nearly 200 pieces of work from 1932 to 1959. Much of this did not touch on Witheridge; nevertheless, he added appreciably

to our knowledge of the manor, the church, and local families.

After his death a tribute to him was published, praising his scholarship, his work for students and his generosity in sharing his learning. He is still remembered today.

SHOPS

In the past half century a number of shops have closed. The Venners' garage at Drayford is no more, and the James' garage in the village closed around the turn of the twenty-first century. John Chapple's garage at the back of the Hare and Hounds has also gone. In compensation John Burd has his garage business down in the Market Field Units. Touts the butchers began in No. 19 The Square in 1949, joined much later with Spar, and ended in 1992. Boundy's boot and shoe shop on the corner below the Post Office closed in the 1960s. Perry's Dairy at Trafalgar Square under John and Millie Williams continued until the 1980s, and there are memories of Millie delivering milk around the village in an old pram. Bert Knight and his son Jack had a wireless shop in West Street, and it is said that accumulators were delivered to customers in the butcher's van. The history of the village bakery can be traced back 200 years. Raymond Reed and his son Paul follow a long line of Churchills and Whitfields in that business. The shop in West Street was a grocer's, antique shop, etc., but is no more. Across from the Church Rooms Percy Bowden, the village tailor, had his business until the 1960s, but he had no successor. The shop in Lower West Street has varied over the years between hairdressing and fish and chips. The newsagent by the churchyard fortunately continues to thrive. The blacksmith held sway where Stoneman Television is located in 2003. The National School is successfully used as the engineering division of Mole Valley Farmers, a farmers' co-operative begun in the 1960s. Down Drayford Road Romantica is a thriving wedding-gown business in 2003 and, nearby, Leach Brothers have their headquarters.

Witheridge garage.

Below: *The bowls club, including:*
Ernest Hutchings, Robert Parkhouse,
Bill Mann, Bill Geen, Bill Morrish,
A.L. Knight, Jack Leach, Andrew
Mackenzie, Henry Taylor,
Sir Douglas McNair, Frank Leach,
William Lake, Frank Lawrence, Dick
Cox, Jim Leach, Harold Parkhouse,
George Palmer, Stephen Selley,
Fred Bryant, Isaac Kerslake,
Hugh Maunder, Bert Cox,
Dai Taylor, Leslie Baker.

Above: *Opening of the*
sports club, June 2002.
Left to right: *Andre Pike,*
Chris Cole, Andrew Ayre
with son Aaron, Terry Ford,
Peter Jones, Terry Cumes,
Nora James, Andrew Ayre,
Colin Pike, Peter Blight,
Steve Wreyford,
Joey Brimacombe.

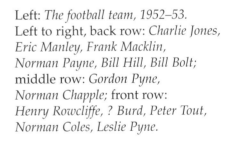

Left: *The football team, 1952–53.*
Left to right, back row: *Charlie Jones,*
Eric Manley, Frank Macklin,
Norman Payne, Bill Hill, Bill Bolt;
middle row: *Gordon Pyne,*
Norman Chapple; front row:
Henry Rowcliffe, ? Burd, Peter Tout,
Norman Coles, Leslie Pyne.

Right: *Football club fund-raising*
1950s. Left to right, back row:
Charlie Jones, Joan Arscott, Stella
Andrews, Tom Tout, Roy Manley,
Frank Macklin; middle row: *Joan*
Aplin, Mrs Greenslade, Freda Tout,
Joan Brent, Norman Coles, Margaret
Coles, Eileen Bryant, Bim Leach;
kneeling: *Pearl Coles, Ann Godfrey,*
Thelma Selley; on floor:
Jim Langabeer, Perce Somerwill,
Les Pyne, Eric Manley, Peter Tout,
Norman Payne, John Greenslade.

The Post Office and Stores, run in days past by Mrs Culhene and Miss Cannon, has a new lease of life. Up in Fore Street Frank Stoneman has a successful electrical firm. Next to the 'Rest a While' Day Centre was an insurance agency. The Day Centre was converted from five garages in 1992 and has proved very popular (comments by visitors are included at the end of this book). There are a number of self-employed people, such as electricians and undertakers; how many can be judged from the pages of *Witheridge 2000*. Perhaps one is worth special mention. A Japanese potter, Keiko Hasegawa, bought Drayford Mill in the 1980s, together with the garage site opposite. She converted the mill into a dwelling and a studio, and built a production workshop across the road. Commercial production lasted only a few years, but her personal reputation as a potter is international. She has managed to survive the floods that from time to time can be hazardous to the people of Drayford.

Until 1977 there was no sports field. Children's play was catered for in the Merryside field given by Miss Mansfield for Witheridge and Thelbridge. Footballers and cricketers had to make do with whatever was available. After the Second World War football was played in a field at Chapner and later on one of the Cannington fields. There was a cricket club in the late 1940s and out at Cobley Farm, near Three Hammers, Raymond Body started his own club. Being of an independent cast of mind, he called the club the Incorrigibles. In 1950 the two clubs combined. Many years before the war the County Council had bought the field known later as the sports field. Their purpose was to use the site for a new school, a fire station and a police house. All these things they did, and by the 1970s the rest of the field was redundant. Others saw it as a potential sports field. The County Council sought to maximise their asset by seeking residential planning permission. Led by the Parish Council, opposition was staunch and well organised, and the refusal of the Water Authority to pass it on sewage grounds won the day for Witheridge. Part of the school area was licensed to the Sports Field Committee, so that a full-size football pitch could be fitted in along the Appletree Close hedge, plus a cricket square in the middle. A building was obtained and opened as a pavilion in 1977. Hundreds of football and cricket matches have been played there. In 2002 a new pavilion was constructed by way of a huge local effort, with no assistance from the Lottery or any other grant source. It is something of which to be proud, and is home to a sports club, whose membership was made open to all, whether sports people or not.

Cricket and football have not been the only sports played in the village. Outdoor bowls thrived from the 1920s to the 1960s, with a quality green, pavilion and flagpole. There were many good bowlers, including some of county standard. However, the

land was not owned by the club and was eventually sold to create the top part of Appletree Close. Sold at the same time was the land on which the three tennis courts were located, which lay between the bowling green and the manse. One court was a touch unpredictable, but the other two had good surfaces, well kept with the help of the original pony roller. Members replaced the pony, but the pony boots remained in the shed for years. In the 1970s the bowling tradition was revived by short-mat bowls in the Parish Hall, which has proved popular and enduring. Badminton has also been enjoyed there, as well as tennis on the hard court nearby. In addition, skittles, pool and darts teams have thrived in the pubs and sports club. Stag and fox hunts and the Beagles (based at Cannington Farm) have long been part of the scene, until interrupted by foot-and-mouth disease in 2001.

Badminton in the 1960s. Left to right: *John Usmar, Winston and Phyllis Maunder, Joan Smyth, Queenie and Gordie Pyne, Angela Maunder, Stephanie Selley, Jill Follett, Pat Smyth.*

The skittles team at the Angel Hotel were league champions in 1980–81. They were also shield winners for achieving the most away wins. Left to right: *Alice Nott, Hilda Dobner, Margaret Leat, Monica Milton, Milly Williams, Joan Yeo, Janice ?, Diane Roberts, Pat Roberts.*

The Firs was built as a doctor's residence in the early 1900s and fir trees planted. The last was felled in 1999.

The Firs in Fore Street was built as a doctor's house around 1900, but when Dr Morton left in the 1970s it seemed to be the end of the village surgery. However, Dr Coffin had other ideas when he came to live at Chapner. He quickly established a surgery across the road from the Mitre, which developed into a full-scale practice. When the old British School became vacant it was acquired and turned into an excellent surgery. Next door, the Firs was made into a care home for the elderly and so enables some of the older residents to stay close to their families and in touch with the village.

POPULAR MUSIC IN WITHERIDGE

In the 1933 carnival the Witheridge Melody Makers played on a horse-drawn wagon as Gordon Reed led the horse along the processional route. The musicians were: Messrs C. Pickard, F. Hitchcock, F. Kingdom, A. Brent and F.W. Kingdom.

At the end of the 1930s music at dances was often played by the local Rhythm Songsters Band.

The Blue Birds in the Angel Room, 1956. Left to right: Cyril Blackford (button accordion), Stan Beer (double bass), Digger Ford (drums), Terry Cottrell (clarinet), Bernard Rewe (tenor sax), John Bryant (piano accordion).

The Hot Spots. Left to right: John Bryant, Terry Cottrell, Jeff Stevens, Bernard Rewe (part-time), Fred Davey, Dennis Knight.

This included Min Blackford on piano, Frank Kingdom on drums, Bill Blackford on accordion and alto sax and vocalist Joan Nott. They played traditional and modern tunes including 'The Lancers', 'The Gay Gordons', 'The Barn Dance', 'Valeta' and 'St Bernard's Waltz'.

In the 1950s dance music really took off in Witheridge. It is the memories of John Bryant that throw light on this period and the years after. About 1954 the Blue Birds were formed by Digger Ford, John Bryant and Cyril Blackford. Later they were joined by Terry Cottrell, and later still by Stan Beer. They began in Chulmleigh Town Hall but soon had other engagements including Witheridge itself. Among them were hunt balls at Winsford, Exford and Hawkridge. For transport they used Joe Churchill's car, Digger's 1938 Austin 12, and John's Austin 7 (when he reached the age of 17 and could drive). John left the Blue Birds in 1958 to complete his military service and was replaced by Peter Boax. The band continued playing into the 1970s and became the Barracuders.

In the 1960s John Bryant started the Hot Spots with Fred Davey and Jeff Stevens. Among their first engagements were sing-alongs at the Gidleigh Arms, but they soon moved on to dances, including those in the Angel Room. Terry Cottrell joined them from the Blue Birds, and they began playing for Young Farmers' dances and hunt balls, which quickly got them more widely known. Next to join was Tony Harper, a drummer from London, whose father was drummer for Ted Heath's Band. It was Tony who taught Keith Gowan the drums. Later there was Johnny Walker, singer and guitarist, and Bob Jarvis, a bass player from Sidmouth. Costs were high; in the 1960s John's accordion cost nearly £200, the public-address system was £600, and the instruments in all accounted for £1,000. Most of the money received went towards the instalments due on the equipment, and yet, when someone tipped off the Inland Revenue, they had to find six years' back tax.

The reputation of the Hot Spots grew, and soon bookings were coming from far afield. Cornwall, Dorset, Bristol, Birmingham and the Rhonda Valley were played and yet they always returned home the same night; four in the morning was not unknown. They became members of the Musicians Union and Equity, as this was a pre-condition of a club booking. Fortunately Keith Gowan's van could take six players and their gear. They could play any kind of music required for the age group. Although he had been killed in the war, Glenn Miller's style was still very popular. There were times when they played as back-up to the likes of Akker Bilk and the Searchers. Their own favourite music was rock 'n roll and Latin American – samba, cha-cha, rumba, tango. (For more on the Devon-based bands of this era, see *Oh No It's Local Rock 'n' Roll*, Halsgrove.)

In 1974 John left the Hot Spots and started Something Different with Mike Herniman on drums and Doug Parish on bass guitar. They started at the

Stag in Rackenford and were soon getting club book-ings in places such as Exeter, Exmouth and Sidmouth.

In 1978 John teamed up with Frank Cregan as the F and J Duo. Frank sang and John was on the organ. They were averaging one or two bookings a week until 1990, when an accident brought the duo to an end.

WILDLIFE

Human influence affects wildlife, so we'll start with trapping and poaching. Moles and rabbits provided sport and income; skins were pegged out on boards to dry. Rabbits also made a useful addition to family meals. In Drayford children on their way to school would check the traps, and reset them if necessary. Rabbits were also dealt with by means of a ferret, net and terrier. Some control was essential, for many winter days had to be spent in casting up hedge banks and repairing rabbit damage. The Little Dart River offered a regular harvest of trout, as well as salmon in the autumn. Lights, nets and tickling were among the methods used. It was said that at one time the whole length of the river within the parish was divided into sections by the poachers, regardless of the fishing rights of the real owners. Youngsters keen to join in were sent packing, but at least one lot found that by letting the water seep out of the sluice gate at the mill end of the leat until the leat was dry, trout and eels could be easily scooped up. Normal eel fishing was known as clatting, in which a long pole with a bunch of worms tied on the end was dipped into the river, usually when it was running high. Eels found this bait irresistible. It is good to record that, after decades of absence, otters are back in our rivers.

Badgers were threatened in the past, and may be so again. At present they thrive; there are a number of setts in the parish, of which at least one has been known for over 70 years. Foxes too have been success-ful, and seem to take more interest in the village itself than was formerly the case.

Local bird life has changed over the years. In the 1960s curlews nested at Stretchdown, and the golden plover and lapwing wintered here, but no longer. The cuckoo was a familiar sound and sight but, again, is no longer. The village swift flock has dwindled from 30 or 40 to under 20, although swallows and house-martins are still numerous. Buzzards are commonly seen, but the dipper and kingfisher can only rarely be spotted along the Little Dart, which also receives water from a number of minor streams including Adworthy Brook, Sturcombe River, Fulford Water and Hole Lake (lake is a local word for stream).

Bluebells thrive in Yeo Woods and elsewhere as do primroses. There are also orchids on Witheridge Moor. Dutch-elm disease took its toll here as else-where, but oak, ash and beech are still a major feature in the landscape. The parish has largely retained its pattern of relatively small fields, their banks topped by hedges of whitethorn, blackthorn, hazel, alder,

beech, ash and holly. Mechanical trimming may have deterred the yellowhammer and others from nesting there, but the traditional skills of hedge laying have not been forgotten. Fortunately, the old harvest of bird's wings is long past; starling wings for women's hats were once popular and the plumage of jays was once in demand by anglers.

Conifer plantations have increased in number, but mixed planting is now becoming more popular. The great pond at Bradford Tracy has silted up, but new areas of water, as at Combe, Dart Raffe and West Yeo Moor, have drawn ducks, coots, moorhens and colourful insects.

Scouts and Guides preparing to tackle the Two Moors Way in 1990. Left to right, back row: *Sarah Vincent, Rosemary Austen, Laura Vincent, ?, Richard Yabsley, Mark Prince;* front row: *Naomi Austen, Marie Burston, Rachel James, Alan Lake, Matthew James, Kevin Edwards.*

Some of the traditional public footpaths have been kept, such as across West Yeo and Adworthy's, and the Witheridge Mill leat path. There are also some newly designated paths, as at Dart Raffe. The Two Moors Way enters the parish from Thelbridge and passes through the village, using part of the Village Trail; it passes the Parish Hall, goes down almost to the river, runs up the valley and to the road at Bradford Moor Cottages on its way to Creacombe and on towards Exmoor.

WATER

Until the arrival of mains water in the late 1940s, the village was often short of water, even after a reservoir was built near Lakelands, fed by a pump in Thelbridge parish. However, at times there has been too much when the Little Dart has flooded, as those living in Drayford well know; within the last ten years a caravan was carried away down there and left impaled on the parapet of Drayford Bridge.

WEATHER

Global warming has been much in the news in recent years, and there may be some evidence in Witheridge to support the idea. The great freeze of 1947 is still

Bradford Tracy Lodge, with listed lavatory, 1990s.

Floods near Witheridge Mill, 1998.

The Little Dart River dry at Bradford Bridge in August 1976.

A helicopter brings yeast for Raymond Reed, the baker. It then took Ivan Spedutti and Ron Lewis out to their bulldozers to clear snow in 1963.

remembered: the tops of telegraph poles just visible above the snow and the Drayford wedding party that took two days to dig themselves up to the hill to Thornham Chapel for the ceremony. In 1963 snow came again with a vengeance. Roads were blocked, and when a link with the outside world was established, tractors, trailers and link boxes with their churns congregated each morning in The Square awaiting the milk lorry. The landscape took on a surreal but beautiful appearance, for the winds had cleared the snow from the fields, which therefore shone like mirrors, and the roads and ditches were piled high. Once the sheep had been dug out, they were fed hay and roots in the fields. As the years passed snow became rare, and winter frosts became less frequent. The year 1977 was a drought summer and standpipes were installed throughout the village,

adding an extra place for a neighbourly chat. There was some snow the following winter, and plastic bags were much in use for sliding down the nearest slope. From then on winters seemed to get milder, and most would hazard a guess that rainfall has increased.

WITHERIDGE SILVER JUBILEE CELEBRATIONS, 1977

The Witheridge Jubilee Committee hoped that everybody would attend to make this an occasion to remember. All children receiving presentation mugs had to have their names registered with Mrs B. Alleyne, 17 Fore Street, phone Witheridge 416.

In addition to the events outlined below, a concert by the South Molton Town Band and Church Choir was held on Thursday 2 June at 7.30p.m.

Programme of events held in celebration of the silver jubilee, 1977

Monday 6 June

Bonfire at Merryside from 7p.m.
Hot dogs and a sing-song.

Tuesday 7 June
12.45p.m.   *Children's jubilee procession. Assembly at Chapner and proceeding through the village.*
1.45p.m.   *Service at the sports ground conducted by the Revd B. Gales.*
2.00p.m.   *Opening of the new sports pavilion by Councillor David Venney.*
2.15p.m.   *Children's sports followed by stool-ball match.*
4.00p.m.   *Presentation of mugs to children at the Parish Hall.*
4.30p.m.   *Free tea for all.*
9.00p.m.–1.00a.m.   *A dance to the music of The Red Stars. All Welcome. Admission 50p. Licence applied for.*

WITHERIDGE SCENE

In 1983 the Parish Council carried out an appraisal, by means of a questionnaire to all households, in an attempt to learn more about what people wanted for the future. One of the things most commonly mentioned was a local newsletter to appear quarterly. The first issue came out in the spring of 1984, under the title 'Witheridge Scene'. The first editorial panel was Francis Venner, John Usmar, Keith Edwards, Les Norgrove, Dick and Betty Alleyne and Deidre Day. The A4 format soon gave way to something smarter, thanks to the help of Ron Clark, a printer from Oxford, who came to live in Witheridge. In 18 years it has flourished and in 2002 was produced by Ron Clark, Margaret Rutland, Nora James and Harry Anderson. The 1984 advertisements give a flavour of the local trade of the period.

THE FLOWER SHOW

For many years around the turn of the twentieth century there was a thriving Flower Show. In the 1980s a new garden club was formed, which has become successful and popular. Spring and summer shows are held, there is a programme of monthly meetings (often with a speaker) and garden visits are made. For example, the visit to Marwood Hill in summer 2002 was a particularly memorable evening. The Witheridge in Bloom Committee does a great job in planting troughs, tubs and flower-beds around the village, aided by volunteers who plant many hundreds of daffodil bulbs, including, by kind permission of Thelbridge Parish Council, the triangle at Chapner Cross.

SCHOOLS

The two schools in Witheridge came together in the 1960s with new premises, although the infants continued to use the old British School for some

time. Tony Parnell was head teacher of the combined school, followed by Claire Shelley and Andrew

The Princess Royal opened the new Romantica workshop and warehouse in Drayford Lane, November 2001. With her is Mr Mike Waddington who runs the firm with his wife Sally.

Children on their way to see the Princess Royal.

Riley. Numbers have ranged from 60 to 100, but the school continues to play a vital role in the community, which supports it well.

'REST A WHILE' DAY CENTRE

For a long time there was a terrace of thatched cottages that stood opposite the Mitre. In 1964 these collapsed and fell into the road. They were replaced by a row of garages. In 1992 far-sighted co-operation between the owner and a local group, led by Francis Venner and Frank Beer, resulted in the conversion to a Day Centre. Although basically for the elderly and handicapped, it is well used by a cross-section of the community. Visitors are always made welcome; their comments appear at the end of this book.

THE TELEPHONE

Witheridge gained a telegraph service by the 1890s, but it was not until the 1920s that the telephone was established in the village. When it came, the manual exchange was sited in the Post Office. It is said that Hugh Maunder, of Middlewick, was the source of this initiative; his number was Witheridge 2. Witheridge 1 was the exchange itself. The Witheridge Transport Company had 3; the surgery was 5, and Rodd's butcher's shop 7. As the number of phones in the village increased, so numbers expanded. The surgery today is 860205, and No. 19 The Square (once the butcher's) is 860207.

TOWN CRIER

In 1990 Miss Peggy Miles, chairman of the Parish Council, started the St John's Midsummer Fair, for which, it was decided, a town crier was required. In the summer of that year a competition was held in The Square, judged by Freda Tout and Joan Pearce; they chose Frank Housam. That afternoon Frank attended a town-crying competition in South Molton to learn his duties. One week later the village saw their first town crier, albeit in borrowed clothes.

Frank and Mary Housam in Canada, 1993.

Each crier is robed differently; Witheridge chose the green and gold of St John. By September 1991 an Exeter tailor had made the full set. In that year, the award of the best-dressed crier at Topsham was won. This led to the world championships in Shanklyn, on the Isle of Wight, where Witheridge came seventh out of 107 entries.

In 1992 Witheridge acquired the right from the Ancient and Honourable Guild of Town Criers to hold the Devon County Championships at the St John's Fair. During the 11 years that Frank has been town crier, with Mary his wife as escort, they have represented Witheridge worldwide and won trophies in Canada, Australia, the USA, etc.

In 1995 Roger Merit of Lincoln recorded the loudest cry at 106 decibels. Later that year Frank broke the record with 110.8 decibels. Later Roger regained the record with 112.4. In 1994 a coachload of supporters went to Skegness and witnessed Frank and Mary win three of the available trophies, namely 'Best Dressed', 'Conviviality' and 'Media'.

Frank has been adopted by the National Caravan Club, as parade leader and proclaimer for the British contingent at international rallies throughout the world. The 2003 rally took place in Barcelona; usually over 30 countries are involved.

WEBSITES

There are two websites that may be of interest to those people wanting to learn more about Witheridge. Genuki is the site with historical information. The Witheridge site itself covers an extensive range of topics. Subtitled 'A Gateway to the Two Moors Way', it is extremely well put together, beautifully illustrated and has picked up many awards. It has thousands of hits from this country and around the world (see www.genuki.org.uk and www.witheridge.devon.com).

THE DRAMA GROUP

Begun in 1952, the group's founder members included Freda Selley, Dorothy Weaver, Toz Gibson, Betty Way, Marion Tarbox, Charlotte Henrich, Tom Tout, Les Bourne and Betty Bourne. Their first production was *A Lady Mislaid* in the Angel Room. The stage managers were Frank Sellars and Fred Bryant, the lighting was by Bill Knight, the prompt was Hilary Powell and the music was provided by John Churchill. The *Gazette* reported that 'the first production of the new drama group delighted audiences at Witheridge.'

From then until 1964 the group presented an annual play in November. There was no stage, so each time one had to be constructed from beer crates and anything else that came to hand. Audiences were enthusiastic, led by the cheerful figure of the vicar, the Revd J.A.S. Castlehow, in the front row. Press reports by the *Gazette's* 'Argus' were largely favourable; any criticism offered was always constructive. Stalwarts of this period were: Raymond Body, Freda Knight ('Polly Prompt'), Freda Tout (producer), Denzil Ayre (stage manager), Frank and Winston Stoneman (electrics), Mary Malseed and Margaret Cox (make-up), Fred Woollacott (stage sets). Among others who helped were: Betty Way, Sylvia Boundy, Margaret Rutland, Marion and David Crane, Mr Holmes, Sir Douglas McNair, Peter Smyth, Kit James, Mrs Jordan and Geoffrey Cox.

Mary Housam makes a presentation to Peggy Miles on the tenth anniversary of St John's Fair, 2001.

The play Miranda. *Left to right: Freda Selley, Betty Way, Charlotte Hunsich, Marian Tarbox, Tom Tout, Toz Gibson, Betty Bourne, Les Bourne.*

The drama group put on Wild Goose Chase *at the Angel Room.* Left to right: *Fred Woollacott, Liz Stoneman, John Alleyne, Peter Smyth, John Williams, Pearl Woollacott, Diana Manning, John Usmar, Queenie Woollacott, Pam Follett.*

Drama group, 1965. The first play to be performed in the Parish Hall, after 11 plays in the Angel Room, was entitled The Noble Spaniard. Left to right: *Geoffrey Cox, Pearl Woollacott, Francis Beer, Margaret Rutland, Peter Smyth, Liz Morton, John Alleyne, Dawn Stephens, Fred Woollacott.*

The last play performed at the Angel Room was *The Fish* in 1963. It was the last for two reasons: one, because the room was at last refused a fire licence and, two, because the new Parish Hall opened in 1964, with greatly improved facilities and flexibility. The first play there was a costume drama, *The Noble Spaniard*. Annual plays continued into the 1980s, and after that came a range of shows such as pantomimes, plays, concerts, variety shows, etc.

Play rehearsals were held in various venues, including the Mitre, Vine Cottage, and, memorably, in the attic of the Angel Hotel, where a space of 10sq.ft was made more hazardous by the bowls on the floor, set to catch the drips from the leaking roof. Play readings took place in members' houses.

A final note: there used to be last-night parties in Vine Cottage, followed by unsteady moonlight walks down the road towards Labour in Vain.

ADDRESS ON BEHALF OF THE CHAIRMAN OF WITHERIDGE PARISH COUNCIL AT THE TWINNING CEREMONY IN CAMBREMER, FRANCE, JUNE 1978

Mr Deputy, Mr District Councillor, Mr Mayor, Chairman/Chairladies of the Twinning Committees, Ladies and Gentlemen.

I am proud to be here today representing Witheridge Parish Council on this notable occasion in the history of Witheridge and Cambremer. I bring you the heartiest good wishes from the Chairman of Witheridge Parish Council. He would dearly have loved to be present here today, and greatly regrets that it has not been possible for him to do so. I bring you also sincerest good wishes and congratulations from the whole Council.

It is perhaps, on an occasion both joyful and solemn, right to seek links between us in history, and it is true that we do not have to look far. Before I left Witheridge to come here I happened to look at names on our war memorial to those from Witheridge who died in the two world wars, wars in which our two great nations fought and suffered for our democratic ideals and for the freedom that we treasure. Some of the men whose names are on our war memorial served in the Devonshire Regiment – a Regiment whose fame is not unknown in the fields of Normandy, and whose motto 'Semper Fidelis' – 'Ever Faithful' is not the worst motto to have in our hearts and minds today.

I have pleasure in congratulating all those who have been so active on both sides of the Channel in all the work that has led to this twinning ceremony. I congratulate the officers, the chairladies, the chairmen, the secretaries, the treasurers (very important, the treasurers), the members of the committees, and all the people who have contributed to this venture by their efforts and their support – especially the people because in the last analysis this is what twinning is all about – this meeting together of people, of children, of young people, of fathers and mothers, of grandfathers, grandmothers, of people from all walks of life joining together in equality and friendship.

Twinning with Cambremer. Left to right: *M. Grandval, Mlle Francine Messague, Bill Stoddard, Fred Woollacott.*

Twinning visit to Cambremer, France, in 1978.

It is of course right that the leaders of Calvados and Devon should meet together, that our national leaders should meet together, that our nations should join together with others in the European community, that we play our part in the United Nations – how much more right it must be for us, the people, to meet each other and learn to like and respect each other – person to person, family to family – and to understand each other – how important this is now and in the future.

In conclusion, I express my gratitude to you all for the magnificent hospitality of Cambremer, and I look forward to welcoming you at the return ceremony at Witheridge.

Le Dixième Anniversaire de Jumelage a Cambremer, Mois de Mai 1988

Monsieur le Deputé, Monsieur le conseiller municipal, messieurs les maires, mesdames et messieurs, les Présidents du comité de Jumelage, Mesdames et Monsieurs.

Je suis venu comme représentant du Conseil de Witheridge pour assister au dixieme Anniversaire du Jumelage entre Cambremer et Witheridge, ce qui est un exemple de co-opération et d'union entre nos deux peuples.

Je vous apporte les salutations et les meilleurs voeux du président et vice président du Conseil Paroissial de Witheridge. Ils auraient bien vouluêtre [sic] présent ici aujourd'hui et regrettent sincerement que ce ne soite pas possible. Je vous apporte aussi les félicitations et les meilleurs voeux de tous les membres du Conseil. Nous ésperons que les sentiments d'amite et d'entente continueront pour le future.

Le dixième anniversaire est un occasion heureux pour tous nos citoyens.

Le Conseil Paroissial de Witheridge prend du plaisir a

vous présenter avec ce plateau gravé pour commemorer le dixième anniversaire du Jumelage.

CUB SCOUTS, 1973–85
Recollections of Nora James.

In 1973 Janet Symons and I started the first Cub pack in Witheridge. We were supported by a committee with Roy Cole as chairman, Mr Stoddard as treasurer and Lin Buckingham as secretary. We met in the Church Rooms and started off with about 12 boys from Witheridge, but later with boys from Rackenford, Lapford and Worlington joining, we moved to the Parish Hall. We were part of the Crediton District, which included packs from Crediton, Okehampton, North Tawton, Bow, Sandford, Chulmleigh, Chagford and Tedburn St Mary. These were our opponents when we held Football, Athletics and Fun Days, a Swimming Gala, quizzes and other topical events. St George's Day Parade was the highlight of the year, always held at either Okehampton or Crediton on the Sunday nearest to St George's Day (23 April). A memorable day was in 1981 when deep snow at Witheridge and deeper at Okehampton meant the parade had to be cancelled.

At their weekly meetings the boys worked to gain badges for a number of crafts – gardening, woodwork, cooking, cycling, etc. – and many in the village were enlisted to help in these achievements. By 1980 numbers had increased to 29, and a note in the minutes read 'no more boys to be admitted – the maximum for 2 leaders is 24'. Luckily at this time Margery Vanstone joined us as a trained uniformed Scouter, which was wonderful for us and the boys.

The first Sunday of the month was always Church Parade, and we tried to have an activity after each service. We took the Moors walk north to Rackenford, south to Washford Pyne, and followed the Little Dart to Worlington. If it was wet we went to Tiverton's swimming-pool. Our favourite venue was Eggesford Forest, where the Forestry Commission allowed us to have our 'Cub Wood'. This we planted with tiny beech trees the size of pencils. We often went down to weed and tend our wood. This was planted in the scheme 'Plant a tree in '73'. Nine years later the council minutes read '7 beech are to be planted in Witheridge, 2 in East Close, 2 in Butts Close, 2 in Fore Street and 1 in Chapple Corner'. These were originally planted by the Cub Scouts in Eggesford in 1973. Large trees now! Eggesford was a wonderful place with a very large tree that sheltered us from many a wet picnic – trees to climb and an old castle relic with the River Taw to get wet in as well.

Each pack took turns to provide a site for the annual district camp. One year in our turn we camped in Mr Manning's field by the river and another year we camped in Lady Stevens' field at Worlington. We held gang shows at the Parish Hall and several years organised the bonfire celebrations to swell our funds, and often put a float in the carnival. The Cubs did some of their own fund-raising, collecting newspaper, stored at Witheridge

Below: *Guide Kathy Harrison receives her Baden Powell trefoil, 1987. Left to right, back row: Nicola Coffin, Deborah Vanstone, Michaela Nott, Rosie Cole, Sheila Lloyd (divisional commissioner), Georgina Pratt, Olivia Green, Lin Buckingham (Guide leader), Karen Ayre, Joyce Vanstone (Brownie Guider); front row: Gail Elston, Rosemary Austen, Clare Gillbard, Gail Beddoes, ?, Sarah Vincent, ?, Victoria Hutchens.*

Above: *To celebrate the 75th anniversary of the Scout movement, 75 Guides, Brownies, Scouts and Cubs gathered in the Parish Hall in 1982.*

Above: *Brownies, 1999. Left to right, back row: Kimberley Leach, Charlene Chapple, Emma Ashelford; front row: Nina Chapple, Elizabeth Copeland, Lisa Burrows, Fiona Iddles, Catherine Iddles, Sadie Leach.*

Left: *Scouts at St Boniface Jamboree at Crediton, 1980. Witheridge Scouts won the Saxon House Competition, building a house of wattle and daub, with a roof of rushes. The team included Tom Feiling, Neil Buckingham, Matthew Risdon, Andrew Leat, Michael Powell, Richard Hill, Michael Hill King and his brother, Matthew Kinnel and Stewart Price. Scout leaders at the time were Phil Risdon and Nick Timson.*

Left: The Scouts' Ethiopian Expedition, 1989, was documented by Matthew Risdon for the BBC TV's local news, who supplied camera and film. The team included Matthew and Neil Buckingham and Rosemarie Cole. They worked in a school and helped refurbish and equip a clinic in a remote area of Wolega Province. They presented a cheque for £1,200 to the Cheshire Home near Addis Ababa for handicapped children. On return and after all expenses were paid, they sent a further cheque for nearly £1,000.

Right: Mount Edgcombe Scout Jamboree, 1986. The Service Team's first year of Venture Scouts. Left to right, back row: ?, Matthew Risdon, Michael Hold, Paul Pincombe, Adrian Cregan, ?, ?; front row: Jackie Hold, Deborah Vanstone, Marilyn Cole, Gail Buckingham.

Left: Cubs dressed to represent countries of the world in 1976. Left to right: Dominic Kite, Sean Parnell, Simon Stoneman, Graham Isaacs, Paul Haresnape, Neil Buckingham.

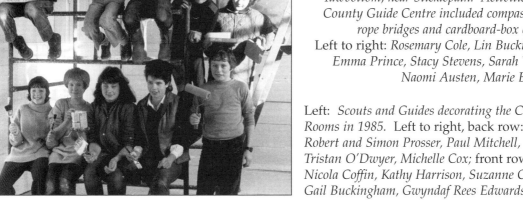

Above: In 1992 the Guides travelled to camp at Tawbottom, near Sticklepath. Activities at the County Guide Centre included compass trails, rope bridges and cardboard-box cookery. Left to right: Rosemary Cole, Lin Buckingham, Emma Prince, Stacy Stevens, Sarah Yabsley, Naomi Austen, Marie Burston.

Left: Scouts and Guides decorating the Church Rooms in 1985. Left to right, back row: Robert and Simon Prosser, Paul Mitchell, Tristan O'Dwyer, Michelle Cox; front row: Nicola Coffin, Kathy Harrison, Suzanne Cox, Gail Buckingham, Gwyndaf Rees Edwards.

garage, and in those days 'Bob a Job' was great fun. We were grateful to Mr Pate, who very successfully ran the 200 Club, and to Iris Webber for organising whist drives at Thelbridge, as well as our own fund-raising committee with jumble sales, draws and bingos.

In 1983 Janet left us to become our District Commissioner, which was a great honour for the pack, but it left us short of a leader again. However, in 1984 Tim Hyland joined us as Pack Leader. By this time the district had been renamed 'Mid Devon District', with a new emblem, namely the Red Devon Bull, designed by Jenny Bidgood. Sadly in 1985, having reached retiring age, I left the pack in the capable hands of Tim and Margery, after 12 very happy years of scouting.

I think 1981 must have been our 'glory year', when at the swimming gala at Exeter with competition from nine packs in the district we won the Swimming Shield, came first in the competition for the 1980 Scrapbook, and won the prize for making a banner. The heading in the Tiverton Gazette *read: 'Witheridge Cubs Do The Hat Trick'. Our crack swimming team then was Blue Ramsay, Paul Vanstone, Gwyndaff Edwards, Lawrence Filing, Richard Temple and Allistair Pratt.*

A RECENT HISTORY OF WITHERIDGE METHODIST CHURCH

With an outline of hopes and plans for the future.

Revd Russell Herbert, Methodist Minister (1999–present) recalls that in 1998 the situation for Witheridge Methodist Church seemed bleak. Sunday-morning congregations had shrunk to about ten worshippers. A recent survey on the building indicated the need for major repairs. The fellowship began to think that the days of meeting for worship at the chapel could be coming to an end. It was decided that the chapel would close and the fellowship would meet elsewhere.

This happened for one Sunday. Suddenly everyone felt that this was not the correct way to proceed. It seemed wrong to withdraw from the centre of Witheridge, where the chapel was ideally placed to

Members of the Methodist Chapel. Left to right, back row: Fred Tidball, Mr and Mrs Bill Thomas, Mr A.L. Knight, Mrs Bert Cox; front row: Mr Burridge, Mr and Mrs Bill Greenslade.

serve the community. So the fellowship resolved two things: first, the existing building, as a historic place of worship, must be restored to a condition fit for public use, and second, this must spring from a vision among the Methodist people to use the building in order to serve the community. The aim would be to make the chapel more 'user friendly' so that it could accommodate a diversity of activities, provide a meeting-place for all ages and take into account the need for disabled access. The Methodist people experienced a fresh sense of vision and decided to draw up a scheme and begin raising the financial resources.

The last five years have been very exciting. The congregation has doubled in size. Local support in raising funds for the building scheme has been tremendous. At the time of writing applications are being made to various national bodies for grants. It is hoped that the premises will be equipped to serve all ages in the community, not just on Sundays but throughout the week. The Methodist people have enjoyed working closely with the Anglican and Congregational Churches of Witheridge and look forward to an ever-deeper partnership in the years ahead.

First prize and ringers' shield at Torrington, 1960. Left to right, back row: Henry Rowcliffe, Reg Headon, Ivan Spedutti, E. Vanstone, John Chapple; front row: Jack Luxton, Tom Kingdom, Jack Twose.

Bell-ringers in the tower, 1963. Left to right, back row: Tom Kingdom, Arthur Bryant, Jack Luxton, Ivan Spedutti, John Chapple, Henry Rowcliffe, Ron Lewis, Jack Twose; front row: John Rowcliffe, Revd Castlehow, Walter Sharland, Gordon Tapp.

Above: *Retirement presentation to Arthur Leat by Bill Stoddard, chairman of the Parish Council in 1976. Arthur was postman for 17 years.*

Above: *A village outing in the early 1950s. Left to right, back row: Eileen Bryant, Margaret Baker, Mrs Criddle, Mrs P. Cole, Betty Bryant, Derek Bryant, Gwen Yendell, Valerie Leach, Hilda Leach, Rene Kingdom; front row: Stella ?, Christine Cole, Mervyn Leach, Michael Leach, ? Kingdom, Brian Kingdom, Michael Kingdom.*

Left: *Conservatives and Miss Witheridge, 1960s. Left to right: Frances Bowden, Pam Follett, Colonel Edds, Marjorie Tucker.*

Right: *An outing in the 1950s was enjoyed by,* outside: *Gladys Leat, Cyril Leat, Winston Pincombe, Gladys Pincombe, Cynthia Grant, Pauline Snow, Linda Dart, Randall Fewings, Mary Nott, Anne Manley, Brenda Winter, Christine Cole, Stella Cole, Rhonwen Kingdom, Derek Holloway, Bill Lewis, Alan Kingdom, Gordon Brewer, Ross Cumes, Mary Holloway, Rosemary Yendle, Joyce Rice, Pat Winter;* in the bus: *Mary Brewer, Ivy Meecham, Olive Yendle, Mrs Baker, Colin Baker, Mrs Pincombe, Derek Ford (Driver), Mr Deakin (headmaster), John Rowcliffe, Dianne Dart, Eileen Grant, ? Ayre.*

Right: *Monday Afternoon Club, 1989. The picture includes: Mrs Jones, Beattie Champion, Hilda Concannon, Mr and Mrs Clark, Betty Bryant, Hazel Elton, Amy Leat, Mrs Stevens, Mrs Bradley, Mrs Luxton, Tom Cook, Mr Frost, Mrs Searle, Mrs Bickley, Queenie Pyne, Mrs Whitfield, Mrs Hodgson, Jean Merritt, Olive Martin, Queenie Ball, Mrs Reid, Mrs Stevenson, Mrs Kingdom, Betty Hender.*

Left: *New Year's Eve fancy-dress party, c.1960.*
Included in the photograph are: *Stephen Selley, Jack Adams, Mrs Squire Cruwys, Mrs Cruwys, Pam Follett, Denzil Ayre, John Usmar, Robin Woollacott, Queenie Woollacott, Pearl Woollacott, Jack Luxton, John Williams, Sheila Follett, Bob Woollacott, Ron Winter, Dave Cumes, Betty Way, Joy Tucker, Sylvia Boundy, Gerald Manning, John Rowcliffe, Gerald Luxton, Bobby Buchanan.*

Right: *Church fête, 1948.*
Left to right: *Edith Burgess, Beatrice Kingdom, Monica Allanson Bailey, Myrtle Criddle, Jill Hayes, Nora Andrews, Joy Tucker.*

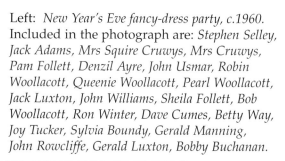

Left: *A Church fête in the early 1950s.*
Left to right: *Phyllis Maunder, Irene Way, Phyllis Adams, Ruby Thorne, Mrs Rowcliffe, Angela Maunder in pushchair.*

Above: *Church Fête, 1976.* Left to right: *Andrew Jones, Alison Brewer* (with bouquet), *Bunty Coffin, Caroline Manning.*

Above middle: *Revd Andrew Jones and Mrs Heather Jones.*

Above right: *Mrs Emily Williams, the chemist's wife.*

Nativity play, 1997.

Above: *Witheridge's church choir at Exeter Cathedral, 1970s.*

Below: *Church Sunday school, 1950s.* Left to right, back row: *George Aplin, Henry Taylor, Robin Woollacott, Fred Davey;* third row: *Fred Woollacott, Mary Payne, Pat Hill (teacher), Frances Bowden, Dennis Bawden;* second row: *Jennifer Sowden, Trevor Champion, Margaret England, Mavis Andrews, Mervyn Leach, Trudy Southcott, Gordon Tapp, Julie Southcott;* front row: *Janet Kingdom, Brian Kingdom, Margaret Baker, Michael Leach, Ann Manley.*

Left: *Royal Observer Corps posing for a photograph that was used on a recruitment poster.* Left to right, back row: *Frank Wheaton, Bob Woollacott, Fred Woollacott, John Usmar, Ron Harvey, Ken Williams, Bill Stacey;* on the floor: *John Alleyne.*

Below: *Millennium street party in West Street.*

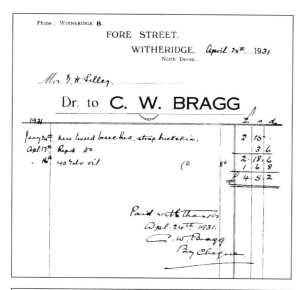

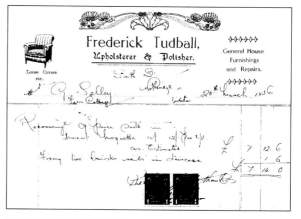

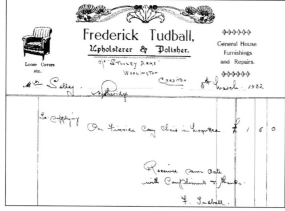

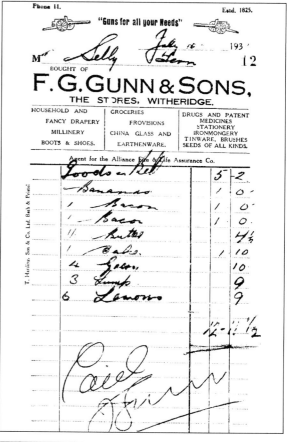

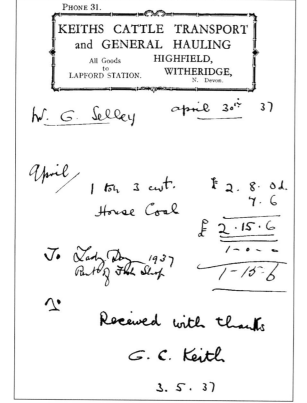

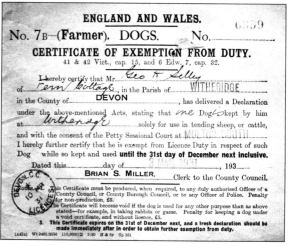

What They Think of Us
Taken from the Vistors' Book at the Rest A While Day Centre

Barnstaple: *We always visit your Fair and receive such a friendly atmosphere.*

Kingsbridge: *Always very pleasant to visit Witheridge.*

Cullompton: *Very welcoming people.*

Dawlish: *Nice to be here again.*

Amsterdam: *Thank you for your hospitality.*

Liverpool: *A very nice place and village community, friendly.*

Utrecht: *What a nice village.*

Brighton: *Good company – will come again.*

Alphen ap Rhein: *Very warm and loving welcome.*

Worthing: *The people of the town are very friendly.*

Gloucester: *Thanks for your hospitality to Two Moors – cold walkers.*

Exeter: *Best tea on the Two Moors Way.*

Swansea: *Lovely weather, lovely village, thanks a bunch.*

Rotterdam: *Warm welcome.*

New York: *What a wonderful time we've had with such kind and hospitable people!*
I hate to leave. Thank you so much for everything.

Essex: *I am so glad that I got the chance to come over here and experience part of the life that*
my ancestors did way back when. I love it here and I will be sure to come back.

Bideford: *Convivial company on this our annual visit.*

Plymouth: *Felt at home almost at once, thanks.*

France: *Merci pour votre accueil chaleureux.*

Subscribers

Peter Acreman, Witheridge, Devon

Sarah and Graham Allum, Witheridge, Devon

Anna and Jonathan Baggs, Witheridge, Devon

Bill and Ria Ball, Thelbridge Cross Inn, nr Witheridge, Devon

Frank and Beryl Beer, Witheridge

Ewart W. Blackmore, Stoney Creek, Ontario, Canada

The Bliss Family, Wandsworth, London

Wallace Boundy, Curriton, Thelbridge

Mr Ivor J. Bourne, Umberleigh, Devon/formerly of Witheridge

Mr Leslie J. Bourne, Feniscowles, Lancashire/ formerly of Witheridge

Mr William A.T. (Bert) Bourne, Kingsbury, Warwickshire/formerly of Witheridge

Gordon T.J. Brewer, Silverton, Devon

Mark Brewer, Sutton, Surrey

Clifford and Gladys Bristow, Witheridge

Graham Clifford Bristow, Exeter

Keith William Bristow, Witheridge

M. Bristow, Witheridge, Devon

David Bryant, Witheridge, Devon

John Bryant, Witheridge, Devon

Dennis Buckingham

Molly D. and Roy R. Bullivant, Witheridge, Devon

K.J. Burrow, Bucks Cross, Devon

Heather Campbell, Gordon House 1987–94

Ann Cann (née Gunn), Crediton, Devon

James R. Chalker, Birmingham, Alabama, USA

Norman Chapple, Exeter

Vera Charles, Brixham, Devon

The Charles Family, ex Mason's Stores – Brixham, Devon

Sarah Child, Rackenford

Yvonne and Michael Childs, Hope House, Witheridge

Geoff Clarke, Waltham, Grimsby

Miss Ruth Clarke, Newark, Nottinghamshire

Mrs Ruby Cligg, Witheridge, Devon

Dennis John Cockram, Witheridge, Devon

Jim and Sue Colston-Reeves, Witheridge, Devon

Mr Michael Connolly, Witheridge

Hilary Copp, Wellington, Somerset

A. and J. Cottey, Little Dart Raffe, Witheridge

Geoffrey Cox

L.W. and I.B. Daniel, Witheridge, Devon

Mrs Heather Dart, Witheridge, Devon

Karen Edwards, Witheridge, Devon

Mrs Dora M. Ellis (née Bourne), Silverton, Devon/formerly of Witheridge

Dr Steve A. Ellis (Elroy), Leeds, West Yorkshire

David E. Evans, Witheridge, Devon

Phyllis Fisher, Dulverton

P.A., S., J.M. Follett

Joyce and Terry Ford, Witheridge

Thomas W. Ford, Camberley, Surrey

Catherine E. Free

Mr D.R. Gard, Hatherleigh, Devon

Mr Eric Gard, Witheridge, Devon

Robert J. Gard, Tiverton, Devon

Ali Gowen, Witheridge, Devon

Mrs Beth Green, Witheridge, Devon

Muriel R. Green, Witheridge

Aubrey Herbert Greenslade, Witheridge

Jim and Roberta Greenslade (née Thomas), Taunton

Margaret Groat (Trawin), Melfort, Sask, Canada

Revd John and Mrs Rosemary Hanna, Witheridge

Dave and Angela Hardman, Witheridge

Rita M. Hayes, Thelbridge

Doris E. Haynes, Witheridge, Devon

Helen M. Herniman, Witheridge, Devon

Alan A. Hosegood, Yeatheridge, Devon

Frank Housam, Town Crier. Witheridge, Devon

Mary Housam, Witheridge, Devon

Simon C. Housam, Tiverton, Devon

Mavis F. Huckle, Witheridge, Devon

Preb. Andrew and Mrs Heather Jones

Jennifer Jury, Blackdog

Bill and Sue King, Witheridge

Paul King, Horseford

Paul King, Horseford

H. George Knight, Pinhoe, Exeter

Mr John and Mrs Hazel Lawrence, Exeter

Ray and Pat Laws

Colin Leach, Witheridge

Joy Gladys Leighton, Glastonbury

Kelvin John Luxton, Witheridge

Neville G.J. Luxton, Witheridge, Devon

Mrs Roslyn Macbride (née Thomas), Durham

John and Mary Malseed, Tooks, Witheridge, Devon

John Manley, Witheridge

Mrs Sylvia Anne Martin (née Davey), Exeter, Devon

Mary, great-granddaughter of Charlie and Mary Gunn